The Out-of-Home Immersive Entertainment Frontier

The Out-of-Home Immersive Entertainment Frontier

Expanding Interactive Boundaries in Leisure Facilities

KEVIN WILLIAMS and MICHAEL MASCIONI

LONDON AND NEW YORK

First published 2014 by Gower Publishing

Published 2016 by Routledge
2 Park Square, Milton Park, Abingdon, Oxon OX14 4RN
711 Third Avenue, New York, NY 10017, USA

Routledge is an imprint of the Taylor & Francis Group, an informa business

British Library Cataloguing in Publication Data
A catalogue record for this book is available from the British Library

Library of Congress Cataloging-in-Publication Data
Williams, Kevin, 1967-
The out-of-home immersive entertainment frontier : expanding interactive boundaries in leisure facilities / by Kevin Williams and Michael Mascioni.
pages cm
Includes bibliographical references and index.
ISBN 978-1-4724-2695-6 (paperback) -- ISBN 978-1-4724-2696-3 (ebook) -- ISBN 978-1-4724-2697-0 (epub) 1. Leisure--Economic aspects. 2. Leisure industry. 3. Popular culture--Economic aspects. I. Mascioni, Michael. II. Title.
GV182.15.W55 2014
790.06'9--dc23

2013045605

ISBN 13: 978-1-4724-2695-6 (pbk)

Contents

List of Figures *vii*
About the Authors *ix*
Preface *xi*

Introduction: Birth of a Genre 1

1 The Structure of Play 5

2 Collapse and Recovery 11

3 Defining the Sector 33

4 The Drive for Immersion 79

5 Social and Co-operative 113

6 Convergence 129

7 Future Trends 141

Conclusion: Living in the Dream 165

Index *181*

List of Figures

I.1	The hypnotic glow of the pinball playing field: Midway Manufacturing Company, Cactus Canyon (1998)	2
I.2	The draw of video amusement: socializing and competition give the genre an appeal for all generations	4
1.1	The Sony Playstation Vita handheld games platform: games are played on handhelds as much as on consoles and computers	6
2.1	The classic video-arcade: a darkened hall full of gleaming lights	14
2.2	NAMCO Bandai BANA Passport card system: near field communication negates the need to swipe cards to collect data	19
3.1	The Cruden BV Hexathrill motion base: it offers a level of simulation capable of training real-world racing drivers or thrilling the most ardent racing fan with an experience unachievable from the at-home console game	57
3.2	The frontage of the popular Chuck E. Cheese emporium: it offers a young clientele a mixture of theme park and arcade with a birthday pizza thrown in for good measure	65
3.3	Injoy Motions' 'Dido Kart 2': digital natives rediscover their love for big gaming	68
3.4	Taking the pop-up arcade to new extremes: this bizarre installation sees original arcade cabinets converted into outlandish experiences as part of a travelling installation 'The Faile Bast Deluxx Fluxx Arcade' in a London Soho gallery in 2010. Created by Faile, Brooklyn's infamous collaborative duo, early pioneers of contemporary street art, it was described as 'creating an explosively immersive installation'	70
4.1	Development of MoCap Games' VR system: combining their leading mechanical motion-capture suit with the latest HMD	88
4.2	NAMCO Bandai's 'Deadstorm Pirates' 3-D shooting experience: 3-D has driven innovation in the movie industry and also found a home in the next generation of amusement systems	95

4.3 Applying technology to the traditional telescope: Western Europe's tallest building, the Shard, uses these revolutionary AR telescopes to overlay information 103

5.1 WallFour Studios' innovative audience-based interactive laser game: 100 laser pointers control the narrative on screen (demonstration at the 2012 Indicade, California) 116
5.2 Alterface's 5Di Interactive Cinema: the audience takes parts in determining the narrative, which generates repeat visits 119
5.3 'Fly 360°' at the 'Fly Zone' gallery in the Science Museum, London: interactive entertainment imparts an educational narrative 122
5.4 Pulsefitness's 'Dance Machine': an interactive game that increases fitness 125

6.1 3-D warping: a model of a house demonstrates 3-D projection-mapping 133

7.1 A prototype large HD touchscreen display: the combination of object / image recognition with such screens is being considered for hospitality, retail and entertainment 147
7.2 Robo-thespian: the life-sized humanoid robot can interact with customers, providing a fully interactive, multilingual and user-friendly platform 157

C.1 Countering the stereotype of solitary and sedentary consumer-game play in a social environment 165
C.2 Inition's vertigo simulator using an Oculus VR dev-kit: a compelling if unnerving example of the power of the immersive experience 168
C.3 DNA Association Logo 173
C.4 Venn diagram of the DOE market (Kevin Williams) 174
C.5 The 2013 DNA/UK Seminar: attendees get to grips with what is needed for a compelling 3-D experience in DOE 175
C.6 3-D-printed sculpture of a visitor: personalized memorabilia is one future application of technology in the theme-park (Disney Research) 177
C.7 Oculus VR's prototype HMD: part of the drive for greater immersion in the game experience 178

About the Authors

UK-born Kevin Williams has amassed a wealth of experience of the past and present of the industries that are defining themselves as key to the DOE arena – after leaving school, he worked with leaders in amusement, commercial and military simulation, virtual reality, theme parks, games software and CGi technology. Possessing knowledge of both sides of the business table as developer, manufacturer and originator, he is one of the elite group of past Walt Disney Imagineers. A well-known commentator in the trade media including *InterGame, Replay Magazine, Vending Times* and the web portal Arcade Heroes, he also publishes his own provocative news service (The Stinger Report) and is a veteran moderator and presenter on the aspects that drive this and related markets. From his position in the DOE sector, he has championed the non-traditional opportunities this sector affords.

Michael Mascioni is a market-research consultant, writer and conference planner in digital media. He has undertaken research projects on such topics as DOE, video games, interactive TV, online entertainment and interactive compact discs for such companies as the IMAX Corporation, Sony Pictures, HBO, Paramount Communications, Thinkwell Group and Image Entertainment. He served as a senior analyst in the broadband entertainment group at Strategy Analytics and as a research associate in consumer electronics at LINK Resources. He has written articles on digital media for such publications as *Funworld,* Daily DOOH, Digital Signage Today, *Digital2Disc,* Internet Evolution and *Technology Review.* He served as the project manager of the 2012 DNA/US DOE conference and programme manager of the 2013 DNA/UK Seminar. He was programme director of the Intertainment conferences on interactive entertainment and managing editor of the A&A Monthly newsletter on Interactive Entertainment.

In co-authoring this book, both Kevin and Michael look forward to opening up the discussion regarding the opportunities and future developments of the DOE sector and providing a detailed commentary on what is seen as the next big development in the application of digital technology to virtual environments.

The Out-of-Home Immersive Entertainment Frontier endeavours to offer readers a glimpse into an innovative universe of entertainment and immersion. Both authors would like to personally thank the leading lights and innovators interviewed for this book, who have helped to create a groundbreaking publication: without their help and support this would not have been possible.

Preface

In writing this book, both authors have endeavoured to create the first publication to assess the implications of the evolution and expansion of immersive media in leisure facilities and highlight the multifaceted nature of interactivity in those facilities.

Charting the scope of the digital out-of-home entertainment (DOE) market not only tells the tale of the emergence of the digital-game narrative outside the home but also of the creation of technologies that can entertain, educate and inform unlike any other medium. From its first deployment in arcades and theme parks, the digital-entertainment platform in public-spaces has generated a draw unlike any other, unshackled by the price and development limitations of its at-home counterparts.

This book – the first in a series on the establishment of the new interactive entertainment narrative outside the home – charts the emergence of this technology and especially how it has been adapted to a broad range of applications. Touching not only the conventional pay-to-play amusement and attraction industries, DOE technology has also started to be deployed in the retail market, marketing and promotion, sports and leisure and even museum and visitor-attraction sectors.

Along with the technology, the methodology of gaming has had to be tailored to the out-of-home environment. The term 'gamification', meaning the application of elements of game-play to the development of content for this environment, has come into common usage. Fundamentally, the sophisticated modern audiences that populate all the venues described (and more) are familiar with the elements of play. They have known the internet and digital technology from birth: they are 'digital natives'.

Timeline

It is important to know the key events in the evolution of out-of-home entertainment. We have supplied a timeline here. They will be discussed at greater length in the main text:

1894	Kinetoscope (first coin-operated film-amusement system)
1895	'Phantom Ride' (one of the first immersive [themed] film experiences)
1931	'Pilot Trainer' (first interactive simulator-amusement attraction)
1962	'Sensorama Simulator' (the 'experience theater', a prototype coin-operated film-viewing system with physical effects)
1968	Sword of Damocles (first head-mounted display virtual-reality viewing system)
1971	'Computer Space' (first video game)
1972	'Pong' (first commercially successful video game)
1974	'Puppy Pong' (first free-to-play video game for retail application)
1977	Chuck E. Cheese (facility combining food and amusement)
1977	'Doron SR2' (first capsule-type entertainment simulator)
1982	Dave & Buster's (facility combining amusement hall and restaurant)
1983	SEGA 'SubRoc-3D' (first 3-D video game)
1984	'Tour of the Universe' (first simulator visitor attraction)
1985	Buzztime (first hospitality-based networked competition game system)
1985	'Exidy Vertigo' (first motion-based video game)

1986	'Captain EO' (first 4-D theatre experience, combining 3-D and physical effects)
1987	'Star Tours' (first simulator theme-park attraction)
1988	Atari 'Hard Drivin' (first 3-D polygon-graphical video game)
1989	WonderWorks (first interactive science attraction facility)
1990	BattleTech Center (first networked simulator game facility)
1990	NAMCO 'Galaxian 3' (one of the first digital interactive audience-based attractions)
1991	'Virtuality' (first virtual-reality arcade machine)
1992	NAMCO WonderEgg (first theme park with digital attractions)
1992	Tectrix 'VR Bike' (first interactive digital exercise cycle)
1993	SEGA 'AS-1' (first interactive capsule-type entertainment simulator)
1994	'Aladdin's VR Adventure' (VR HMD experience demonstrated to over 45,000 guests over 14 months)
1994	'Ridge Racer' (first texture-mapped video game)
1994	Joypolis (first indoor theme park with digital attractions)
1996	KidZania (first child-orientated role-playing amusement centre)
1998	'Aladdin's Magic Carpet Ride' (first interactive networked VR attraction)
2000	uWink Bistro (first restaurant facility using self-service and entertainment technology)
2002	TimePlay (first interactive cinema experience using touchscreen terminals)

2004 Positive Gaming 'iD'ance' (first wireless multi-player dance game)

2005 'MagiQuest' (first facility-based interactive live-action, role-playing game)

2005 Flight Experience (first airline flight-simulator facility)

2007 i-Way (first VIP facility with spa, restaurant and racing simulators)

2010 'StreetMuseum' (one of the first uses of augmented reality in a museum)

This book seeks to debunk the myth of a complete dichotomy between the digital out-of-home interactive entertainment and at-home consumer interactive entertainment markets. As it demonstrates, there is significant interplay and synergy between those markets, and the increasing involvement of consumer-game developers in the DOE market is a clear testament to that synergy.

Introduction
Birth of a Genre

Excitement, fun and complexity are the defining elements of play and interactive entertainment. Modern pastimes such as reading, art, sport and entertainment media have grown as a distraction to the drudgery of modern life. Nowadays games attract a sophisticated audience.

The formative years of young adults are spent in emulating their elders and developing the skills needed to take their positions in the adult world, and play is a major part of this process. Instilled in our growth to maturity, play has come to define our spare time and proved to be a strong diversion. Leisure, hobbies, recreation and entertainment have also become established as profitable business areas.

The video-amusement industry borrows its language from fun-fairs and carnivals, end-of-the-pier and carnival game experiences and theme parks, pinball parlours and arcades. Dropping a coin into a slot to experience a short distraction in an entertainment environment is as old as the bagatelle board and skittles table of the Victorian era. The immediacy of 'pay-to-play' supplies much of its the appeal.

The narrative element of play explains how a brief distraction can be monetized for a wider and more sophisticated audience, one familiar with the language of play but also with virtual worlds. Charging individuals for more and more short periods of time on a game in order to hone their skills has made the operation of interactive entertainment systems a highly profitable business venture, whether in speakeasies, pinball parlours, video arcades, gamebars or the latest location-based entertainment (LBE) facilities.

Figure I.1 **The hypnotic glow of the pinball playing field: Midway Manufacturing Company, Cactus Canyon (1998)**

The digital out-of-home entertainment (DOE) sector looks to commercialize gaming experiences in areas that would not normally been expected to produce repeat visits. With the addition of 'gamification', passive non-interactive audience experiences are transformed into undertakings that the player can influence to achieve goals and rewards, which compels them to return and continue their progress.

Other applications include the addition of leagues and tournaments, familiar from sporting sectors, such as bowling, which gather players into leagues and award prizes and incentives to compete. Competition also can be supported by micro-payments – small incremental inducements to keep playing – and other ways to improve the player's position.

Where at-home console games offer the players the comfort of their own homes, the public-play environment offers a social atmosphere and an opportunity to use dedicated hardware unique to the entertainment experience. As many are now recognizing, DOE offers a playing universe that takes up where the sedentary and transient consumer games sector left off.

Figure I.2 The draw of video amusement: socializing and competition give the genre an appeal for all generations

Chapter 1
The Structure of Play

Members of Generation X will remember their first at-home video-game experiences, as they migrated from darkened arcades to their living rooms and played on black-and-white screens. From this grey world the audience for digital entertainment has grown and grown, but it is with Generation Y (born between the early 1980s and the early 2000s) that we see an audience familiar with digital gaming that has also migrated from arcade machines to embrace the emerging game-console scene.

This transition brought with it a perception in the popular media that arcade products were somehow dated or defunct. The secretive nature of the video-amusement industry has proved its worst enemy in its attempts to promote itself in the modern market. It is difficult for the consumer-game media to penetrate the research and development (R&D) curtain, and this has made it easy to dismiss the video-amusement industry as irrelevant. The reality is that video amusement is an integral part of popular culture. Even those too young to remember arcade gaming in its heyday are drawn to the appeal of public-space (out-of-home) gaming and the well-known titles that established the genre of video gaming.

There are many examples of how video amusement is still proving popular even though the original producers are languishing. Microsoft borrowed most liberally with their Xbox Live Arcade (XBLA), the digital market place for users of the home-game platform provided a virtual arcade for them to build and populate with recreations of famous video-arcade machines. Likewise, invoking the popularity of classic arcade titles still generates great revenue, with NAMCO Bandai profiting from the 1980 release 'Pac-Man' and vast sums being spent on the smartphone version of Taito's 'Space Invaders'. The imagery as well as the games are used as brands in their own right.

Figure 1.1 The Sony Playstation Vita handheld games platform: games are played on handhelds as much as on consoles and computers

The re-emergence of the DOE scene has not received the same popular coverage as the at-home consumer-game sector has, but things are about to change. Even as the consumer scene looks forward to the launch of the eighth generation of home video-game consoles and hopes that it can address flagging game sales, there is an interest in looking beyond the restrictions of a box plugged into the player's television to entertainment that offers a greater level of innovation on new dedicated entertainment platforms.

While some in the consumer-game media may call the arcade industry dead, the reality is that the sector has evolved to match the changing audience.

Adam Pratt, author of *The Arcade Experience: A Look Into Modern Arcade Games and Why They Still Matter*, commented on the future:

> *It is not without its challenges, but I see those as obstacles to be overcome, not impassable barriers. What I mean by that is that everyone involved in the industry needs to stop holding back and shoot for creative and innovative vision behind our projects, whether that is through game development, distribution or site operation. Granted, it really has to start with innovation in development, as there is only so much creative space available to the lower channels. Unless we get into development ourselves, there is only so much we can do to attract players and keep them in the venue.*

Pratt describes the audience of his online service, Arcade Heroes, as:

> *A lot of amusement industry people from every aspect of the market, but there are a number of players too. In all honesty my goal is to reach out to the players, as at the end of the day if they are uninformed and not seeking out new content, that doesn't provide the life-blood that the rest of the sectors ultimately rely on. Arcade Heroes may fill a niche of the gaming news market, but there is nothing to say that it has to remain niche. There will be changes in the future to improve upon what is in place as a way to reach out to players and bring more to the fold.*

The new arcade model in the West places machines not in the centre (as with the traditional arcade venue) but as a secondary revenue stream in a site crammed with different attractions. Many of the new family entertainment centers (FECs) fill the gap between traditional and modern, with video-amusement machines sitting alongside redemption-ticket and carnival games. Other facilities have large brand-new amusement attractions in pride of place to draw in a transient audience. Likewise facilities that would not normally consider adding a video machine are looking at an entertainment element.

According to Pratt, the drive toward DOE development is

> *somewhat difficult to [explain], but I think it goes along the lines of not all amusement is DOOT [digital out-of-home technology], but all DOOT is amusement. Amusement has many mechanical items and games that may not fit into the exact definition of Digital Out-of-Home Entertainment, but perhaps Analog Out-of-Home Entertainment.*

Venues now seeking to include an entertainment mix are looking both at the new aspects of amusement platforms (machines unlike the traditional 'black box'), but also at new DOE hardware. With this drive to improve their use of the modern entertainment platforms, facilities are striving to offer the public amusements that tie in with social experiences and even with applications on smartphones.

The modern out-of-home entertainment experience must appeal to a changing customer base. In this environment, games need a greater level of 'play' and sophistication, such as achievable goals and scoring to increase repeat visits. From the amusement hall, the interactive game experience has migrated to all aspects of modern life and leisure.

Gamification and the DOE experience can be found in shopping malls in marketing and promotions (retail-tainment), such as projected floor screens that allow the player to play simple games incorporating the company's brand; in the use of innovative narratives for museums, science centres and visitor attractions (edutainment), such as theatres that allow audiences to watch films with 4-D effects; and even as an encouragement to exercise and rehabilitation (exergaming), such as special networked dance mats hooked up to giant screens where movement and exercise are all part of the game. These are a few of the examples we will explain in more detail later in this book.

Beyond the machines themselves, the structure of the game in the DOE environment can been broken down into three core components: the more traditional amusement approach where the player pays for a set number of lives or time to complete the game; a free-to-play model that allows the player to partake in mini-games offering a quick gaming fix; and the attraction approach, an extended game-play experience linked to an audience-based narrative. All three of these approaches offer a much more intense play narrative than their earlier alternatives. The return to popularity of DOE and the application of new technologies have led to the development of new gaming narratives.

How this new play narrative could be placed into facilities was discussed during a recent keynote presentation, 'New Reality for Location-Based Entertainment', at a Digital Out-of-Home Entertainment Network Association (DNA) conference: Randy White, CEO of White Hutchinson Leisure & Learning Group, presented the concept of 'staycation', referring to the new tendency of people to have their holidays at home, as budgets (and belts) are tightened, and how it was fuelling interest in DOE. (The term 'staycation' was coined in 2003.) To capture this audience, facilities had to offer the same level of entertainment as that found at the major venues to which consumers had previously travelled to visit. With DOE, a smaller venue can offer a bigger entertainment punch.

Speaking about his observations, White stated:

> *Our research clearly shows that the staycation trend surfaced back in 1997 and continues to advance to this day. The financial downturn only accelerated the trend, making the year-to-year change pronounced enough to get noticed.*

White's views on the future of the entertainment experience include clear links between out-of-home entertainment, mobile entertainment and LBE. The modern audience is immersed in a digital forest that comprises four-screens (television, laptop, tablet and mobile phone). There is a need for the out-of-home experience to prove equally as compelling. Entertainment is no longer dependent on location or what White calls 'high fidelity' – a term he uses to distinguish a high-quality experience (such as a live music performance) from a cost-effective equivalent (such a CD of the performance). The danger lies in offering a DOE experience that falls in the middle (known as the 'fidelity belly') and is neither one thing nor the other and thus fails to attract the disposable income and leisure time of a highly pressed audience.

According to White, there are three ways DOE operators fall into the fidelity belly:

- they have older facilities that have not been updated in all aspects of design and operation to provide a modern high-fidelity experience;
- they develop a new venue without understanding that it requires a high-fidelity experience to compete in today's entertainment market; or
- they develop a new venue as cheaply as they can.

White goes on to say, 'the digital out-of-home entertainment approach is essential to location-based entertainment, provided it is properly applied and used'. When questioned if DOE, in his eyes, was just a flash-in-the-pan or something more concrete, he affirmed:

> *DOE is here to stay. We now live in the digital world, and digital technology will continue to advance and become fully integrated into and essential to just about every aspect of our work, home and leisure lives.*

DOE is changing the structure of gaming from pay-to-play to free-to-play. We will look more closely at the traditional model of the amusement business and how it is evolving into the modern DOE sector later. The business model of the Western amusement industry has been streamlined since the 1980s, with many aspects now focused on a single point of sale. This means a direct sales approach has become predominant.

The hardware required has also changed the nature of the business. Venues that follow the new approach see video-amusements and the other genres of prize and redemption gaming as a secondary revenue stream. FECs, bowling alleys, laser-tag, batting-cages, roller-skating rinks, mini-golf, ice rinks and obviously cinemas, all profit from video-amusement, but the model needs modernizing to embrace the next generation of technology and establish new audiences and increase revenue.

The new generation of technology is defined not just by new amusements and attractions but by the concentration of more immersive entertainments in wholly DOE venues, offering a level of social game play unique to the public play environment. This new experience is aimed at a target audience familiar with gaming on consoles but also drawn to repeat visits to a specific venue or location.

Chapter 2
Collapse and Recovery

Video Amusements: Collapse and Recovery

For some individuals, it is difficult to perceive that digital out-of-home entertainment is anything more than just a grand way to describe the black box with flashing lights that has come to epitomize arcade machines. While the heyday of the video-amusement arcade may have passed, video amusement is still a worthwhile business. Video-amusement's popularity in Japan has allowed corporations such as SEGA and NAMCO to generate significant revenue. Even some of the smaller companies such as Taito and Capcom have proved successful. While many may argue that this is unique to Japan, the video-amusement business still finds a place in the West in mixed machine placements, as mentioned earlier.

In its search for new investment, the video-amusement business has had to be mindful of developments in the modern market. More industries looking to incorporate a DOE component means that the traditional video-amusement business faces competition from the attraction, retail, hospitality and museum sectors. The coin-operated-amusement industry has charted the growing sophistication of their customer base, from bagatelle to electro-mechanics to digital to video.

In the 1970s, video-amusement hardware proved a difficult commodity: the complexity of the new technology strained business models and operators were scared that video was too much of a novelty. In 1972, operators feared that the TVs would be stolen from their 'Pong' cabinets, but their tune soon changed in the face of video's phenomenal popularity: the first explosion of this new technology.

Video amusement soon became a serious business. North America produced Atari, led by Nolan Bushnell, who was untainted by any of the issues that saddled the traditional amusement trade at the time: he had never worked in an amusement park but came fresh from producing the first video-arcade title 'Computer Space' for Nutting Associates. Its failure, and 'Pong's success, would result in the founding of a new breed of amusement manufacturer that would re-shape the industry.

The experiences of those early days were similar to those of the current transition to DOE. Speaking with Nolan Bushnell – who describes himself as 'just the guy who created the first commercially successful video game in the amusement industry' – we asked what the video amusement industry is to him:

> *I always saw the coin-op sector acting as an interesting bridge between the research laboratory and the home, allowing technology to migrate between the two. Technology is generally very expensive at first and having it in public venues is a means to get it in circulation and so reduce that expense.*

The second explosion came from an emerging sector, Japan, which moved out of North America's shadow and developed new video technology and made it its own. This period saw great changes: in 1976, Kee Games introduced the first microprocessor-powered game; in 1978, Taito Corporation took inspiration from their previous electro-mechanical games and applied it to the new medium of digital gaming, launching 'Space Invaders' (also made possible by the microprocessor).

With 'Space Invaders' and its vast popularity, the amusement trade had to recognize video amusement as more than just a flash in the pan after 'Pong'. Video-arcade history records the impact on popular culture that the game in all its variants would have: the coin shortages in the vicinities of the cabinets and the near addiction of the players.

Gaining special insight into the thinking of one of the most influential Japanese factories at the time, we spoke with Akihito Shoji, senior vice president of online and arcade divisions at Taito Corporation. Discussing the influence and legacy of 'Space Invaders', Shoji commented:

> *The arcade game created a worldwide boom, with 2013 marking its 35th anniversary. We consider 'Space Invaders' as Taito's brand symbol, and we use it as a corporate character, which is widely used in our business, including the sign boards in Taito Station, our game arcades*

in Japan. Also there are various kinds of licensing agreements on 'Space Invaders' throughout the world. We regard 'Space Invaders' as our most important content, marking an evolution in media as games have proven. It is a long lasting icon and unforgettable experience for all of our customers across the globe.

The demand for the Japanese game would see US manufacturer and distributor Midway Manufacturing (a Bally Company) license the game and claim it as their own, revealing the seamier side of the amusement trade with brands being copied in a scramble to supply the hunger for the next and better video release. The tinkling cashboxes fuelled a revolution in development – what would be christened 'the golden age' of video-arcade games. The traditional amusement trade restructured itself to support licensing, production, distribution and operation.

Though harder to identify with just one product, the third key explosion in video-amusement games would be a pyrrhic victory for the industry. The advancement of computer graphics imagery (CGI), which superseded the 2-D game experience, ushered in a brand new perception of video amusements. Borrowing directly from the simulation industry and scaled down for arcade application, the new CGI system started a near fatal 'arms race' amongst companies producing video games in the early 1990s. Games such as SEGA's 'Virtua Formula' and 'Virtua Fighter', which provided gaming in virtual environments, would drive a hunger for 3-D game experiences.

With the need for more and more CGI performance, the drive for cost-effective technology claimed video-amusement developers unable to compete in the high-stakes game of R&D. But what was good for amusements was also good for consumers. The technology originated with NAMCO (and their 1995 'Tekken' and the System 11 architecture) in collaboration with Sony Computer Entertainment (with support from Evans & Sutherland) and would also be instrumental in establishing the PlayStation console, a relationship that continues to this day.

At this point, the video-amusement industry in the West entered what has been perceived by some as a death spiral. Some observers claimed that the console-games industry stole its audience, which reverted to at-home play. However, the reality is more complicated.

Figure 2.1 The classic video-arcade: a darkened hall full of gleaming lights

Video amusement lost direction and focus as more and more expensive CGI hardware and lavish game platforms sent many video-arcade operators bankrupt. Where one or two failures could be withstood in the golden age, the vast sums spent on installing the latest simulator racer or shooter could be crippling if the game did not prove popular. Operators were unwilling to gamble on the games' success and were distrustful of a video-amusement industry that placed all the risk on them. With collapsing revenues and a lack of investment, the Western video-amusement industry turned its back on its traditional model and began playing second fiddle to the new entertainment-facilities revenue stream.

When asked about his views of the slump in video-amusement, Bushnell stated:

> *I see many in the arcade scene perceived the business to be over when the arcade and home games equally had the same performance of graphics. This view is not properly thought out and seems to totally miss what the arcade scene has to offer. Recently I have seen everyone*

in the business jump onto the redemption bandwagon just because you can't give teddy bears through screens! The offset of the video-game business is that originally a lot of operators use to say, 'hey I can fix the relays and plugs on my pinball machines easily, so that's what I want to spend my time doing'. So when they saw 'complicated' video arcade games come along, they let other people handle that stuff, so they let the camel nose under the tent and lost control.

Going into more detail, Bushnell continued:

The thing that has to be remembered is that the public is bored easily and is fickle – what entertained them yesterday might not today. The sacred duty of all in the games business is to push the innovation envelope. The danger is when the business stabilizes for a period, and those in it think this is how it will always be and are surprised when it moves on for more innovation. Fundamentally, video is a display technology, period, and I feel the best is yet to come.

Going on to observe what interested him in new trends, he observed:

My youngest son is dealing with Great Wolf Lodge with a game concept called Virsix [covered later in this book], an interactive adventure for use in hospitality, malls, movie theatres and other public venues. This kind of thing is really exciting and shows how innovation can still add to the fun.

The modern video-amusement industry is now a lumbering beast, wounded by the collapse of the late 1990s. Traditional operators are finding it impossible to invest in ever more expensive dedicated amusement hardware. The industry has reverted to mixing ticket-redemption machines for young players with video-amusements in such venues as bowling alleys, family entertainment centers and some cinema locations: arcade gaming has turned into an impulse entertainment.

America still has video-amusement specific developers, one of the most prominent being Raw Thrills, founded and led by Eugene Jarvis, a veteran developer of pinball and video amusements (working previously for Atari, Williams and Midway). Raw Thrills' partnership with major distributor Betson Enterprises ensures a strong foundation from which to release games.

Asked about the survival of the current video-amusement market, Jarvis stated:

> *Stagnation has been slowing, replaced by resurgence, thanks to a drive toward the unique experience of arcade gaming. There are some arcade companies that want to be the 'jukebox' of the same games from home in an arcade package. Other developers are looking toward offering hot compelling content 24/7.*

He went on to say:

> *The industry is searching to find unique interfaces and compelling intellectual properties. The development need is to create 'eye candy' that players demand in their arcade games. Development from this hot crucible produces unique games, such as the 'Golden Tee' concept or the 'Buck Hunter Pro' concept that are located in different locations than the traditional arcade experience, such as sports bars. Arcade gamers are hungry cannibals firing up the barbecue with the meat of new ideas!*

But there is another vibrant market. The Asian video-amusement scene is a stark contrast to what the Western industry has become. With successes in the late 1980s, the Japanese came to dominate: Taito, SEGA, NAMCO, Konami, SNK and Jaleco are just some of the companies that released internationally popular 2-D video games that became household names in what was seen by some as a second golden age. This dominance was cemented by a standardization of how games were released. Thanks to introduction of the JAMMA (Japan Amusement Machinery Manufacturers Association) Standard in 1984, the game is contained in a PCB (printed circuit board), rather than in the whole machine, and can be replaced easily if a title wanes in popularity. This quick swap-over process (emulated by the console-cartridge industry) allowed for greater sales of games and wider innovation.

However with the arms race in CGI, the JAMMA Standard lost ground against large dedicated simulator-style hardware, and expensive machines were installed and replaced once they fell out of fashion. At the same time, many of the Japanese factories had also become major operators of machines, running their own amusement facilities.

Asian developers continued to invest in out-of-home video gaming long after Western ones had began to concentrate on the at-home market. That investment produced new developments in the social game experience that epitomized the video-amusement scene in Japan, a culture of socializing and group activities fuelled by the enjoyment of video gaming. Though overlooked by many who have charted the evolution of the game community, Japan ignited what some have seen as the third wave of arcade popularity.

Konami Digital Entertainment (KDE) has proven themselves a powerhouse of innovation in video amusement, with a long pedigree of applying original thought to their games. Their Bemani initiative changed the perception of play completely. In 1997, when KDE released 'Beatmania' in Japan, the Western amusement market dismissed the quirky musical game as a 'Jap-only' title. But what was missed by an intransigent Western trade was the emergence of a brand new genre.

With the release the following year of 'Dance Dance Revolution' (DDR) a totally new way to play video games was inaugurated. The game was played standing on a platform divided into different coloured sections. The players stepped on the sections in response to the music and prompts on the screen. The more accurately they did so, the higher their score. Called 'Dance Stage' in Europe, DDR overcame trade indifference and proved a smash hit in the West. Soon new players were invading the arcades and gyrating to the music. Countless updates and versions of the game appeared, creating what seemed to be the love-child of the electric toy Simon and the board game Twister.

With this success, KDE became a serious player in the international video-amusement scene and released a host of games under the Bemani label. As Pratt mentioned in *The Arcade Experience*, the Bemani brand has remained a strong cash cow, and, as such, a new 'Beatmania', 'Guitar Freaks' or 'DrumMania' is released about once or twice a year. They have introduced a few new music concepts to the market such as 'uBeat' (which to the amusement of the internet is called 'Jubeat' in Japan), 'Reflec Beat' and 'Sound Voltex Booth'. All involve new ways of hitting buttons to the rhythm of the music, generally with a touchscreen of some kind or, in the case of 'Sound Voltex', a couple of spinners and buttons. To Konami's dismay, these ideas are always being copied by Chinese companies, who seem to be safe as long as they stay in China.

The Japanese video-amusement trade has continued to refine its approach to social gaming. Manufacturers in Japan have also become operators, opening facilities where people can play their games and others in an enjoyable atmosphere. The traditional amusement venue in Japan has undergone a metamorphosis with the inclusion of dedicated social networking spaces.

Along with innovative games, the Japanese factories also started to connect players directly with each other – taking the highscore chart to the next level –

by incorporating network play and online registration. SEGA released their Amusement Linkage Live Network (ALL.Net) system in 2001 and were soon supporting more than 2,000 facilities in Japan, using the architecture that brought networked tournament systems to a selection of the company's new releases. 'Virtua Fighter 4' was the first game to be supported by the service (called VF.Net for the game), which allowed four players to play against each other and supplied the player networks, mobile-phone reviewing and player's cards.

But it was not just SEGA games that got the ALL.Net treatment. NAMCO Bandai licensed the architecture for use on their games, including their popular fighting series 'Tekken', making ALL.Net the largest player network in the amusement sector. However, rather than just being a Japanese phenomenon, the system has also been converted for use in the Western market. In January 2013, NAMCO America made 'Tekken Tag Tournament 2 Unlimited' (TTT2) available in the West.

NAMCO offers a JAMMA-compatible PCB kit that can be used in a wide variety of JAMMA cabinets with high-definition (HD) displays, supported by TEKKEN.Net. NAMCO America has created a website for US players (based on the Japanese original) with unique territory rankings and customizable player characters accessed by BANA Passport cards.

Ushering in this new era, Katsuhiko Mikami, product and sales support for NAMCO America, revealed the thinking behind their effort to educate the traditional US amusement trade about the value of networked machines:

> *For us, TTT2 is the challenge to introduce 'network using game' into the US market place. As you know, more and more games that have 'online' features are released in Japan. We at NAMCO adapt some games from Japan to the US market. Probably for the future, if we don't start incorporating online features now, we may not have new games in the US. So TTT2, one of the most well-known video games is a good timing to start our new strategy in US.*

Asked whether this is just an experiment or a dedicated move, Mikami stated:

> *Yes, I would say this is experiment by* **NAMCO** *so far. As I stated above, we will have more and more network games in the future. Before we start late, we try to do something for this sector as much as possible.*

Figure 2.2 NAMCO Bandai BANA Passport card system: near field communication negates the need to swipe cards to collect data

Regarding the question of the major hurdles that NAMCO faced in undertaking this move to the West, Mikami said:

> *I think it is 'tradition.' When I worked in Japan, and NAMCO Japan started the network-using game business, customers were all saying that it would be impossible to accept that kind of business scheme that not only buying game but customers still need to pay 'network fee' per month or per play to venders. But since NAMCO Japan has tried to keep the income of the game by giving new courses, features, characters etc., via online, and players came to think that online made the game more enjoyable, operators had changed their minds into 'online has good aspects'. Then they came to understand the game little by little. In practical steps, all the location needs at least one NBLINE Router, which is a dedicated router with our NAMCO network system.*

Having come from the Japanese video-amusement scene, Mikami was asked what his views of the American scene were. He stated:

> *As you know, the US arcade market is shrinking little by little. If we continue the same traditional way of business as we have done for years, the trend will continue, and sometime in the not too distant future there will be no more arcades. Considering this situation, we at NAMCO are trying to introduce new kinds of games not only to the US, but all over the world. Since we merged with Bandai Group, we have a lot of resources to develop new things. We have a large group of companies and will take good advantage of these resources and keep challenging new things.*

Other factories in Japan have experimented with their own systems, though not all are gaining the momentum that was achieved the first time with SEGA's ALL.Net. Taito invested time and resources in a network infrastructure that allowed players to compete in real time, and their 'Taito Net Entry System' (NESYS) gained the company a foothold in the sector, with the racing title 'Battle Gear 3' in 2002. The BG3 series initially used a unique ignition key as the players' card. The system was superseded by the NESiCA Card, which contained the player's identity and accumulated points. NESiCA points are redeemable as credits for games and for specific items within the game.

Commenting on this, Takafumi Fujimoto, producer in the R&D department in the AM business division at Taito Corporation, stated:

Taito's NESYS is the basis of our network business, and it is a system open to the third parties of TAITO Type X series. NESiCAxLive is a content download system that works over NESYS, offering a wide range of games from classic retro titles to the newest version of well-known titles. This wide selection of games covers player preferences. The operators highly appreciate the revenue-share model as, after an inexpensive start-up package, the new titles and the upgrades will be delivered free of charge to all the clients' [terminals] automatically. It also offers an advantage that was not possible with the conventional way of exchanging the game board, in that all the players, even in the remote areas, can start playing the game on the release date.

Regarding this new business model, Fujimoto was asked if Taito saw their NESiCA points as virtual money that could replace the traditional coin-box. He stated: 'We are going through a planning phase on the usage of NESiCA points, so as to improve the benefit of both operators and players.'

Akihito Shoji posited a future possibility:

Ever since the introduction of smartphones and tablets, people's way to play or enjoy games changed dramatically. The new devices continue to show remarkable progress all the time, and we foresee a time when all games can be played on the smartphones and the tablets. However, even after this advanced equipment become ubiquitous, it won't be possible to reproduce the 'real' feeling or the 'touch', which the arcade games can offer nor the feeling of participating in the real place where the friends gather.

Shoji went on:

The arcade games can create extraordinary experiences in the ordinary life of the players. The 'reality' and 'touch' in the 'real place' is unique to the arcade games, and this value becomes more precious as the game devices gets more universal and more common in daily life. In addition to this value shift, the arcade machines are often connected to the network recently and there are fundamentals that make it easy to connect the arcade games with various online services. Our plans for future arcade games are to exploit their unique qualities and plan those games with smartphones in mind from a game design and business perspective, thus offering people more attractive experiences.

KDE was one of the first companies to fully deploy an operational IC-card online-tournament service across their whole amusement line. Launched in 2002, the e-amusement system comprised a dedicated server, online network and player IC-card, with an account accessible from the player's mobile phone or PC. By 2005, the company integrated the service into the e-amusement IC-pass-card system revealing that they would only produce amusement content that supported the infrastructure 100 per cent (with an installed base at that time of over 40,000 connected systems).

The company extended the features of the e-amusement infrastructure to include a save-and-continue feature, allowing players to carry on the game where they left off. This feature can be activated by the IC-card or the player's mobile phone using a special app. The creation of micro-payments for services and features in the game has been constantly upgraded in the e-amusement infrastructure. In 2003, KDE launched 'ee'MALL', which offered a place to acquire virtual items using virtual credits accrued in their account (predating the use of achievements in the consumer sector by some time). The system finally terminated in 2006.

The company replaced the e-amusement pass card with the Pay Smart Enjoy Life (PASELI) system in 2010. This IC-card system combined player data for games and tournaments and is also an e-payment system, using virtual credits which can be topped-up with real money. Topping-up the card allows operators to monetize the games, providing on ongoing secondary stream of revenue after the primary purchase of the game. Other factories followed suit. In 2011, SEGA launched their AiME card system, superseding the ALL.Net cards and allowing multiple games to be stored on one 'near field communication' (NFC) card. NAMCO Bandai are supported on their own BANA Passport, which employs the same architecture. The AiME system is part of the move toward a virtual credits system, with the player able to accrue points on the card (as with the BANA Passport) and then redeem them in the game.

There are numerous elements of the Japanese video-amusement scene that are different from the Western one: connected online smart payment systems is one of them. Taking away the perceived 'cash' aspect of the traditional video-amusement business and opening up alternative sources of revenue has been hard to swallow. However with a dwindling audience base that is nevertheless growing increasingly sophisticated, the international video-amusement industry has had to grow up and embrace new thinking.

The need for new investment saw Japanese video-amusement factories pool their resources and change their tactics, establishing the Japan Amusement Machinery Manufacturers Association in 1981. Membership was decimated by the upheaval in the arcade scene, but, under new direction, the association has attempted to move with the times and embrace promotion, even changing its name to Japan Amusement Machine and Marketing Association.

With the change in name came a consolidation of approach: the association sought strength in numbers by merging with shopping-centre and park-equipment groups. Another major development in the Japanese video-amusement business was the launch of two major trade shows a year. In 2013, a new event called the Japan Amusement Expo (JAEPO) was introduced under the tag-line 'We Love Arcades!' In 2013, the industry collapsed under pressure including the fall-out from the 2011 Tōhoku earthquake and tsunami, a crippling financial environment and a general malaise in the DOE scene as the public spent its disposable income on at-home console games.

The dominance of the Japanese factories has also come under threat in recent times from the high cost of manufacturing, which has triggered a shift toward using Taiwanese and Chinese companies to build machines. China, in particular, has taken full advantage of the situation and has started to develop its own original video-amusement content. One of the Chinese developers that has gained major recognition is Universal Space (UNIS). Having lived in the shadows, supplying specialist manufacturing services to many family entertainment centers (FECs), UNIS is now able to release its own video games on the international market.

Steven Tan, general manager of UNIS, commented on what the new Chinese video-amusement developers brought to the scene:

> *I think Chinese developers expect the amusement scene to grow in a different way from perhaps the direction envisioned by the Western world. The Chinese are more exposed to Japanese products as well as their own local market. Within these countries there is a vibrant pool of resources and talent from which to access different ideas and new concepts. ... We want to move forward, promote original ideas, and develop new concepts. This ethos comes from the top, company ownership and through senior management.*

Regarding the learning curve of working in the US, Tan stated:

> *The US, and for that matter, the UK and European markets, already have in place a high benchmark in terms of standards that the operators expect. UNIS has been involved in the USA market since 2000 and during this time our focus has been solely around games that are suitable for indoor family entertainment centers. We have been working actively in this market to understand the level of expectations of a 'plug and play' ready game.*

He added:

> *Although a game concept might be unique, there is no compromise in the West on quality, service and support. We have been learning over the past decade to listen to our distributors and the operators, heed suggestions and implement them where feasible. But we still have room to grow. There will always be a learning curve for us, as there is in any industry. As soon as you think there isn't one, then I suggest that you shouldn't be working within that industry anymore.*

Regarding future aspirations in the DOE arena, Tan said:

> *UNIS's passion is in the development of its products. Our slogan 'Fun is universal' echoes the culture that our core staff embrace. The amusement sector is a global business, and therefore our long term aspiration is to take the UNIS family of products across the globe, establishing long term, sustainable business relationships with our buyers and operators alike. We will continue to listen to our customers, improve within, and become more established globally with, our brand.*

While many attempt to paint video amusement as a failed market, the reality is that even in the West, video gaming in the public sector is still incredibly popular. The difficulty in finding state-of-the-art facilities have compounded a feeling of terminal decline. However, the old protective infrastructure of distribution and operation, which strangles innovation, is being discarded, and a new approach that takes its cue from DOE is being adopted to establish a new video-amusement industry from the wreckage of the old.

A debilitating element of the traditional video-amusement industry has been the price of a gaming session. For an entertainment industry dealing in cash at the point of play, this has stayed surprisingly consistent while the price of equivalent entertainments has risen. In 1972, 'Pong' offered one credit for 25¢ (equivalent to $1.36 in 2013); in 1994, 'Daytona USA' would require four coins, $1, a play on average ($1.48 in 2013). In comparison, cinema has seen a rise in average price from $4.08 in 1994 to $9.00 in 2011. While a console game in 1994 was $40, in 2011 the latest big title was $60. But the video-game is still priced at about $1 a play.

However, video-amusement has migrated away from dealing in cash-to-play, with modern amusement facilities depending on swipe-cards: cards loaded with credits and topped-up when depleted. This has allowed the large FECs and entertainment facilities to support a better business model. This revenue does not return to the manufacturer, but is retained by the operator of the machines. For manufacturers, exclusion from this source of revenue is another contributory factor to the demise of their industry and has seen them consider operating their own hardware, as they do in Asia. The use of network-based video-games has seen factories charging operators and players a 'network fee' as a means to bolster income and gain access to the revenue stream.

The amusement sector has started to embrace more advanced means of handling payments, following transport and retail industries in using smart payment infrastructures. Where the physical swipe-card system has traditionally been a feature of FECs, a new level of sophistication is beginning to appear. Systems including radio-frequency identification (RFID) and NFC are being used in Japan, along with 3-D scanned barcodes (quick response code) that do not use the magnetic strips on the card, but can be connected to sophisticated back-of-house infrastructure. Very precise control of pricing and promotions can be obtained: prices can be lowered and special promotions offered during quiet periods, ensuring better use of the facility. This establishes a drive toward a greater sophistication in the cards and the handling of cashless payment lead by companies such as Core Cashless.

Theme-parks have also started to adopt a new visitor-payment and ticketing infrastructure that embraces the next-generation of e-payment systems and leads to greater monetization. Walt Disney Parks and Resorts have built on the group-visit infrastructure with the new 'MyMagic+', which has links to a website and mobile app, allowing visitors to plan and personalize their visits to the park. At a reported cost of nearly $1 billion to develop, Disney hopes to offer, on arrival, a mixture of the app and the new 'FastPass+' system, which will revolutionize the exploration and experience at the park. All this is combined with a RFID wristband (MagicBand) that acts as a tracking system, with ticketless entry / e-payment to parks and services.

Another park resort beginning to use revenue-enhancement technology is Universal Studios Japan. The corporation is working on a closed-loop prepaid electronic payment (e-money) system called 'Wonder Money', which is a mobile app service acting as a site-based 'mobile wallet', allowing visitors interactive capability with e-money point-of-sale (POS) terminals throughout the park to purchase goods and services and reduce time spent in queues (through new Customer Relationship Management [CRM] systems). This infrastructure – with support from NEC Corporation – provided Universal with the ability to update the payment infrastructure with contactless IC-readers that support NFC – vital to personal e-payment systems – dramatically changing how guests experience the venue.

One of those now focusing on revenue enhancement for clients, by delivering specific programmes that bring measurable improvements, is Lilly Development Partners, founded by E. Brooks Lilly. Regarding the application of smart payment in the location-based entertainment (LBE) scene, Lilly stated:

> *The ability to accept nearly every form of 'cashless & contactless' payment at the attraction's entry gate or point of play is paramount. Tomorrow the device at the point of pay must accept both barcode on a wristband, card, or smart phone screen and NFC or RFID credentials borne by the same kind of credentials. Why? The choice of payment method is no longer an either/or decision, but rather a question of where and how the guest has stored and linked their money to a credential. Simply put, we must accept barcoded PassBook on iPhone, NFC on Android, and RFID in our bank cards, or suffer lower per capita spending.*

Asked to speculate on future links between players and venues, Lilly commented:

> *Five driving forces of player-linking have emerged in the digital era. The systems behind the entertainment must perfect multiple links to the player and that relationship must exist on five planes:*
>
> - *payment: link the player to multiple forms of payment, including aggregation of changes;*
> - *privilege: enable entitlements and access to features, functions, locations and entry;*
> - *profile: catalog likes, needs, conditions and groups / affinity relationships;*

- *promotion: encouragement for revisits, couponing, aggrandizement and call to action;*
- *performance: scores, ranking, rewards, earning, recognition and esteem.*

For equality of play, this link must also accommodate tiered play fields and handicapping.

There is one model of the video-amusement business that does not involve players paying for their entertainment directly. In recent years, a number of video-amusement projects have used 'in-game advertising' and product placement to pay for the machines' installation. One recent example has been 'Winnitron 1000', an independent free-to-play video-game cabinet featuring new games specially created by independent game developers in the Winnipeg area and hoping to attract others from around the world.

The Winnitron 1000 platform has been created as an open-source video-amusement platform for developers to showcase their skills and to become active in an independent video-game community. The idea grew from concepts first presented at the 2010 Indie Game Jam, Winnipeg. Initial prototypes using salvaged arcade cabinets were followed by a full-production version located in a number of hospitality facilities throughout the city and constantly updated with new independent games. The company aspires to have cabinets in Vancouver, Seattle and even Brazil.

The more traditional free-to-play model is also being applied in retail-tainment applications of DOE systems. It is difficult to monetize such systems as interactive floor projection systems or touchscreen devices, so the application of a free-to-play approach using venue and sponsor advertising has become the norm. Where the in-home console-game industry has found it difficult to create viable revenue from in-game advertising, the digital out-of-home (DOOH) advertising sector has turned to gamification as a means to gather 'eyes-on-screen' metrics to evaluate effectiveness.

Apart from the difficulties of self-operation and the demands of the Western video-amusement trade for connectivity, developers have managed to monetize their games. One of the leading lights of a connected future in the North American sector is developer and manufacturer Incredible Technologies. The company is famous for their social golf video-game series, 'Golden Tee'. First launched in 1989, the track-ball controlled game established its popularity in taverns and sports-bars, in part by the inclusion of a lucrative competition element. 'Golden Tee LIVE', launched in 2005, marked the creation of a networked tournament infrastructure, allowing players to accrue points and win cash prizes. Incredible Technologies charge an additional fee for players to compete in prize tournaments, while deriving subscriptions from operators. Somewhat belatedly, the video-amusement industry discovered the concept of tournament play and connectivity as a new revenue stream to bolster its failing business model. Scott Morrison, vice president of marketing at Incredible Technologies, gave us an idea of how the company sees tournament infrastructure developing:

> *Giving the player an experience that is not readily available at home is important to the success of a commercial amusement device. The ability to win with skill is one method of achieving this goal. Because rewards are based on skill, it is a challenge to offer formats that intrigue, engage and reward players of all skill levels. IT continues to explore new ways to enhance the out-of-home entertainment experience.*

Looking towards that future, Morrison commented:

> *Our strength is with location-based entertainment, where our main focus remains. We are constantly looking at new ways to incorporate current technology and player habits into a platform or activity that engages this audience.*

Going into more detail on how Incredible Technologies has moved beyond traditional amusement into the hospitality sector, Morrison stated:

> *Certainly the longevity and consistency of 'Golden Tee Golf' and 'Silver Strike Bowling' have elevated them beyond a simple amusement device. Much like pool tables and dart boards, they have become more of an industry staple and long-term revenue source as opposed to a typical video game that requires frequent route rotation. However their main purpose is still to entertain and engage players. Since 2000 we have mailed over 1.3 million Player ID Cards. We estimate that over 1 million unique players (both registered and casual) will play at least one game this year, and 250,000 unique players play at least one game each month.*

One aspect of the Western video-amusement scene that is changing with the development of social-tainment applications is 'food-and-fun' experiences. A maturing gaming audience has allowed a new brand of hospitality venue to be developed. Nicknamed 'gamebars' or 'pinballbars', facilities that marry a bar environment with classic video-game machines have gained momentum, with a number opening in the West. They are ideally designed to make the most of the revenues available from staycationers. The mix of alcohol, entertainment, social atmosphere and the mystique of arcade gaming exposes a new audience to the allure of video-amusements, though it represents only one aspect of the resurgence of DOE, it is proving a compelling one.

The social element of DOE also includes social gaming. A key trend in the video-amusement sector is the development of social iOS game apps for public-space play. App games for online and mobile game decks condense the game experience down to a simple play experience that uses the same criteria as those that originated in the amusement sector (unsurprisingly, many classic arcade titles have been downloaded as apps in their own right).

Recently million-download social-game apps like 'Bejeweled', 'Temple Run', 'Doodle Jump' and 'Fruit Ninja' have been converted into video-games. Large flatscreen presentations and even multi-touch interfaces hope to offer a compelling new platform for these games. The simplistic game play is seen as an update of the traditional mechanical prize game: video-game apps are turned into video-redemption (videmption) games that require skill to win redeemable tickets.

Videmption is part of the profitable redemption-ticket scene that allowed the video-amusement industry to survive during the hardest of times. Redemption games offer players tickets dependent on their skill that can be redeemed for prizes at the venue. It is a derivation of the carnival pay-for-prizes element of fun and a classic element of the carny transposed into FECs, amusement and entertainment venues. The traditional games offered a simple mechanical-skill experience, and, with to the popularity of the social app games, have been updated to suit an audience that is already familiar with touchscreens and video-game narratives.

Facing an upheaval in the traditional video-amusement business, some developers have found adopting a new approach to business as impossible as continuing with the one they know, even considering adding gambling machines (video-lottery terminals and sweepstakes). At the same time, other industries are seeing the benefits of incorporating the new kinds of DOE hardware into their businesses and are also looking to steer the market toward their own needs. Avoiding the traditional video-amusement approach, they are creating brand-new breakaway business models, capable of supplying the DOE needs of the hospitality, retail and leisure sectors.

Trends

More than just trends, the new forces that are shaping the video-amusement scene are changing the perception of video amusement completely, not just reshaping the platform the players use but also redefining the business models.

PLAYER CONNECTIVITY

As seen in Japan, with networked gaming infrastructures like ALL.Net and NESiCA, adding a social element to game play is a good way of ensuring repeat visits. The development of satellite terminal games in the Japanese sector seems to be the video-amusement factories' answer to the Asian PC Bang sites (large-area networked PC-game venues), with games such as SEGA's 'Border Break' and KDE's 'Steel Chronicle' played on special networked cabinets offering multi-player action.

Internationally, the networked game experience was driven by the need for more repeat visits from audiences willing to pay for their gaming sessions. Social network technology will play a big part in this development, with mobile phone, e-payment and more and more social apps used to enhance the player's experience. Prize competitions are an important element of the modern video-amusement scene. While the at-home console sector has fixated on achievements and virtual currency, the DOE scene is able to deal in real payment for wins amongst real players, a factor in establishing its credentials with a sophisticated audience.

PHYSICAL INTERFACE

Video amusement has driven innovation in player interaction with the game environment, as all of the interfaces that have been popularized by consumer gaming originated in video-amusement. In 2001, KDE's 'Police 24/7', using their MoCap (motion capture) game system, ushered in the body-movement game experience that would later go on to be popularized by Nintendo with the Wii console in 2006.

The future of DOE will see an increase in the number of new and innovative interfaces, including greater force-feedback and gesture recognition. It should be remembered that entertainment venues offer better spaces to 'get physical' in. The aspirations of the at-home console scene to drive motion capture in games seem to have dulled, as players tire of having to avoid furniture and injury while getting physical in the conventional home.

GREATER IMMERSION

The need to break free of the restrictions of just a box and a screen has driven manufacturers to greater lengths with their dedicated video-amusement machines. As discussed elsewhere, the LBE market drove the development of individual-player capsules and pods for use in interactive networked gaming experiences. NAMCO Bandai created their own networked pod attraction to offer this compelling experience ('Mobile Suit Gundam' launched in 2006).

Many video-amusement manufacturers used theme-park attractions to populate their indoor facilities in the 1990s and re-evaluated the mixing of large amusement experiences in a small footprint. Developers in both Japan and America have designed mid-scale attractions: stand-alone enclosures that cover the same foot-print as six or eight conventional cabinets, with restricted play time.

Speculation is rife on how popular this trend will be, as the consumer-games industry has constantly thrived on originality. How the video-amusement business will manage to monetize the simple 'casual' experiences on offer from game apps is still not known.

No matter how much innovation is on show, the video-amusement trade is a shadow of its former self as a result of the much more diverse modern gaming environment, marked by a highly sophisticated audience in the majority that is now able to get their 'gaming fix' from their home game systems and mobile decks. How to turn this popularity into numbers playing in social-tainment environments is an interesting problem for the new DOE sector. But where video-amusement has focused on a 'traditional' approach to pay-to-play entertainment's loss of relevance, new technology and business approaches are emerging to feed a market hungry to play.

Chapter 3
Defining the Sector

The Immersion of Entertainment

Pay-to-view technology can be traced back to the original moving picture 'film show', the coin-operated Kinetoscope, or peephole kiosk ('What the Butler Saw'), which pre-dated motion pictures as a mall-based experience with its own arcades.

The first immersive simulator experience embraced the (then new) medium of film, such as Robert Paul's rocking movie house patented in 1895 and including such examples as a spaceship. Typically the film content for these experiences was of moving vehicles, such as a train or street car, known as a 'Phantom Ride'.

Many electric amusement venues showed 'Hale's Tour' (originated in 1905) offering an audience of 72, a simulated train trip, including painted scenery and a film backdrop. This compact attraction proved popular, with 500 installed across America by 1907.

Another example that used physical effects and a movie-picture presentation appeared in 1962, when US inventor Morton Heilig developed the Sensorama Simulator, dubbed the 'experience theater', which involved a physical experienced triggered by a special 3-D film, all housed within a prototype individual viewer. Though the concept was embryonic, it held the nub of an immersive experience.

This technology was fuelled by the multi-sensory technology revolution. The ability to use physical seat effects, triggered by a 3-D film, was developed just as digital technology became cheap and reliable enough to produce what many see as the first 4-D film, Walt Disney's 'Captain EO' in 1986.

Currently, the 4-D film experience has become the preserve not only of the large theme parks but of the new generation of entertainment venues looking to use the latest digital out-of-home technology. The popularity of 4-D film systems in the attraction and leisure sectors is partly due to the innovative experience they can offer to a large audience but also because of the physicality achieved by the effects they produce. Along with smoke and smells, lighting, vibration, tickling and even snow and bubble effects can be created in the theatre. Six-DoF (degrees of freedom) motion platforms provide a high level of immersion – achieving literally the first 'mixed reality' experiences. Borrowing from Hollywood, the latest CGI effects are available to create compelling film content. The 4-D experience is a 'passive' film experience that is competing with 'interactive' games in the public-space entertainment environment.

A distinctive aspect of 4-D installations is their ability to provide the modern 'experience theater' (ranging from two seats to thirty) in retail, leisure and visitor-attraction sites, without a specially constructed theme park. The only real requirement for these installations is a high foot-fall (throughput) to fund the investment. Known by some as mid-scale attractions, the draw of these installations is linked with their enclosures, which are 5m wide, 4m long and 3m high. This is the same size as eight deluxe amusement pieces, but the revenue generation of an eight-seat 4-D theatre is far greater than the individual pieces.

Manufacturers of 4-D and 5-D theatre can, in many cases, trace their roots back to military and commercial simulator developers. For example, Simuline Inc. is an entertainment off-shoot of the military-simulator company Darim Control Technologies. Simuline has shifted from previous alliances with amusement developers such as SEGA towards using their advantage to address cost, effectiveness and flexibility. The company has deployed their 'X-Rider' system, a 6-DoF, four-passenger enclosure (which can be scaled up to eight seats) with a 3.8m screen offering 3-D visuals supported by physical effects including wind blowers, snow and bubble effects, water sprayers and strobe lighting, across over 15-countries. Simuline's growth has mirrored that of interest in 4-D entertainment, and they recently announcing their '4D Chair' platform. In 2010, the company saw the majority of its shares acquired by Seoul based conglomerate CJ Corporation.

With extensive cinema-business holdings, including film production and the largest multiplex cinema chain in South Korea with some 680 screens, CJ Corporation's addition of Simuline to its business portfolio is the kind of move that others in this sector will soon be considering. The cinema chain is already offering guests the '4DX' cinema seat to watch certain action movies – the heave, roll and pitch of the seat following the action on screen.

Easily configurable, compact enclosures have proved popular in a number of markets, including those of Eastern Europe, Turkey and China. A number of manufacturers have gained traction in Russia, such as Total Interactive Technologies with some 200 units of their '5D Theater' system in Russia and the Commonwealth of Independent States (CIS) – a four-seat enclosure sitting in a compact envelope. Another provider is Amusement and Edutainment Technologies (AET) with their '5D Cinema AVATAR' in two- and four-seat configurations. The AET system promotes a 'Wow effect' and has been placed in high foot-traffic locations like train stations, shopping malls and leisure entertainment venues. Clearly, emerging markets represent a key audience for these DOE systems. Along with Eastern Asia, Central Europe is embracing new stand-alone attractions based on 4-D enclosures, such as 'Cinema 6D' by Italian Effeci Group and '5D Cinema' by Ferretti Industries.

Another aspect of 4-D development, beyond the smaller enclosures, is modular seating systems that can be flexibly deployed, rather than being installed in a set cinema environment, allowing the developer to create the right mix of seating to fit the venue's profile.

One of the early pioneers of the 3-D and 4-D theatre scene, SimEx Iwerks combined two legendary developers and originators of large-format attractions. In its heyday, Iwerks was famous for such innovations as 'TurboRide', a two-rider motion seat module, and envisaged offering 18-, 36- and even 50-seat motion-theatre enclosures. Along with the seat system, the company has their own cabin and open-motion platform theatre systems – products like the 'Atlas' can accommodate 300 riders an hour.

In 1993, Iwerks Entertainment broadened their investment into motion-simulator systems, large-format 3-D films and 4-D experiences, with a plan to develop interactive systems for the location-based entertainment sector. The first interactive concept developed was 'Virtual Adventurers', providing a network of up to four six-player vehicles, each with their own control device. The first adventure was 'The Loch Ness Expedition' and the vehicle was arranged as a submarine. Production prototypes of 'Virtual Adventures' were installed at the Nauticus Maritime Museum in 1994 and at the Foxwoods Resort Casino in 1995.

The authors were able to speak with one of those at the heart of 'Virtual Adventures'. Michael Haimson, was product manager for interactive attractions at Iwerks Entertainment. Asked what the important aspects of the 'Virtual Adventures' design were, Haimson commented:

> *Each of the six players had their own unique user interface that impacted the virtual world that they were in. There were no passengers. The vehicle was designed to be generic. It could have been a submarine, a boat, a spaceship, a land rover, etc. Theoretically, multiple adventures could be made available during a single day with a simple software change. The seats were arranged so that a family group of 2 or 3 could sit adjacent and share tasks within the experience.*

It was known that Iwerks had negotiated with Twentieth Century Fox to license the 1986 sci-fi film *Aliens*, to be developed as a possible second adventure for the platform, although internal difficulties at Iwerks and eventual delisting from Nasdaq, put paid to 'Virtual Adventures'.

Regarding the demise of the project, and the collateral damage, Haimson said:

> *The development budget is not that important. But the high product cost made the business model work only in installations with fairly high and fairly consistent traffic – even during the weekdays. The main product cost was the very expensive image generators that were required. Although the product cost was on par with roller coasters at about the same throughput, the experience was not considered the same enjoyment level. This made it a hard sell for high-end family entertainment centers with primarily weekend traffic and also for amusement parks that use their main attraction budget for roller coasters as anchor attractions.*

He went on to say:

> *While the cost issues were a significant hurdle, I feel the biggest lesson learned is that the quality of the experience was quite dependent on the enthusiasm and interpersonal dynamics of the ad hoc six-person team in each of the four vehicles in an adventure. Since most family groups visiting attractions are either 2, 3, or 4 persons, the vehicle would almost always have strangers sitting together. And the dynamics of strangers varies widely based on the culture with which the people were raised. We actually discovered that having an employee in the vehicle to help and encourage the players made a huge positive difference – but also at some extra operations cost.*

The ability to offer a flexible but also reliable 4-D system for the widest variety of facilities drives many of the leading developers in this sector.

MediaMation is a leading supplier of effects (EFX) theatre systems. The company works for major attractions that use their 'X4D' motion-effects system, supported by special physical-effect systems linked to the film content. The company provides a package that can be placed in theme parks, museums, science centres and attractions worldwide.

We asked Dan Jamele, vice president and chief technology officer at MediaMation for his opinion on the market:

> *The 4-D theatre market is still a growing and expanding venture that provides an experience unattainable at home. Its combination of high throughput, fast ROI [return on investment], and ever changing content options makes 4-D a very desirable addition to parks, fun centres, and other entertainment venues.*

Regarding the elements shaping the market, he stated:

> *Really, the growth we have been experiencing comes from our long track record. We have been working with simulators for over 21 years now and have seen trends come and go. We took the best elements from all the various projects and systems we have been involved in and have successfully combined them into a product line that serves customers with a wide range of needs, budget, and goals. Key to this is, of course, our full digital servo motion systems that set our products apart and allow us to produce a truly entertaining experience in a 4-D setting.*

When asked if there was a shortage of 4-D film content to feed this emerging market, Dan stated:

> *That is a tricky question. Certainly there are some really good films out there. However, they don't always lend themselves to a 4-D experience as much as they are simply entertaining short films. The result is that at times, people are simply adding some effects to a movie that don't make a lot of sense. Similar to 3-D movies that came out and some were just bad 3-D used for effect only. For us, a good 4-D movie needs to combine a story, great motion action scenes, and logical 4-D effects so the effect adds to the movie, rather than seeming 'forced' or just a 'gag'. So, to answer your question, I would say that there is a limited number of really good ride or attraction films that work really well with 4-D motion theatres. I have seen a lot of really bad and cheap films, as well as good ones, but finding that balance*

> *between a good film, and the proper budget to produce and still not price it out of the range of many theatres is a difficult task for the film producers. Hopefully, as costs to create CGI and 3-D continue to drop, we will see more quality content at prices that work for a majority of attractions.*

Concerning the question of oversaturation of 4-D systems in the market, Dan commented:

> *Certainly, We've found that. Just look at the number of companies displaying 4-D options at the 2012 IAAPA show [International Association of Amusement Parks and Attractions, the leading international trade show for the theme-park and attractions industry]. The trick, as always, is to distinguish yourself with quality, experience, service and price. However, for the general public, good 4-D motion theatres are still a unique experience and draw crowds. Coupled with a good movie and the proper venue, I think the future is still very strong for 4-D theatres.*

Concerning the shifts in the market following the introduction of interactivity, he stated:

> *Yes. It's still new and at present has been relegated to 'shooting gallery' type interaction. But similar to traditional movie theatres, there is a majority of people that simply want to be entertained and that will still be the driving force in the market for a while (non-interactive). As the interactive part becomes more organic to the movie and process, I think that we will see more and more of it.*

The ability to offer a recognizable attraction that generates a large throughput, whilst also being cost effective and reliable is the aim of the new generation of 4-D theatre developers. One example is Kraftwerk Living Technologies GmbH, which developed such next-generation attractions as 'Marvel Superheroes 4D' located in London's Madame Tussauds. But beyond 4-D theatre and mid-scale enclosures, Kraftwerk has championed the digital-dome concept: using planetariums supplied with new content to give what the company calls 'fulldome' experiences.

Re-proposition of existing installations ('retro-fitting') is an aspect of many of Kraftwerk's attractions: for example, they incorporated the latest technology in the new attraction 'Arthur 4D/5D' at Futuroscope in France. In this case, the term 5-D is used to define the motion-seat component of the 4-D experience. Fully configurable motion seating (5-D seats) and in-seat effects provide the audience with a very immersive experience.

Not all applications of 4-D have individual-effects seats in an auditorium or enclosure. One of the first developers of entertainment simulation experiences in the public sector is also one of the oldest developers of a cabin-based approach: Doron Precision Systems launched their first entertainment simulator (the 'SR-2' system) in 1977, offering 12-bench seating and a 16mm-film presentation in a motion-based enclosed cabin, which became a stalwart at county fairs and carnivals.

Doron has extensive interests in simulator vehicle training, including for law enforcement personnel – the entertainment division continues to represent a fraction of the company's key business. Since the 'SR-2', Doron has developed the 'Transport 6', as the name suggests, a modern six-seat version of the enclosed cabin theatre and motion platform, offering a varied library of motion-ride experiences for a diverse audience at many venues, ranging from museums to shopping malls. Along with the cabin-based systems, Doron developed 'Doron Active Theater', an enclosed 4-D theatre system.

Another corporation with both a background in commercial simulation and links to the first successful theme-park motion-simulation attraction is Walt Disney. 'Star Tours' was launched in late 1987 within the Walt Disney Theme Park operation, based on a commercial simulator motion base with a cabin theatre mounted on top (based on the original 'Tour of the Universe' attraction of 1984). This led to the 'SR-2's success in the multi-million-dollar e-ticket attraction market. From this point, developers with links to the original 'Star Tours' attraction strove to create a less expensive version.

From this development background, the UK company Simworx emerged with a dedicated selection of entertainment simulation systems. The company's 'Stargazer' combines seven seats placed on an open-motion platform, deployed in theme parks, museums and science centres. The company has also developed their 'Dimension 5D' – motion seats with a vast array of different 4-D effects, suitable for a variety of locations. Simworx has emerged as a defining force in the next generation of 4-D, with over 180 systems in the field.

We asked Terry Monkton, managing director of Simworx, what the key elements shaping the company's development were. He commented:

> *Constantly keeping technology up to date, in particular AV [augmented reality] systems, and, in addition to offering turnkey solutions, also providing custom attractions as and where necessary. New film content is also key, and we are fortunate to partner with first class film producers that continually introduce new films in the market place.*

Regarding the likely key elements of future business, Monkton observed:

> *Undoubtedly, one of the key factors is constant technical development. The sector moves fast, and it is important to have a cycle of new product offerings every few years or so. In addition to 4-D theatres, we offer a range of dynamic simulation attractions, and have embraced dark-ride technology which gives us a position with clients in that we can be flexible to their needs now and in the future. We have a new large-scale simulation product, totally unique to the industry which has been developed and manufactured.*

It was revealed that Simworx's new projects were being introduced in mid-2013 with a first installation and a launch of a new product to the industry scheduled for IAAPA that year.

One aspect of the growth of 4-D has been the ability to call upon strong ride-film content. In the early years of the sector's growth, the film content was live-action and offered extreme scenarios, but with the advancements of digital 3-D modelling and live action, it has been replaced by a greater level of sophisticated 3-D rendered films. The CGI that has revolutionized special-effects in film and TV has also fed the hunger of numerous independent studios for 4-D theatre.

The circulation of content has seen specialist 3-D and 4-D content providers, such as nWave Pictures who developed CGI for TV commercials, migrate into making full-length films and 4-D film experiences. Other companies like UK-based TheJuice are also leading the charge to offer stand-alone attractions a wide selection of content, not only their own but also from other new animation studios.

The move towards interactive theatre has led to the integration of amusement gaming, themed attractions and stand-alone operation. Combined into a easily marketed package with the highest possible return on investment and a recurring investment path, interactive content is able to generate repeat visits with a simple swap-out at the click of a mouse.

The amusement scene has been the instigator of many of the innovative applications now gaining in popularity. SEGA, in partnership with motion-platform developer MOOG, created an interactive capsule attraction, the 'AS-1' (Advance Simulator-1), in 1993. It was an eight-rider cabin simulator including a unique game element: each rider had a trigger grip to interact with the game and drive the narrative. The concept opened the door to the idea of audience-based interactivity. One of the interactive rides launched on the 'AS-1' platform was 'Michael Jackson: Scramble Training', continuing the singer's affinity with entertainment technology innovation, since his 1986 involvement with Walt Disney's 'Captain EO'.

Triotech, a Canadian corporation with a background in innovation, has become one of the leading developers in the field. Originally, the company focused on video-amusements, developing a number of innovative arcade titles, before turning to mid-scale attractions, launching first their 'XD Theater' accommodating four to thirty visitors and incorporating the unique motion seat (using motion actuation by manufacturer D-BOX Technologies).

Having established a compelling stand-alone 4-D theatre environment, the company went to the next level, creating an interactive version of their enclosure system. Under the 'XD-Dark Ride' brand, the company offers an audience-based shooting-game experience within a stand-alone package. Players are encouraged to compete, with high-scorers picked out during the game and offered a unique keepsake of their success, similar to the ride pictures captured on roller-coasters.

The need to bring a high level of immersion and entertainment to a digitally sophisticated audience has shaped new developments in the traditional attraction sector. Where the extreme rides have attempted to become more extreme, the more conventional attractions have started to embrace interactivity to establish a more compelling experience and generate repeat visits as players strive to get higher and higher scores.

The dark-ride genre unites elements of traditional attractions with the latest in interactive entertainment. The dark-ride, haunted-house or ghost-train attraction is a stalwart of the carnival and funfair. Moving audiences through scenarios in vehicles has proved a long-lived and reliable attraction.

It originated with the successful walk-through 'Noah's Ark' and evolved into the 'Amusement Railway', a dark-ride vehicle system first patented in 1929.

The dark-ride achieved more prominent success when Disneyland opened 'It's a Small World', highly colourful animatronic (animated mechanical/ electrical) characters in themed environments that the audience travelled through in a boat. The attraction – like a lot of the original Disneyland concept – was developed for the 1964 New York World's Fair and was capable of handling a large throughput of visitors and offered an original application of traditional fairground attractions. It was based on Disneyland's 'Snow White and the Seven Dwarfs', a track-based dark ride developed by WED (Walt Elias Disney) Enterprises in 1955.

Dark rides grew in popularity. One of the leaders in developing a wide variety of themed dark rides became Sally Corporation. Founded in 1977, the corporation specializes in both the animatronics to populate the environments, as well as the vehicles and themed environments. One of the visionaries behind the dark-ride business, John Wood, chairman and CEO of Sally stated:

> *Sally Corporation pioneered the development of the interactive dark ride. We first introduced the concept with 'Ghost Busters' the dark ride back in 1986. With the development of the relatively simple and inexpensive black light attractions like 'Ghost Blasters', 'Scooby Doo' and the 'Great Pistolero Round Up' we made it affordable for both the small and the larger parks. At present, we have over 50 interactive dark rides out and operating.*

Regarding DOE, he says:

> *I think it will be vitally important for the future dark rides. Adding a game feature to ride and park experiences is happening regularly now, and digital media allows for amusement park attractions to become much more competitive and exciting.*

Over a period of time, a 'shooting gallery' element was added to the dark ride, and it was only a matter of time before the attraction went digital. Sally are working on their own digital interactive approach with their 'VIPER SixD' demonstrator that was presented to the amusement trade at their popular conferences.

Wood went on to say:

> *We at Sally have been interested in putting 3-D video into dark rides for over 20 years but, when Alterface came out with video interactivity and Disney came out with 'Toy Story: Midway Mania!' we began investigating digital interactivity more earnestly.*

Reflecting on the new digital applications, he commented:

> *Trends in the immersive themed experiences are often stimulated by Disney and Universal. The industry pays close attention to the trend setting attractions they develop and often strive to create similar ones in their parks.*

Again, following big e-ticket attraction success ('Men in Black: Alien Attack' and 'Toy Story: Midway Mania!'), the ability to offer an interactive attraction with a high throughput of visitors that can fit into a variety of floor spaces generated a resurgence of interest in the technology. One of the developers of interactive dark rides (iDR) has been Belgium-based Alterface. All their attractions unite digital game screens with interactive theatrical effects, using the company's 'CinemAtion' architecture, such as the 'Kingdom Quest' iDR at Legoland Discovery Center Dallas. The technology took one step further in using autonomous vehicles to transport the players (developed by ETF Ride Systems and their 'Multi-Mover' trackless dark-ride system).

To take advantage of the popularity of the iDR genre and the possibility of installing it in a wide range of facilities, specialist developers have come together to offer a single source for the innovative technology. Sally announced their partnership with Alterface in order to establish the next-generation of iDR systems, and, already, work has started on their next 3-D attraction 'Justice League: Alien Invasion 3D' for Warner Bros. Movie World. Commenting on the affiliation, John Wood noted: 'Alterface's vast experience with interactive video has allowed us to transition from tangible environmental experiences into virtual experiences without a tremendous research and development expenditure.'

Through another marriage of convenience, Triotech has built on their success with the 'XD Theater' business and turned their interactive multi-player technology towards iDR. With this move, they have announced a partnership with Zamperla, the legendary Italian attraction designer and manufacturer, and are working closely with the company on the new generation of iDR installations for a variety of facilities, from theme parks to large retail attractions.

Speaking with Gabi Salabi, vice president of sales and business development at Triotech, we asked if he felt this new generation of development in the market was important:

> *Absolutely. The iDR will become one of the anchor and featured attractions in major leisure centres. It delivers a very rich and multi-dimensional experience that differentiates itself from other traditional rides.*

Concerning the diversity of venues that are considering IDR, Salabi commented:

> *They will vary mainly from larger FEC brands to amusement parks. Ultimately, the investment decision will depend on three main criteria: the client's budget, space constraints and the daily capacity they are seeking.*

Regarding the key elements Triotech brings to the Zamperla relationship, Salabi stated:

> *We are excited about our partnership because it brings together two companies with complementary experience and knowhow. Our competitive edge is our real-time, interactive technology and licensed content. On the other hand, Zamperla has a tremendous heritage and expertise in building innovative and reliable ride equipment.*

With this new relationship in mind, Salabi was asked what technologies are being considered for the future application:

> *We are working on some very exciting new products that will really attract the attention of such institutions as science centres and museums. We want to keep innovating and pushing the envelope in all areas of out of home interactive entertainment. It's still too early to let the cat out of the bag!*

Other developers joining forces to capitalize in this sector include De Pinxi, with an extensive background since 1991 in creating interactive experiences in leisure and education, who have announced a partnership with Lagotronics, a designer and manufacturer of a unique modular system for dark rides.

The two companies are working on iDRs with a combination of (3-D) virtual and actual targets in one ride. Both pedestrian and vehicle dark rides are linked to a social network infrastructure, supporting real-time video captures and integration with Facebook.

Chinese companies have also looked at iDR as a new area of business. Playfun Culture and Technology are proposing to build what they call a '4-D dark ride', a 5,000m^2 iDR with six screens, animatronics and a 370m track with a unique 180°-rotational eight-person vehicle. Other developers have also been researching their own iDRs.

IDRs also have many advantages for operators: they can be produced in a range of sizes and can accommodate high audience throughput; they offer a repeat-play element, as guests try to beat their previous scores, and their interactivity provides a different experience every time; and old games can be swapped out at the click of a mouse and updated with the next release.

The Trends

As a progression from 4-D, many have called this new sector 5-D, 7-D or even X-D. Full-motion interactivity and physical effects have been seen as the defining features of the multi-sensory technology revolution in entertainment. Developers are focusing on other sensory effects for the audience. AR is one such development, a superimposed 'heads up display' for use in a number of games, such as driving games with a shooting component.

Interacting with the audience through sensory effects has a long tradition, such as the 'Scratch & Sniff' (Smell-O-Vision) of the 1960s. The use of special scent distributors within the theatre during 4-D experiences is best illustrated by the use of such effects in the edutainment 4-D experience at the London Science Museum ('Legend of Apollo 4-D'). More advanced olfactory dispersal systems are in development, and it is expected that unique individual dispensers will be more widely used in 4-D experiences, including in smaller enclosures.

How the audiences view the visuals is another concern for manufacturers of 4-D systems. From the crude cardboard red-and-green 3-D glasses of the 1950s to the latest RealD lightweight polarized glasses, developers have striven to offer stereoscopic representation of the images on screen without encumbering the viewer. James Cameron, writer and director of the 3-D movie *Avatar* (2009), has already been linked to claims that the planned sequel will be screened using a glasses-free 3-D system (nicknamed 'Free-D'). The entertainment theatre scene is working on their own version.

Providing each member of the audience with their own personal viewer or screen has also been considered. In the late 1990s, Ham on Rye Technologies (discussed below) developed a head-mounted-display (HMD) virtual-reality (VR) technology. Their theatre system mixed live performance with a ride. As HMD technology has advanced, the possibility of personal viewers has re-surfaced. Aardvark Applications have developed their 'Immersa-Dome', a hemispherical display in front of the viewer integrated with a seat that produces vibration effects.

Sensory technology is also contributing to the latest generation of theatre systems. As well as personal visuals and audio, audience members can also experience virtual motion. Galvanic vestibular stimulation, as provided by the experimental motion-sensation helmet from the University of New South Wales and other researchers, induces the perception of motion by manipulating the liquids and hairs within the inner ear (the vestibular organs). Although this is still in its infancy, it is not hard to imagine an all-encompassing visual, audio and motion system. The savings made by doing away with the expensive motion platform could totally change the 4-D experience.

But the future of immersive experience theatre lies far beyond passive experiences, as demonstrated by iDR. Adding a game element to the experience makes repeat visits more likely and monetization easier.

Entertainment's Retail Dimension

Locating games so that they attract the largest throughput of players is a concern for all game operators. One aspect of the coin-operated-amusement sector since its heyday of the 1930s was the placement of mechanical gaming machines in taverns and bars in the civilian sector, as well as on army bases, such as Post Exchange (PX), and bars, during the inter-war years.

Retail – and in-particular hospitality (restaurants, bars, hotels/motels and resorts) – has proved capable of deriving a useful secondary revenue stream from video games, by tapping into the audience already circulating within their venues. Video-games were initially seen as impulse-play opportunities. It was only after the placement of the first successful video-amusement system ('Pong') in Andy Capp's Tavern in South California that their true value was realized. The first fault-report to Atari from the tavern revealed an improvised cashbox had overflowed and was jamming the machine and has gone down in folklore as testament to the arrival of the video-game market.

At the pinnacle of video amusement, empty retail units were improvised into video-game rooms: colloquialized as 'arcades'. Shopping malls in the 1980s were populated with dark sticky floored temples to the glowing black boxes of the video game. Games also found homes in convenience stores, cinema foyers and transport terminuses, sucking the coins out of the pockets of youths addicted to the latest arcade masterpiece. But with waning popularity, video amusements were side-lined to a secondary revenue stream for FECs, hotels, bars and leisure locations.

To address this decline, attempts were made in the 1990s to build on the growth in CGI, immersive technology and gaming experience to increase the appeal of video-amusements. What became known as location-based entertainment (LBE) venues were inspired by an explosion in computer-simulation technology driven by the need for new military simulations fuelled by the Cold War. Simulator networking (SIMNET) trainers were the first practical man-in-the-loop team-mission rehearsal trainers, used at centres such as the US Army Armor School (USAARMS) multi-component training brigade, with their M1/M1A1 Abrams crew-training systems. These M1 and M2 SIMNET modules offered an innovative and cost-effective large-scale and real-time networked simulation platform to train crews, especially in the requirements of the modern close-combat combined-forces battlefield.

The computer entertainment scene also embraced the simulation experience, especially the uniquely immersive nature of the technology. One of the very first out-of-home applications of simulation technology united the themed environment of the laser-tag venue, a board-game level of sci-fi narrative and a simulation network within cut-down modules (reminiscent of the M1 SIMNET units). Launched in 1990, the BattleTech Center offered between 16 and 32 pods for players to do battle in a virtual environment, piloting giant virtual Mech's (robotic battle machines). This would become the model for all sim-centers: players paid their entrance fee, booked their pod and received a tutorial and mission briefing. They would then be taken to their pods and compete in a networked environment. Afterwards they would receive a mission review on a monitor and a mission log sheet to take away. In 1994, Virtual World Entertainment (VWE) developed a SiteLink service that allowed competition between sites all over the country.

VWE had over 30 sites installed across the globe with success following. It was reported that the Yokahama BattleTech Center sold 30,000 tickets in its first month of operation. *Wired* reported that the average player was 24½ years old. The modules evolved into sophisticated 2.7m long capsules, with immersive wide-angle collimated (WAC) display, military-style instrumentation CRTs and advance CGI, known as 'Tesla' cockpits, designed by FROG in 1995. Perceived as the fourth generation of the simulation entertainment, the system managed without expensive CGI hardware, as the Tesla used an innovative new PC graphics-accelerator board (Pixel-Planes) from UK developer Division Limited.

In a rare interview with the visionary behind BattleTech and the VWE empire, the authors spoke with Jordan Wiseman, founder of the role-playing-game publisher FASA Corporation, whose off-shoot Environmental Simulation Projects would go on to become VWE. Asked if the detailed BattleTech universe (through books and board games) defined the LBE approach taken at the beginning, Wiseman stated:

> *No. My original approach in 1980 was that the players would all man stations on the bridge of a starship, and thus it was a co-operative game. A couple of years later I showed these designs to Paramount who I had a good relationship with due to the 'Star Trek' roleplaying game that I had designed and published and they were very supportive of my building it using their brand. As I got further into design and the years rolled by I realized that the common space and interdependences of the players would be very intimidating for strangers and thus changed the design so that each player piloted their own ship. When we were finally able to fund the hardware and software development it was due to the success of the Battletech board game and thus I figured it was best to build on that success.*

Asked about the influences behind the original concept and how much SIMNET influenced the first approach to Battletech Centers, Wiseman replied:

> *None. When we started the Battletech Center development in 1987 SIMNET was not known or maybe not even started yet. Later, I think in 1991 or so we worked with a major military contractor who was bidding on the CCTT project who reached out to us because or tech/ solutions were a fraction of the cost of what Simnet had done.*

Wiseman was asked what had made them go to FROG to create the Teslar:

They were the hot design studio at the time and Tim Disney [director of VWE and grandnephew of Walt Disney] really wanted to work with them. They came up with great conceptual sketches, but didn't add much value in how to merge the realities of the game tech and manufacturing costs so we ended up doing all the real industrial design work ourselves.

Regarding what fundamentally hindered the deployment of the VWE concept, which only ever reached about 30 sites, Wiseman observed:

There are a couple of factors. The first Battletech Center was small (5,000-ish sq. ft.), cheap to build, and could be operated by one employee when at low throughput. This made the centre continually profitable to operate, but as we rolled out the Virtual World Centers they became more elaborate and thus more expensive to build and operate. In the first year of operations, the centres were always wonderful, but after the novelty wore off and we dropped to the steady state level, many of them were not profitable. Another key factor affecting our operations was my insistence on always improving our tech and experience, because I was looking to stay ahead of competition that only really existed in my head. Our experience was so far above anything else at the time that we should have concentrated on developing more games for the existing tech rather than constantly reinvesting in the same games on new tech.

On whether the LBE approach championed by VWE could rise again as part of the new DOE approach, he stated:

I believe that there is nothing on the planet more entertaining than other people. We are social animals with millions of years of evolution providing us much more social information that can be conveyed in person then can be sent across the internet, so we will always congregate in physical spaces. We also love immersion into situations and worlds that take us away from ours and what LBE was always about was combining these two primal human needs. And so yes I think that the opportunity exists for new forms of digital LBE to be successful.

He concluded:

People have no need to travel to a location for processing power, as their homes and pockets are now populated with supercomputers. But people will travel for personal social interaction and physicality, and

> *thus what excites me are concepts which capitalize on the computing power that consumers already have in social and immersive settings.*

It was the physicality of the experience that fired many to emulate the environment created by BattleTech.

Wiseman was reported as having said in 1992 that with VWE 'our goal is to create a legitimate entertainment format'. An explosion in the development of LBE facilities seemed to vindicate this: CGI hardware developers working with theming and game experiences, hoping to copy the format. Military image-generator (IG) manufacturer Evans & Sutherland (one of the first computer-graphics companies) were one of the first at the time to sense the downturn in defence-industry spending and attempt to diversify its experience in virtual-world rendering, hoping its vastly expensive IG hardware could be camouflaged in the development costs of planned LBE sites. One of the first high-profile and sudden failures, supported by E&S in 1992, was Lucasfilms division Rebel Arts's attempt to create a retail project based on the Star Wars universe with networked two-player 'Mirage' capsules. The project (under 'the ultimate reality' tag) never got past the prototype stage, foundering under astronomical cost ($500,000 for the IG alone), although parts of the wreckage would be recycled in a later amusement collaboration between SEGA and Lucas (the 'Star Wars Arcade' simulator in 1993).

Another concept using E&S's 'Extra Reality' was the 4-D cinema corporation Iwerks Entertainment's six-player 'Virtual Adventures' system (four network pods for a planned 24-player experience), part of the planned, 5,500m^2 Cinetropolis entertainment venue with Foxwoods Resort Casino. But again the concept fell at the first fence.

Evans & Sutherland continued its move from military simulation to virtual entertainment following the failure of 'Virtual Adventures' with a totally original concept. The company created a hang-glider simulator of their own called 'VirtualGlider': the pilot lay prone with their head in front of a special screen representing the virtual environment and piloted using special controls. By 1997, the company had sold some 22 units in North America, Europe and even Hong Kong. But E&S would eventually remove themselves from the DOE scene as their expensive hardware was superseded (while retaining a stake in edutainment through their original planetarium business).

Commercial high-performance-computer manufacturer Silicon Graphics Inc. introduced the 'Magic Edge' concept along with a number of other applications at that time. 'Magic Edge' was a jet-flight simulator with special motion capsules: twelve 'Hornet' simulators competed in networked air combat. The first site opened in 1994, and a special partnership with amusement giant NAMCO led to sites in Southern California, Japan and Australia, but a mixture of complicated business model, expensive and temperamental hardware and bad management led to its demise.

NAMCO's investment in LBE was to bolster the interactive element of their planned entertainment-venue empire. In 1992, they developed their own amusement theme park (ATP) called NAMCO WonderEggs, a mix of indoor theme park and upscale amusement arcade. Many of the attractions were originally developed for Osaka Expo '90 (re-launched three times in Futakotamagawa, Tokyo). Other Japanese video-amusement factories would undertake development of their own flagship ATPs, but it would be SEGA Amusement who would manage to establish a chain of venues under the Joypolis brand in 1994.

Described as 'theme parks in a box', ATPs blossomed under SEGA's stewardship, and the company eventually opened six Japanese sites and went on to build more in England and Australia. However, it was the introduction of the ATP concept into America (as department-store-sized entertainment venues) that produced a feasible entertainment venue within the retail environment. SEGA partnered DreamWorks and Universal Studios to create the SEGA Gameworks chain of venues.

SEGA Gameworks borrowed heavily from other LBEs at the time, such as Canada-based Playdium Entertainment. A few of the original Joypolis mid-scale attractions were re-engineered to suit Western audiences. Gameworks commandeered a Universal Studios sound-stage and transformed it into a model of the envisaged concept, inviting Hollywood luminaries and entrepreneurs to offer their opinions. Once stabilized, the Western concept would lead to 17 Gameworks across the USA, although the hoped-for 30 sites never materialized, and the operation collapsed in 2004. The wreckage was acquired by a management buy-out company with no links to the original creators.

Having failed to find a means to partner SEGA in importing the Joypolis concept into American, the largest entertainment corporation, Walt Disney Company, undertook its own plans to develop an ATP concept called DisneyQuest. Disney's 'Imagineering Division' commissioned immersive interactive attractions for their target audience. They experimented with

AR, VR and immersive displays for facilities they hoped to establish in major cities all over the planet, but further work was halted after the first facility in Orlando (1998) and the second site in Chicago (1999) were weighed down by their exorbitant costs. However, the original Orlando facility is still open (one of the longest running LBE venues).

Joe DiNunzio, previously senior vice president of new product development at Walt Disney Imagineering commented on what he felt was the fundamental reason why SEGA and Disney could not work together on a US Joypolis: 'Most directly, both companies saw a significant market opportunity that they wanted to exploit on their own.' Regarding why the largest entertainment company could not strike the right formula and get it to work, he added:

> *I don't believe there is one answer to this question, as it was complicated, and I am sure different people involved would give you different answers. The first factor in my mind would be the fact that after the launch there were a number of changes in the parent company and the market that altered the calculus on investment in the business, including the appetite for risk and the patience for return on capital.*

Looking at what DisneyQuest achieved and speaking of the aspects from the project relevant in today's market, DiNunzio postulated:

> *There are many, but three that I would focus on are the WDI team's incredible ability to (1) create co-operative and immersive digital experiences that are shared by multiple players in real time and space – as exemplified by 'Pirates of the Caribbean'; (2) focus on compelling gameplay at the core of the experience, regardless of the technology being used – as exemplified by 'Lost Treasure of the Incas'; and (3) conceive of experiences that take traditional rides and make them interactive and personal – as exemplified by 'Cyberspace Mountain'. The knowledge gained from creating DisneyQuest has been incorporated into Disney's next generation of theme park experiences all over the world.*

Regarding the projects he undertook after leaving Disney, DiNunzio still found DOE relevant to his new endeavours:

Across our work as entrepreneurs and consultants we are finding new and ever more compelling ways to connect people by combining digital technology with physical places.

Numerous projects have been attempted to create a profitable ATP concept for the Western sector. SONY Entertainment invested in a plan to build 100 facilities, creating a SONY LBE division to develop the Metreon site. The first opened in San Francisco in 1999, and another two sites in Germany and Japan were created, but the concept was abandoned. Other corporations in the entertainment sector viewed LBE as a means to attract repeat visitors through gaming experiences: Q-City (Q-ZAR), BlockParty (Blockbusters Entertainment), StarPort (United Artists Theaters) and Funscape (Regal Cinemas) are just some of the failed concepts. This high rate of attrition would sour interest in ATP and LBE projects for some time.

While some corporations aimed to attract new audiences and promote their brand through locations with themed entertainment attractions, the immersive entertainment simulation came full circle, as companies were hired by the very military that had spawned the technology. The US Army created the Virtual Army Experience (VAE) (also called the Army Experience Center). Originally developed as a travelling inflatable space comprising numerous entertainment simulators depicting stylized combat roles, a $9m permanent location covering 1,300m^2 was opened in Philadelphia in 2008, acting as a recruiting sergeant for an audience immersed in entertainment simulation.

The marriage of military simulation with entertainment experience continued in the establishment of the location-themed retail entertainment unit. One of the earliest applications was modelled directly on another aspect of the SIMNET infrastructure: the simulation experience created for fighter pilots. Fightertown USA was developed by Kenny Aero in 1992, and, like the military air base it was located next to in Forest Lake, California, it offered air combat simulation. Although on a greatly reduced scale, the simulation was very authentic for the time.

Many commercial and defence training corporations were enticed by the opportunity to 'beat their swords into plough shares' with the early 1990s downturn in defence spending after the end of the Cold War. As mentioned regarding IG developers, a number of commercial simulator manufacturers turned to entertainment. Veda Incorporated took their full-G bias-motion-base technology used in jet-flight simulation and turned it into an extreme entertainment application creating Chameleon Technologies for the project. They launched the 'Chameleon' in 1994, a entertainment system with six enclosed pods rotating round a central hub, each pod able to pitch and dive to create elevated g-forces, the two players in each pod steering and shooting and all six pods networked in an interactive game.

A mobile virtual reality entertainment (VRE or VE) with a $2.4m price tag including $400,000 for the IG alone, the 'Chameleon' was presented as the 'ultimate video game' and obtained a high-profile installation at Six Flags Over Texas amusement park in 1995. But its incredibly high price tag and complicated hardware lead to only a few installations, although the platform would affect the growth of the LBE approach, muddying the waters regarding the best business model for this entertainment environment. Though Veda would leave the market eventually, the centrifugal approach would be emulated by others, including Walt Disney.

Likewise, the more authentic simulation experience has found a home in the themed venue sector. Beyond the military, the simulation of motor sport offered a rich vein for LBE. One of the innovators of the concept was Silicon Motor Speedway (SMS), a company that began by taking the arcade game 'Hard Drivin' from Atari in 1988 and developing it into a trainer simulator for law-enforcement personnel. From this, a breakaway company developed a NASCAR racing simulator. Using a two-player full-motion racing-car simulator, the company would go on to open over 10 facilities in North America. But eventually a lack of software updates and working capital forced the operation to close.

We asked Bill Donaldson, president of Race Cars USA, LLC, a company that has emerged from SMS, about the demise of the first attempt. He stated:

> *The Silicon Motor Speedway product was actually quite remarkable and far ahead of its time. The patented hydraulic platform and the customized features for the retail market were far ahead of any competition. However, the main drawback was that the experience was limited to NASCAR race cars and 6 oval race tracks, and the company was never in a financial condition to be able to continue to create and offer new tracks, cars and game features to sustain their thousands of customers over the long term. The result was a declining revenue model*

> *year after year, and with mall leases and labour costs increasing each year the end result was accumulated debt.*

Asked about the new approach, Donaldson revealed:

> *The Race Cars USA business model today differs primarily in three areas: (a) the vast amount of content that we can now offer to the customer (wide variety of race tracks, race cars and game features) as a result of the new software interface technology that we recently developed: (b) the high resolution graphics within the software matched with HDMI [high-definition multimedia interface] projection or screens allows our product to be current with today's high definition standards for computer graphics; and (c) the capability of racing online with other racing centres across the country or in international markets allows for our customers to be able to compete against a large field of competitors as opposed to only ten or twelve that can physically meet at one racing centre at a given time.*

Giving a perception of the modern market, Donaldson commented:

> *The challenge for the LBE market today is offering an interactive product in the out-of-home space that is difficult if not impossible to achieve within the home market using a PC or console. We believe Race Cars USA has such a product as the cost and space requirements make installing one or more of our simulators prohibitive for the vast majority of the home market. An attraction such as ours will push consumers out of the home to a virtual racing centre for an experience that is impossible for most to achieve at home.*

Commenting on the new technology shaping this sector, he said:

> *I would not suggest any particular technology is vital to the sector, but I will say that the continuing technological advances and downward curve on pricing is important to allowing the LBE products to compete with home products.*

Many of the attractions that originated in the Japanese ATP sector are now receiving reinterpretation.

While this account of the LBE sector may read like a litany of failure, interactive, networked, immersive experiences have continued to draw interest from players. However, the initial expense of the technology necessary to supply them has stymied all attempts to develop a workable business model until recently.

Simulation Centres: Next Generation

As the Cold War brought simulation technology within reach of commercial entertainment developers, the success of the at-home console-games industry produced cheaper CGI technology and games content that could be used in future immersive simulator experiences. While the military-simulation sector fuelled LBE's emergence, the commercial-simulation industry still had a part to play, in particular the professional motor-sports industry and its growing dependence on highly realistic racing-vehicle simulators (both open- and closed-wheel racing cars). Cruden BV, a developer of motor-sports motion simulators with a background in military simulation, has adopted its platforms to the entertainment market, including one for the I-WAY simulator centre in Lyon, France. Opened in 2008, the venue offers a VIP-club environment for members with 18 motor-racing simulators, supported by restaurants, bars and even a spa.

Frank Kalff, commercial director at Cruden BV commented on how the company has focused its technology into the entertainment sector:

> *Cruden is very focused on the attractions market. We devote approximately 50 per cent of our business and product development activity to this market. We succeed in making this professional technology suitable for an entertainment application with our user-friendly operating software and by adapting software to suit attractions' needs. For example, we offer customers fresh updated tracks including fantasy tracks such as I-WAY's moon race. We offer data analysis so guests can work on improving their times and dynamic spectator views with opportunities for local advertisers to buy space from the attraction owner. In terms of marketing, having been members of the International Association of Amusement Parks and Attractions and exhibitors at the IAAPA Attractions Expo for 11 years, we are an entrenched part of the global attractions community. We undertake media relations and advertising in the attractions media, have created an attractions-dedicated section on our website and formed relationships with master planners, architects and theme park equipment specifiers. We achieved an installed base of entertainment systems of between 40 and 50 in the attractions business.*

Figure 3.1 The Cruden BV Hexathrill motion base: it offers a level of simulation capable of training real-world racing drivers or thrilling the most ardent racing fan with an experience unachievable from the at-home console game

When asked what factors drove Cruden in the entertainment market, Kalff stated:

> *Unlike other motor-sport driving games, we can guarantee guests that they are driving the exact same professional equipment as Formula I drivers. The whole system – the hardware, including motion system and cueing, the visuals, the vehicle models – are the same; it is realistic, accurate and highly sophisticated. The fact that we are selected by the high-end simulation centres such as I-WAY and Ferrari World Abu Dhabi gives the market faith in our product durability and support, and, particularly with I-WAY, which has been running the longest, the fact that the simulator centre can be a sustainable business.*

The company sees their software as not just a game: 'It is professional grade, which creates a level of realism that guests will not find in games, hence it creates a unique experience.'

The immersive racing-simulator environment appeals to players of all ages and has become a growing aspect of the prosumer scene. 'Prosumers' are professional consumers prepared to spend whatever it takes to have the very best of their chosen hardware. Rather than being satisfied by using their console joypad, prosumers go to great lengths to recreate realistic racing cockpits and wrap-around screens (commonly referred to as their 'game-rig'). The 'sim-racing' scene includes everything from the conventional PC set-up to the highly realistic simulator enclosure, with players competing over networks in highly realistic circuit-racing competitions.

Developers of software content for the sim-racing sector offer an open-source of networked realistic racing environments, which have engendered consumer applications and, as their sophistication has increased, have started to be applied in commercial installations. One such developer is Sweden-based SimBin. In 2009, the company established an operation called RaceRoom Entertainment, creating not only a professional networked variant of the game software but also establishing over 15 RaceRooms across Europe and North America, offering a retail-unit-sized simulation venue, with 12 to 30 mid-spec racing systems in each one supported by RFID-based multifunctional smart-card membership and competitions. A number of other independent developers of racing retail venues have also made headway across the international scene to offer a commercial sim-racing environment.

Sim-racing represents an interesting example of the consumer-game experience migrating to prosumer home use and then out-of-home, a perfect example of the boundaries of the social play experience. The sim-racing home sector has seen many followers create elaborate homemade simulators offering a high-level of fidelity to the racing experience. The latest server-based network had individuals racing simultaneously in competition. Where the conventional game console leaves-off, the sim-racing (as well as the sim-flying) community excels and reveals the limitations of at-home play for those wanting a more immersive experience.

An example of the networks that support the sim-racing community is iRacing, which offers an on-line racing community with a membership of over 35,000, in 2012, 40 official series and 400 private leagues across 100 countries. However, the at-home PC-based motorsports simulation scene is only one aspect of sim-racing. With the decline in popularity of sim-racing at home, the LAN-gaming scene came to the fore in the mid-1990s, to be followed by the DOE venue.

The ability to offer a racing experience as compelling as (if not superior to) the at-home PC experience has seen open-source content providers licensed to provide suitable racing experiences for the DOE sector. Image Space Incorporated (ISI), a software developer specializing in simulator architectures, computer IG and entertainment systems integration, has seen their mixed-class road-racing, ultra-realistic PC title 'rFactor' used on a number of DOE platforms (including Race Car USA, BlueTiger and others).

There is one aspect of the sim-racing sector that is only recently being explored as a luxury experience for a very particular clientele. EXcape Entertainment Group is taking this approach, which focuses on the high socio-economic lifestyle market and, in order to attract this market, has created two delivery channels: 'experiential' marketing, supporting luxury brands and a stylish venue chain (called Race Fight Club [RFC]).

The experiential marketing platform involves an exclusive presentation as an effective way to build brand with the target audience. EXcape Entertainment offers a networked PC-based racing package, experienced through the use of the 'Hyper Stimulator' chassis kit, replicating the driving position of a racing-car cockpit, with the latest force-feedback steering peripherals. The light-weight but highly specialized 'virtual racing cockpit' provides a professional entertainment platform for high-profile corporate events and VIP presentations.

One such example was the recent commission for the grand opening of the S$65m eight-story building housing the Audi Center in Singapore, the automakers' premier facility in Asia in 2012. As part of the ceremony, eXcape was commissioned to supply a dedicated racing environment for VIP visitors to compete in and hence to extend the entertainment value of visiting the new facility (luxury retail-tainment).

James Fiorillo, CEO and founder of eXcape Entertainment Group spoke about the unique presentation their brand offers:

> *We are not a wizz-bang amusement company. Aspirations, a sense of learning, a sense of doing something real, the whole range of emotions that comes from a reality based experience including the human interaction is what we focus on.*

The 'Hyper Stimulator' chassis is a unambiguous but highly sophisticated chassis, and Fiorillo was asked how this competed with the more 'extreme' motion-based racing-simulator platforms:

> *Motion platforms are not real, cars don't move that way when you race them and pro drivers hate motion platforms for that reason. They are more for gaming-oriented setups.*

EXcape has built on its efforts, supplying experiential marketing, brand promotion and event planning in Asia, and are looking to support this with the development of its first series of Race Fight Clubs. Offering a total-immersion entertainment experience, the idea is to create a multi-zone venue with the race stage-area complementing the cafe-bar and edutainment elements of a highly themed social space. Fiorillo was asked how appealing RFC is to their target audience:

> *The chassis we are using physically surrounds the user and draws them into a compelling and fun experience. This has been combined with a specially designed entertainment environment that has been tailored for a much more sophisticated audience than drawn to traditional location-based entertainment sites of the past.*

Currently on the drawing board, RFC is commencing a major investment process to roll out a chain of facilities, initially in the emerging markets of China and the Middle East, but also with aspirations further afield.

Taking the expertise needed to create commercial simulation and applying this to entertainment has continued to be seen as the way for new developers to enter the sector. Trans-Force is the international edutainment division of Russian Transas Group, the marine- and aviation-simulation system corporation. Transas, along with ship's bridge simulators and maritime platforms, has also investigated the application of their technology to the entertainment sector, having opened a number of interactive theatres and media cafes. The company also developed 'Orion' and '5D Attraction', offering four-seat interactive motion-simulator capsules for attractions and edutainment.

The easily configurable, compact, 4-D enclosure has also appeared in interactive versions, first applied in the amusement sector with the eight-player 'Cyber Dome Super Shooting System' from SEGA in 1992 and later with the internationally released NAMCO 'Galaxian[3] Theater 6' in 1993. Inspired by the 28-player attraction created for the Osaka Expo '90 and NAMCO's WonderEggs theme park, 'Theater 6' offered an enclosure 5m wide, 4.9m long and 2.4m high in which six players shot at a screen in an interactive space narrative combining pre-rendered and real-time graphics. In 2012, Russia-based Yotto Group, working through EXOFilm, launched their '6D Cinema', which offered interactivity in a 4-D theatre. The four-seat motion-based ride system incorporated joysticks for each rider to interact with the game content on a large 8m by 2.5m curved screen in a 5.5m wide, 5m long and 3.5m high enclosure.

The stand-alone simulation facility has not vanished with the evolution of the LBE sector. One exponent has been able to successfully build a dedicated air-combat simulator called Flightdeck. Located in California, some nine jet-fighter simulators offer networked air combat alongside a Boeing 737 flight simulator. The venue also offers players not only a place to experience the true simulation environment from training to flight but also an observation area (Officers Club) where players can watch the virtual combat and relax. The site offers guest packages and private events management.

In an interview, Paul Wigboldy, founder and president of Flightdeck, commented on how much the modern LBE sector has changed:

> *In our arena, flight simulation, as in other types of LBE facilities, I believe the advances in both hardware and software have resulted in a deeper immersive experience. For example, we've had customers say they experienced motion during their simulated flight when, in fact, our simulators are static.*

Going on to describe the fundamental Flightdeck experience, Wigboldy said:

> *We're providing people a chance to be a pilot and experience what it's like to fly a jet aircraft – whether it be a fighter pilot in an F-16 doing 800 knots in air-to-air combat or the co-captain of a Boeing 737 commercial airliner attempting to land at JFK. Our average customer is male, middle income and higher, between 18 and 80 years old.*

Finally, Wigboldy was asked to speculate on the future of LBE:

> *I can't speak for the sector as a whole but, for our specific section of the sector, with technology continuing to advance, I feel the sky's the limit! There, I had to say it. Seriously, I really do feel this way. One of the biggest challenges at Flightdeck is staying abreast of the technology changes. The future looks very positive for the companies that keep up with the next, next thing.*

The value of the simulation experience as a component of a retail-unit has not been lost on conventional retail chains. In 2011, Mad Catz Interactive, a provider of accessories for consumer video games, acquired a simulation-service company that could trace its roots back to the original Kenny Aero, Fightertown USA operation. V Max Simulation was acquired to offer Mad Catz Saitek's range of flight-simulator accessories an entertainment-centre component as an additional element of their business. A Saitek flight centre (Fightertown) with refurbished Air Force simulators was opened in Chino, California.

The retail-unit-sized entertainment facility has continued to be a lucrative one for flight-simulator operators. As well as fighter jets, piloting commercial airliners has proven popular. Australian based Flight Experience has established ten facilities in six countries including Hong Kong and France (first opening in Melbourne in 2005), offering the opportunity to take control of a virtual Boeing 737. The company welcomed their 100,000th customer in 2011. Other developers such as the European iPilot have also started to provide virtual jet-pilot simulator experiences.

It has to be remembered that, while the traditional stand-alone amusement venue may have been superseded by the FEC, the bowling alley was one of the first to see video-amusement as a complement to their main business, and it has continued that love affair. Where others have cooled to the coin-operated amusement platform, the bowling scene has proven a loyal redoubt.

Now, with the evolving of the audience, the bowling scene has seen some major developments, creating strong entertainment spaces to complement their updated bowling experience.

An example of the new approach to the bowling experience is epitomized by Round One, a Japan-based leisure corporation with bowling alleys incorporating extensive indoor amusement at over 100 sites in Japan. This is a state-of-the-art approach to the video-amusement and bowling component: at its opening, the Los Angeles venue of the first Round One in America housed one of the biggest arcades in the USA. The popularity of amusement venues in Asia has not diminished, and some FEC developers have broadened their coverage: a division of amusement developer LAI Games, the Timezone chain has over 280 locations in Australia, New Zealand, Indonesia, Singapore, the Philippines, India and Vietnam and entertains over two-and-a-half million customers. Their primary audience are parents with young children, followed by young adults.

Prominent executive, Sonaal Chopra, CEO of Timezone, mentioned in discussion how the company has redefined its approach to amusement, offering

> *unmatched value for a money spent ... with more than just an amusement site, but more like a mid-scale attraction venue that helps bonding among families, among friends and delivers memorable fun.*

This is an example of the value of providing a strong entertainment experience in a local package.

Looking to the future of the stand-alone amusement environment, he stated:

> *I see further emphasis and importance of destination entertainment formats. I see internet playing a key role in amusement, with a demand for attractions going forward. I don't see much future for high-priced simulator and video product that eats out of operator cashboxes*

This last comment seemed to mirror concern that some of the 'amusement network' systems include an operator subscription that reduces traditional coinbox returns. Chopra went on to confirm that Timezone has their eye on the future of visitor experience through their venues: 'Our Internet Platform under development will enable customers to engage with the store remotely via any browser interface, tablet or handheld. This will be unique in the industry.'

Whereas the ATP concept may now be side-lined, indoor, themed entertainment sites are still being developed as a component of the future regional entertainment experience aimed at the modern staycation audience. Merlin Entertainment has developed indoor family-entertainment venues, Legoland Discovery Centres: the first site opened in Berlin in 2007. Now with six locations in Europe, North America and Japan the operation has not only created a passive-entertainment venue split into various zones, but as has embraced a 4-D theatre component and an iDR approach, offering a flexible high-throughput attraction able to be accommodated in the average 3,000m^2 floor space of a centre.

While many of the entertainment venues using DOE technology follow traditional lines, there are some innovative approaches to the interactive digital experience in a resort setting. MagiQuest was first launched in 2005, the brain child of developers linked to the failed Sony Metreon (under the new company name Creative Kingdoms). Taking their knowledge of themed environments and interactive narrative in a free-flow venue, they created a live-action role-playing experience. Players of all ages (and sexes) use their wands (also called 'magis') to cast spells and interact with the game. The IR (infra-red) emitting wands were movement tracked and if used correctly unlocked achievements and allowed the player to amass skills. MagiQuest became very popular for a diverse audience, and Creative Kingdoms was bought by Great Wolf Resorts (America's largest family of indoor waterparks) in 2010.

By 2012, the MagiQuest component of Great Wolf Resorts had proven to be an incredible draw and celebrated selling their millionth MagiQuest wand (a special magi handed to a seven-year-old female player at the Great Wolf Lodge in Williamsburg). In growing the operation, Creative Kingdoms had taken the foundation of MagiQuest and developed a suite of experiences for a variety of facilities.

New interactive adventures included 'Story Explorers', in which players used specially equipped plush toys to decide their character's next move; 'CompassQuest', in which players used special compasses to find clues and complete puzzles; and 'DinoQuest', in which players became virtual palaeontologists using special devices in the world's first interactive dinosaur adventure. Creative Kingdoms, with their strong background in child-orientated content, aimed for wider application in themed entertainment venues.

Figure 3.2 The frontage of the popular Chuck E. Cheese emporium: it offers a young clientele a mixture of theme park and arcade with a birthday pizza thrown in for good measure

Hospitality: Feeding the Hunger for Fun

The marriage of fast-food and video gaming is an old one: from the arcade machines in pizza parlours in the 1980s to the merger of Pizza Time Theater and ShowBiz Pizza to create Chuck E. Cheese (CEC) in 1984. CEC has become famous as the epitome of the children's party room combined with a pizza restaurant and redemption-game and video-amusement area. From Nolan Bushnells' original concept in 1977, CEC has become the most public face of digital entertainment in a hospitality context. America's Incredible Pizza Company has a 1950's theme with redemption- and video-games, and there is a wide selection of new concept venues of varying sizes entering the market.

Nolan Bushnell commented on how much the current CEC venues have changed from his original aspirations:

> *I think that the real problem is that Chuck E. Cheese has been seen as running out of gas – it got a little greedy and is finding it hard to attract a new audience. Just look, if you are a 30-year-old family guy with kids, you can hardly afford to go out to these venues, they have been filled up with little machines that just eat up your tokens and are not fun. Families find that they are spending all their money on tokens for this experience, the venue is charging too much to get those few tickets, and so they don't get any repeat visits or returning visitors. As a result, they are just shooting themselves in the foot.*

He went on:

> *Regarding the smaller concept FECs prototyped in the market, my view is that 'big' will pull people across town, 'small' won't. If you go to an amusement site, then you want to be in the middle of chaos. When I ran Chuck E. Cheese, we tried small-sized facilities and they never performed. The factor to be aware of when you have a large facility is you can afford a good manager, while a small site can't afford to support the same salary for a good manager. The difference between a good manager and a poor one is around $20,000 a year, but if you try and save that kind of money you get nothing but your head up your ass, against superb results, that includes working machines, clean restrooms and happy paying customers.*

Beyond tomato sauce and cheese, a wider diversity of restaurants has come to see video-amusement and more advanced mid-scale attractions as complementary to entertaining patrons and encouraging a longer dwell time. Another exponent of the popular perception of 'food and fun' is Dave & Buster's (D&B), with over 60 facilities comprising a mix of high-dining and bar but, at its heart, a dedicated gaming component with traditional billiard and pool tables supporting carnival and simulator gaming. Where these venues offer a profitable mix of refreshment and entertainment is the use of card-based payment: the D&B Power Card, which can be charged with game credits. Since the merger of Buster's Restaurant and Slick Willy's World of Entertainment pool hall in Little Rock, Arkansas in 1982 to become D&B's, the alliance of the hospitality and gaming has continued.

Speaking with one of those responsible for shaping this, Kevin Bachus, senior vice president of entertainment and game strategy at D&B's, who comes from a background in console games and is one of the four individuals at Microsoft Corporation who conceived the Xbox video-game console system, we asked about the previous success D&B had found running early LBE attractions in their restaurant/entertainment chain:

> *The VWE and Virtuality installations, were spectacles: large-format games coupled with technology that was cutting edge, ahead of their time and brand new to the industry. We had dedicated staff for the attractions that understood the nuances of operating this type of equipment, as well as repairing it. Eventually the 'cutting edge' and newness aspects wore off with both titles and since new software was not available, we determined that they had ran their course. VWE had a cult following with gamers due to its play complexity but an inability to connect to the everyday guest was an issue that we could not overcome. Virtuality was able to connect to the everyday guest but without new game software being developed to drive play, it ultimately lost that connection.*

Regarding D&B's continued interest in aspects of DOE or amusements, Bachus commented:

> *We are definitely still interested in all aspects of DOE and are constantly on the look-out for something unique and spectacular. But I suspect amusements will always be at the core of our guest experience.*

Concerning how amusement machines fit into their big picture, he added:

> *Amusement machines are at the hub of our business. One of the things that makes D&B so unique is the total combined experience of food and fun under one roof. Delivering the latest and greatest experiences to our guests – something they can't get anywhere else – is what they've come to expect from us.*

Finally, we asked what future applications of current entertainment technology the D&B operation is considering to stay relevant in a changing market, Bachus said:

> *I'm trying to pull technology concepts from every connection I've made throughout my career. You never know where the next big hit will come from. Nolan Bushnell once told me that he always loved to spend time in research labs looking at future technology because he knew that arcades could be the link between the lab and the consumer – a step between impractically expensive, complex tests and inexpensive consumer devices. I couldn't agree more.*

Figure 3.3 Injoy Motions' 'Dido Kart 2': digital natives rediscover their love for big gaming

Most recently, a brand-new trend has been seen gaining momentum in the Western market. The bar and tavern sector has been joined by what some have described as 'gamebars' or even 'beercades'.

The maturing of a sophisticated gaming audience comes at a time when staycation is also shaping the retail landscape. The US legal drinking age also played a part in creating the perfect climate for this new breed of entertainment facility. The draw of the retro arcade scene combined with the social experience of the bar saw the creation of the gamebar, which attracted an audience enthusiastic about the classic arcade but also 'digitally native', comfortable with their leisure time spent in surroundings that mixed gaming and hospitality and even happy to embrace elements of a nightclub. One of the new exponents of this environment is Insert Coin(s) Interactive Nightlife, a facility seen as the progenitor of the bar–arcade hybrid, with some 60 vintage arcade cabinets housed in a nightclub-style location and a number of booths to play console games. Another example is Barcade, with trendy and attractive bars at sites in Brooklyn and Philadelphia (and another due) 'decorated' with classic games (combining bar and arcade atmospheres). The mix of video amusements is carefully tailored. The operators revealed that they only included video games made between 1970 and 1990 (over the years this has been extended to include releases up to 1993). The original Barcade environment is jealously guarded as new start-ups attempt to capitalize on the popularity of this mix of nostalgia and social entertainment. Hospitality and amusement venues are embracing the new digital entertainment systems, the successors to traditional pool tables and shuffleboard.

The founder and CEO of Insert Coin(s), Christopher LaPorte, commented on how he felt the chain fitted between arcade and nightclub:

> *While we offer bottle service and DJs, I wouldn't call Insert Coin(s) a nightclub just yet. The term is off putting for the gamer scene. To be a nightclub in the traditional sense is to adhere to stringent guidelines that alienate the general consumer. The arcade aspect is in my opinion covered in the truest sense by the 60 cabinets we currently house in Las Vegas. But like so many of the 'barcades' enjoying success today, it's based on the nostalgic aspect that caters to the 30-something crowd. It's why we strive to fulfil a new segment in the nightlife market with our interactive nightlife concept. They're not just arcades, but console-gaming experiences, which a younger audience has more relevance to, allows us to introduce this sector to the arcade experience.*

Regarding how best to describe this new sector, 'gamebars' or 'beercades', LaPorte stated:

> *As a generic term, I think this is our best bet. We currently enjoy over 25,000 guests a month into our 6,600 sq. ft venue. To be labelled an arcade, we'd be missing the boat on attracting that wider audience. With the use of motion-sensor gaming in our Minneapolis location and our focus on retro console gaming with our bottle-service sector, we will continue to utilize our trademarked interactive nightlife, but for up and coming bars/lounges incorporating gaming as an additional entertainment factor, then yes, 'gamebars' is 100 per cent accurate.*

In defining their concept, LaPorte turned to the state of the amusement business from his perspective:

Figure 3.4 Taking the pop-up arcade to new extremes: this bizarre installation sees original arcade cabinets converted into outlandish experiences as part of a travelling installation 'The Faile Bast Deluxx Fluxx Arcade' in a London Soho gallery in 2010. Created by Faile, Brooklyn's infamous collaborative duo, early pioneers of contemporary street art, it was described as 'creating an explosively immersive installation'

The traditional arcade is dead. The family fun center is the only model that can be truly sustained without the alcohol quotient. Until the American culture adopts the arcade scene in the way Japan embraces it, it is difficult to showcase new arcade technology for a number of reasons: (1) the size needed for some of these newer machines. You're almost required to own large spaces to house such cabinets with the advances in multiplayer arcade machinery whether it's a racing or shooting titles. Right now, with the size of my venue, it's difficult to introduce these machines when it affects my maximum occupancy thus dipping into my liquor revenue; (2) the cost of these machines. With classic cabinets ranging as low as $500 to the absolute highest

$3,000, to spend around $10K a machine for a Tekken Tag Tournament 2 machine when the general audience is content playing such a title on a PS3 or Xbox 360, even the hardcore gaming audience is content by providing MadCatz arcade sticks to replicate that experience.

Commenting on where Insert Coin(s) sees its digital entertainment coming from in the future:

My vision of Insert Coin(s) is to avoid following suit with the traditional family fun center so no skee-ball, crane machines, or sports-oriented games. I'm looking at more small-space entertainment options and touchscreen gaming with the popularity of mobile gaming, i.e. 'Angry Birds'.

LaPorte went on to describe their audience:

Casual gamers equal a wide variety of clientele. Age range from 21 to 45 with a 50/50 split male-to-female ratio. My goal is to introduce this crowd to the hardcore gaming and arcade scene we are all trying to revitalize.

The development of new opportunities for 'food-and-fun' in the West has not all been left to newcomers: some recognized and respected names are re-investing in the combination of digital entertainment and hospitality. NAMCO Entertainment, the US division of the Japanese amusement factory and game publisher has an extensive background in facility development, along with their conventional video-amusement business. In 1997, the company signed an agreement with Skyline Multimedia Entertainment acquiring the XS Entertainment 'cyber arena' facility brand, a mixture of restaurant, nightclub and game zone – the first facility opened as XS Orlando in 1999 to mixed reviews and was eventually side-lined and closed.

In 2010, NAMCO Entertainment reviewed its extensive entertainment-centre business that, including Time-Out, Aladdin's Castle, WonderPark and other amusement facility chains and partnered theatre, restaurant, bowling and retail operations, comprises over 1,000 locations (one of the largest amusement operations in the USA) and undertook an extensive R&D project to create a brand new 'destination entertainment concept'.

David Bishop, executive vice president of NAMCO Entertainment, who is responsible for formulating this project, commented to the games portal Polygon:

> *It's no secret that we've been exploring a number of new business models and noodling the future of out-of-home entertainment for several years now, and our current planning does include an 'upscale' restaurant with 'entertainment elements'.*

Still veiled in secrecy at the time of this book's writing, sources have suggested that the project has been codenamed 'Level 256', although this was yet to be confirmed. A name rumoured to have been chosen in homage to the infamous last levels of NAMCO classics 'Pac-Man' and 'Dig Dug'. Rumours suggest that this may be one of the most ambitious LBE projects seen in the USA for the last 10 years.

The project has been referred to by some sources as a 'restaurant-centric' concept, with food as the primary motivation for the audience and the entertainment element acting as a focus. Special attention has been given to creating the right mix of digital entertainment, with unique attractions as well as machines from the company's extensive catalogue redressed to suit the facility's atmosphere. Although it is at an early stage of development, and much still needs to be defined, this new operation has been envisaged as a move towards establishing an international chain for the corporation. Bishop went onto say:

> *We've been working with an established American restaurateur, as well as some other really talented external professionals, to develop the concept. But the project is still in a relatively early stage of development.*

This represents a glimpse into the investment still being poured into DOE in hospitality.

The global financial conditions have placed even more pressure on the conventional retail sector to attract larger audiences and increase dwell time and spend. The shopping-mall sector has looked at 'entertainment anchors' to generate the magical '3-hour duration' at a mall: cinemas, restaurants, bars and entertainment. With the growing sophistication of video games and connectivity at home, the retail sector has looked to new means to draw audiences to their product, and the use of retail-tainment has grown.

Best described as wrapping the promotional message in an entertainment package, the skill is in achieving the right mix of game experience without ramming the marketing message down the player's throat. Even consumer-games have left their comfort zone of the living room and ventured into the retail scene. Commercial deployment of console-game systems in entertainment venues has created unusual mixes such as John's Incredible Pizza Company's food-and-fun concept PLAY^2, Interactive Sports Bar and the Californian Powersurge Video Fun & Fitness. These sites see a hospitality element with console-game systems available in purpose-built enclosures, attracting walk-in traffic and the all-important private events.

Although already used to a limited extent, 'pop-up video' arcades have emerged as promising alternative entertainment and marketing vehicles for developers and operators of traditional video-arcade games and unconventional independent game developers alike. Many factors account for the increasing attractiveness of these arcades: major shifts in the video-arcade market are prompting greater marketing experimentation, pop-up video arcades are generating greater interest from independent game developers as well as established arcade-game developers and operators, and new and more portable technologies such as tablets are exerting greater pressure on arcades.

For now, arcades are primarily positioned as promotional platforms and do not represent a significant source of revenue, though they will likely have a substantial marketing impact in the near future. Two main kinds of game initiatives and systems seem suitable for pop-up arcades: repurposing of video-games as promotional applications in cabinets and the installation of hybrid arcade systems combining console and free-to-play games, similar to the hybrid systems found in the kiosk and digital-signage sector.

There will be a natural evolution towards pop-up arcades from pop-up stores and pop-up experiences in the hospitality sector. Newer 'eat-ertainment' venues, such as gamebars, may also open up key new opportunities for pop-up arcades. Retail locations and visitor attractions will likely generate the most revenue for pop-up arcades, while independent operators, such as gamebars, will yield significant revenue for pop-up arcades over the long term.

John Gerner, managing director of Leisure Business Advisors, sees two key opportunities for games in pop-up arcades: an opportunity to showcase brand new games developed by young game designers, especially because they can be offered at low cost in those settings, and an opportunity for operators of established games with multiple machines to deliver their games in new venues during fallow periods. From his perspective, pop-up arcades allow video-game operators to 'try out new game ideas at much lower risk, typically in vacated retail space'. In essence, he views pop-up arcades as game 'incubators', that can spawn much needed game innovations allowing the video-arcade business to 'compete effectively with sophisticated home game systems'. He believes that 'merged' physical–virtual pop-up arcades could offer a 'good option' for video-arcade operators intent on 'experimenting with new ideas'. In his view, another factor favouring an increasing role for pop-up arcades is their suitability for alternative payment systems, such as via smartphones.

One of the major players in pop-up arcades is SEGA America. For its pop-up arcade near the 2011 'Comic-Con' show in San Diego, the company transformed a mixed co-op retail space called Industry Showroom into an arcade offering a multifaceted entertainment experience comprising music, merchandise, games and serving as an 'oasis' for gamers, allowing them to enjoy the ambiance of a lounge, explains Jared DeVincenzo, president of marketing, Genome Project, which helped develop the space for SEGA. As Kellie Parker, senior community manager for SEGA America, explains:

> *We were intrigued by the idea of a pop-up arcade, because it was a chance for us to set up the space exactly how we wanted, from layout to decor to hours of operation. We were excited to see so many fans of all ages visit our arcades and are really pleased with the results.*

According to Parker, 'games that are easy to pick up and play for a few minutes tend to work the best' at the pop-up arcades, and 'our "Sonic the Hedgehog" games are always extremely popular' in those arcades. DeVicenzo found that sports, horror and comic-based games were the most featured and popular games at SEGA's 2011 pop-up arcade in San Diego, such as 'Sonic the Hedgehog' and 'Captain America'. Music featured prominently in the arcade, with a DJ stationed near the entrance, and prizes were offered throughout the day. On-site screen-printing of customers' favourite game posters was also available at the site.

As DeVincenzo explains, SEGA chose the space largely out of necessity. Given the difficulty in securing exhibition space at Comic-Con due to high demand, SEGA sought an alternative space to showcase their games. He sees benefits from pop-up arcades for all parties concerned. For operators of pop-up arcades, the spaces are particularly attractive, as they afford 'reasonable rental rates'; for retail landlords, pop-up spaces allow them to make good use of vacant space during slow periods, such as holidays.

Retro games, pinball, fighting games and special cabinets are particularly well suited to pop-up arcades. From a broad perspective, Gerner observed that pop-up arcades blending popular cultures, including music and retro gaming, tend to work well. In general, games offering simple play will fare best in those arcades. In this regard, app quality games are particularly suitable to pop-up arcades, as they are easy to develop.

Independent game developers will increasingly use pop-up arcades as a distribution and promotional platform: for example, Winnitron Indie Arcade Game Network showcases independent games typically for short periods in alternative venues across North America, such as the NYU Game Center.

Another key group bringing independent games to pop-up arcades is Tiny Thumbs, an organization for independent game developers in north Texas. It established pop-up arcades during 2012 to 'bridge the gap between art and technology and offer greater exposure for independent video-game talent around the world', explains Kyle Kondas, co-curator (with Bobby Frye) of the arcades. Tiny Thumbs' first pop-up arcade in 2012 at the CentralTrak Artists Residency of the University of Texas at Dallas drew 'over 200 people', he reports. Its second pop-up arcade was at the Dallas Museum of Art during January 2013.

Admission to Tiny Thumbs arcades has been free, though versions of some games in the arcades have been sold online or via smartphone or tablet apps. Typically, its arcades offer a wide variety of games, including 'puzzle games, side-scrollers, art games and maybe eventually text-based games', notes Kondas.

Tiny Thumbs planned additional pop-up arcades during 2013, including installations at store fronts, 'theme-oriented' arcades and a pop-up arcade 'imitating a drive-in theatre', where games will be projected onto a large screen. Ultimately, it would like to establish its 'own permanent' space, at an 'art gallery', for example.

Kondas underscores the importance of pop-up arcades as a distribution and promotional avenue for independent game developers and notes that 'art audiences' are potentially a major new audience for independent games. He envisions many new showcase opportunities for those games in 'art galleries, restaurants and bars'.

The scope of games in pop-up arcades is likely to expand even further, encompassing more site-specific games and AR games. Considering these developments, pop-up arcades seem well positioned to play a more prominent role in the arcade- and consumer-game businesses in the near future.

This is best illustrated by Walt Disney Pictures and the promotion of their 2010 motion-picture *Tron: Legacy* with the re-interpretation of Flynn's Arcade: a theatrical venue offering the chance to play classic arcade games and imaginary games inspired by the film. Walt Disney use this approach again with their 2012 motion-picture *Wreck-It Ralph,* an animated feature based on the arcade-game experience, supported by a recreation of the fictional arcade game 'Fix-It Felix Jr.' from the movie with cabinets placed in movie theatres.

In any case, these pop-up arcades will likely be increasingly used to test and promote new games and game devices and to provide dynamic new entertainment and marketing opportunities for game developers, publishers and operators.

One application of the pop-up video arcade that has gained traction is the mobile-gaming business. One such example developed by Creative Works, the 'game truck' offers mobile gaming for parties and group functions, using consumer-game content on a big screen in a truck. Accommodating up to 16 players, the truck even includes a social-media blog station with on-board Twitter and Facebook connectivity to share the experience. Here, party entertainment is taken to the players' location instead of the players visiting the venue.

One retailer to add gaming to their mix was GamerBase in the UK. Part of HMV, Gamerbase offered a multi-player gaming zone, with over 50 seats providing networked pay-to-play versions of the latest PC and console games. GamerBase hoped to use the popularity of interactive entertainment to generate longer dwell times in retail outlets, though, sadly, this innovative approach was still tied to the retail venue it supported, and the collapse of the HMV retail empire meant Gamerbase had to extract itself from the mess, aiming to rise again as a dedicated offering.

Another element of the retail and promotion sector to embrace the opportunities offered by DOE is the advertising industry. Digital signage (digital out-of-home [DOOH] advertising) has also embraced an interactive narrative to draw a more varied audience to their messages. As other industries have considered gamification, so has DOOH advertising.

The gamification of advertising and promotions, especially outside the home, is a major diversion from the tradition pay-to-play gaming sector. However, by generating an audience and promoting a message, game platforms can 'pay for themselves' (i.e. be free-to-play). The ability to offer a versatile platform that can be placed in some of the busiest thoroughfares has allowed innovative designs to blossom. One such originator in this scene is EyeClick, a developer of dynamic floor, wall, window and table-top displays that are completely interactive and can be deployed in airports, malls and commercial locations. A game with a simple narrative includes players by tracking their movements.

The DOOH scene has led to a huge increase in interactive terminals allowing the audience to interact and customize their exposure to promotions: ranging from Nespresso stores, with their touchscreen kiosks, developed by IntuiFace, to the Virgin Media store in the Westfield mall in London, containing wall-mounted gesture-control displays promoting the company's various packages and options, developed by Acquire Digital. The next few years will see an increase in interactive promotional narratives, which will change customers' experiences, especially when linked with social-networking applications, and reveal the lucrative side of DOE.

The Trends

The convergence of the DOOH advertising and DOE sectors is producing major growth in innovation, using material and technology from the amusements industry to provide entertainment within a crowded and complicated retail and hospitality market for a sophisticated, digitally native audience.

IMMERSIVE DISPLAYS

The flat-screen display has come a long way from the cathode-ray tube of the 1980s and 1990s. Plasma and LCD screens are finding more and more applications in the display sector, but there is now a move towards more immersive presentations, such as stereoscopic displays. There are also immersive displays using the latest projection technology combined with curved and wrap-round screens. New projection technology, providing greater power and smaller size, is also shaping the new entertainment delivery platforms.

Part of creating an immersive display is offering the highest possible resolution. Unlike the eighth generation of home video-game consoles that failed to adopt 4K high-definition (4KHD) systems – the most advanced imaging technology in the market to-date – the attractions industry has already used 4KHD systems in such features as 'The Amazing Adventures of Spider-Man: The Ride'. Already interactive entertainment systems are entering the

DOE sector as this environment offers a level of immersion unobtainable from systems found in the home.

IMMERSIVE CAPSULE

The latest projection technology, immersive displays, motion-base platforms and audio technology lead many to see the future of the LBE concept as an all-inclusive capsule- or pod-style approach to the gaming experience. As a logical progression from the Link Trainer of the 1920s and the Tesla Cockpit of the 1990s, a new generation of completely immersive single-user capsules has been proposed. One such conceptual design was the 'i-Cocoon' from the collective of designers and architects, NAU.

SIMULATION SICKNESS

The danger of too much immersion has been a concern since the early days of cinema. Now issues such as photo-sensitive epilepsy (caused by flashing lights of a certain frequency) or 3-D headaches are receiving greater attention. The US Army Research Institute for the Behavioral and Social Sciences first investigated nausea suffered by crews using Tank Driver Trainer in 1995. How immersion may have to be rationed is an aspect of future development.

AUDIENCE TRACKING

Through face recognition and eye tracking, DOOH advertising can count the number of individuals who actually see a promotion or advertisement and record how many males and females, young and old look at the screen, and even what part of that screen they look at and for how long. This statistical data can shape a campaign and prove its effectiveness, and it is expected that soon game systems will routinely gather this information, which will allow games to pay for themselves.

FREE PLAY

The possibility that games including extensive promotions could be self-funding and hence free-to-play is an interesting aspect of the future of the market. The at-home consumer-games industry however has faltered in the application of in-game advertising: the returns on investment proved less than promising. Though not generating vast sums at present, appropriately developed and monitored, promotional content could prove a major aspect in the future of DOE.

Chapter 4

The Drive for Immersion

A fundamental element in the future of digital out-of-home entertainment will be the use of an immersive environment to draw the player into a digitally created world that also offers an experience unlike anything available by other means.

Core aspects of the technology derive from military- and commercial-flight simulators. Since the first pilot trainers of 1929, the ability to simulate environments has become a growing industry, accelerated by increased investment during the Cold War and the birth of sophisticated computer generated imagery.

With the increase in visual representation of digitally generated environments superseding the 'model boards' of the late 1960s, digital recreation has moved from simulations of land and sea to outer-space and the imagination. The ability to immerse the user has shifted from recreations of fighter-jet and commercial-jetliner cockpits, tanks and law-enforcement vehicles.

With the greater sophistication of CGI technology, its application has widened to the visualization of computer data and the viewing of virtual worlds and CAD (Computer Aided Design). CGI environments were viewed originally on a monitor, but the more sophisticated incarnations of the late 1960s migrated to the first head-mounted displays (HMDs), allowing direct viewing of virtual worlds.

Migration from the screen to the specialist digital display was also matched by the development of more sophisticated projection technology. After digital-projection technology recreated real-world views for military and commercial simulation, the technology found a home in movie theatres, where it superseded the traditional film medium. The motion-picture industry has harnessed digital-projection and simulation technology to replace models with digital effects, leading to the most sophisticated examples of the filmmaker's art.

The amusement industry was the first to invest in the development of simulators to immerse the viewer in an interactive virtual environment using the latest developments in interactive CGI and video-game narratives. The amusement theme parks created in the late 1990s acted as a home for these new devices, such as the first HMDs offering VR entertainment. Immersive entertainment systems have been increasingly deployed in the marketing and promotion sector, allowing luxury brands to be represented as components of interactive entertainment experiences.

The military had another use for computer-generated environments: target-acquisition systems. These are an essential component of modern military helicopters and fighter jets and superimpose computer-generated target information over the real world (through head-up-displays), thus 'augmenting' the real-world. With the appearance of smartphones, apps which superimposed information over real-world images captured by the camera and orientated using the internal compass and gyro of the devices were developed to provide augmented reality (AR).

AR entertainment apps are still at an early stage of development – they typically include informational tools (directions and locations of interest) – but game apps have also used AR. As mobile phones incorporate a greater level of 'smart' technology through their ability to connect to the internet, they now allow interaction through social media. Location-based information (where the user is and what they are looking at) can be transferred to contacts through social media applications.

Smartphone apps with AR components are becoming popular with venues that can control their use. Theme parks and museums have already added new levels of interaction with their visitors, personalizing their experience at the site. Likewise, retail locations and cinemas use AR apps. Gamification is being increasingly seen as an important part of the customer experience.

Virtual Entertainment Immersion

The cross-over of technology from commercial and military simulation to the entertainment sector has been demonstrated above. The Link Trainer, one of the first pilot-training simulators, had more sales to amusement parks in 1929 than to the US military. Hughes Rediffusion's airline simulator was used in Disney's 'Star Tours', and Martine Marietta's military IG technology was used in SEGA's Model 2 arcade hardware. It is not surprising that the more exotic simulation technology migrated to entertainment applications.

With the development of US military-training technology to support the Apache AH-64 attack-helicopter programme in 1983, a recreation of the innovative Target Acquisition and Designation Sights / Pilot Night Vision System (TADS/PNVS) gave birth to new research in HMD technology (building on the extensive 'synthetic-world' display work by Iva Sutherland in the 1960s). 'Virtual reality' (VR) would enter the vernacular through work at VPL Research in 1984, popularized by VPL founder Jaron Lanier's claim that VR technology was 'a new plane of reality that will thrill everybody'.

VR technology was used in HMDs, flat-panel displays mounted within a helmet that also supplied audio stimulus. The movement of the HMD synched with the displayed visuals of the virtual world. Initially using binoculars and screen-style viewers, technological advancements shrunk the display down to a wearable size. The encumbered viewing technology was combined with tactile interfaces, such as gloves, and hand movements were used to interact with and control the virtual navigation.

VR would be inexorably linked with the perception of future entertainment, in part fuelled by the cyberpunk novels of William Gibson (*Neuromancer*, 1984). The technological developments associated with VR became confused with popular fiction. The 1992 motion-picture *The Lawnmower Man* fired the audience's imagination of what VR could achieve, thanks to the ground-breaking CGI created by Californian visionaries Angel Studios, and led the public to expect more than could be achieved by the available hardware.

UK company Virtuality would become the leaders of VR in entertainment. They began as W. Industries, financed by the video-amusement operator Leading Leisure Organization with software support from Rediffusion, developers of the 'Commander' interactive capsule simulator (at the time called the 'Bandit'). W. Industries were renamed Virtuality and ploughed their own furrow in the application of virtual experience to entertainment, launching 'Dactyl Nightmare', a game based on a TV-programme commission seeking to use the hardware in a game show, in 1991. 'Dactyl Nightmare' used the 1000CU platform, and a jet-fighter game called 'VTOL' used the 1000SD platform. These systems proved temperamental but popular VR demonstrators, and, from these, Virtuality developed a series of cyber-space or stand-up (CS-SU) and sit-down (SD) VR game platforms, refining their patented HMD technology ('Vissette') and leapfrogging from hardware reiteration to hardware reiteration.

Virtuality even attempted to create a chain of location-based entertainment facilities offering networked gaming, under the name 'Legend Quest' and opened a venue at the Tower of London. However, actually generating significant revenue from their VR systems was a constant problem. The products they had developed showed serious overreach and proved cumbersome and unreliable. Only 3,500 units of the first 1000CS platform were ever sold, and the 2000SU platform sold less than half of that, while the last SU-3000 system sold only a handful of working units.

In order to generate revenue and placate investors, the company turned to licensing their technology. One of the companies who signed an agreement with Virtuality was SEGA Amusements, which entered into a laborious R&D collaboration with the UK company that would involve the sharing of their HMD technology and software experience and result in the launch in 1996 of the SEGA arcade game 'TecWar'. The prototype was tested at a number of locations and was shelved after a poor reception. SEGA went on to create a separate VR technology based around the licence, releasing an ATP attraction called 'VR-1 Space Mission' (based on the 'AS-1' motion platform and using HMDs).

Another licence was with NAMCO. In 1996, they licensed Virtuality to create and release a game based on the company's mascot. 'Pac-Man VR' never received a full release and was shelved soon after launch. This came at the same time as an aborted agreement with Atari Corporation to release a home version of 'Vissette' (called 'Jaguar VR') in 1995. These difficulties along with growing concerns about the actual revenue generation capabilities of the hardware forced the company to fold.

Speaking exclusively to the authors of this book for the first time since the failure of this approach to VR in DOE, founder and visionary behind Virtuality Dr Jonathan Waldern said:

> *When you look back at what we were able to accomplish, the myriad of different entertainment titles and equipment experiments, Virtuality was a university of entertainment technology on steroids. It was an incredible journey that was widely reported and something all the amusement industry benefited from at that time. I believe we did a text-book job of being a VR pioneer. We amazed, underdelivered on the promise, scrambled, and ultimately failed. The only difference in our 'Crossing the Chasm' story is that we have picked ourselves up, brushed ourselves off, and are destined to try again. In technology, all the moons must align to deliver a disruptive new communication medium, so timing is often everything. Entertainment is the cookie-cutter application. Here in 2013, twenty years on, I believe the galaxy*

> *is once again poised for alignment. One of our corporate stockholders at the time, IBM used to tell me we were ten years too far ahead. They were wrong by half but now I believe them!*

Regarding his proudest accomplishments in establishing VR and Virtuality in the public space, Waldern said:

> *I think we gave millions of people the amazing sensation of how [immersive person-to-person entertainment] VR will one day appear. It's a new form of communication building on a complex set of iteratively improving technology – but when fused properly, its key effect is the 'product' of the sensory components, not the sum.*

Waldern was asked about the issues he saw shaping the latest HMD technology, especially from his current position as chairman and chief technology officer of SBG Labs, founded in 2003 and pioneering revolutionary work in reactive monomer liquid crystal materials (RMLCM), an all-digital solid-state alternative to traditional optical assemblies:

> *The current approach coming to market this year for VR consumer applications (like Oculus Rift's conceptual headset) uses the very same architecture originated in the Virtuality LBE's nearly twenty years ago – hi-def displays with bulky large field lenses combined with low-latency head tracking and high-performance graphics (albeit higher definition). The fundamental challenge to engineer lightweight HMD optical technology for VR has not changed, except hundreds of millions of dollars instead of tens of millions are now being invested. The Holy Grail is still a wide field-of-view display in a pair of glasses but many of the world's top engineers have consistently underestimated what it will take to deliver this 'moon shot'. Both my team and I have dedicated ourselves to this goal and we believe we are two years away.*

SBG Labs' core business focus is on wide field-of-view (WFOV) HMDs for avionics, industrial and consumer apps, including entertainment.

In conclusion, regarding his involvement with the amusement business, Waldern stated:

> *Our ultimate goal was to internationally link the LBE centres together, but the equipment cost versus return did not pan out. It's a tough business model to resolve unless the equipment cost can be reduced*

> *to consumer-level pricing and or some other club membership model can be implemented. The amusement industry was always been both forward looking and receptive, so perhaps along with the switch to cloud-based capacity, the operator's model can drastically change and deliver the financial sustainability to develop these more advanced LBE unification models. The VR centre concept is a large scale challenge that will require a gaming company with the ultimate in corporate and investment fortitude – so perhaps an Apple, Microsoft, Disney or EA will be the next to try such a project.*

Previous approaches to VR in entertainment included audience-participation experiences. Ham On Rye Technologies developed a new platform called the 'Virtual Reality Theater', which incorporated the latest HMDs worn by a large theatre audience experiencing a virtual presentation hosted by a 'vactor' (virtual actor) in a virtual environment. Audience participation was monitored as they experienced the 360° environment. The system was sold as an interactive marketing theatre to resorts, parks and malls. However, though the system was highly acclaimed and won industry awards, the company found it difficult to monetize the system's popularity and it faded from the scene.

VR proved alluring for a number of entertainment companies. Walt Disney Imagineering ploughed considerable sums into investigating the opportunities that VR offered for an immersive entertainment environment, creating a concept demonstrator called 'Aladdin's VR Adventure'. The experimental system was demonstrated at Epcot Center for 14 months, entertaining over 45,000 guests. This experiment would be later vindicated with a practical production version of the attraction, now renamed 'Aladdin's Magic Carpet Ride'. The unique design of Disney's VR HMD used CRT rather than liquid crystal display (LCD) for a better visual perception, the excessive weight supported by a spring-suspension system (called GatorVision).

Disney installed the productized Aladdin attraction alongside a second new VR attraction called 'Ride the Comix', in which guests wielded swords in combat with virtual cartoon villains. These attractions were part of the 12 installations within the company's own ATP: DisneyQuest. The spring-suspension system (or 'Sword of Damocles') was also applied in the amusement sector. Global VR, one of the last amusement companies with a VR background sold one of the last VR amusement pieces, the popular 'VR Vortex', with its spring-suspension virtual-viewing system, until 2004: by which time VR had lost all of its previous allure.

Vilified by amusement operators saddled with temperamental and expensive hardware that failed to live-up to its promise, VR faded into the background and embraced cost-saving and technological advancements before bursting onto the scene again. Interest in immersion within a virtual environment has re-emerged, and the consumer-game sector has developed a familiarity with traversing virtual worlds through a conventional display, no matter how large or how flat, and the improvements in mobile technology (smartphones and game decks) have led to a wealth of new lightweight displays and advanced motion tracking.

With the popularity of 3-D movies (reaching a peak with *Avatar* in 2009), there was an expectation that 3-D would migrate into the home. However, in reality, consumer take-up of at-home 3-D proved lacklustre, but interest in 3-D glasses and personal-viewing technology gained momentum. In 2011 in Japan, Sony Consumer Electronics developed the 'HMZ-T1', a high-priced personal HD 3-D viewer comprising a visor running two OLED displays and stereo audio. The Sony system was not originally developed as an HMD in the true sense, but it rekindled interest in VR.

In the military and simulation industry, VR was reborn, with the few remaining HMD manufacturers crafting lightweight, but expensive, platforms that were used in mission rehearsals by special forces and law-enforcement personnel. With more cost-effective display-panel technology, the consumer and attraction entertainment industries rekindled their interest in a workable application.

However, rather than taking a conventional path to deployment, the first new VR HMDs have been promoted in the consumer-game sector through an innovative Kickstarter campaign that raised crowd-sourced funding to build development kits for game studios to experiment with. The developer, Oculus VR, and their proposed 'Oculus Rift' HMD have received considerable promotion from leading game-software executives, and, after raising $2.5m from their successful Kickstarter campaign in 2012 (hitting its first funding target of $250,000 within 4 hours), the first prototype dev-kits were rushed into developers' hands in 2013 for $300 each: all in an effort to develop a consumer model with a similar low price. Along with consumer-game developers, it is known that DOE developers have also expressed interest in this new platform.

Speaking to consumer-game trade publications in 2013, at the time of the launch of dev-kit system, Palmer Luckey, founder of Oculus VR, and Nate Mitchell, vice president of product development, spoke honestly about the enormous challenge with the first dev-kits. Mitchell said: 'The Rift delivers in many ways – maybe not on the VR dream entirely, but it's the first step in the right direction', while Luckey went further and said:

> *Developers see it as a good tool for creating virtual reality. It's not the best solution yet, and not the be all and end all of where we want to be. Problems like low latency, precision head tracking and wide field of view have been fixed – naturally over time we'll get higher-res small screens.*

Going on to explain:

> *There were attempts at VR in the past – but the developers are now finally thinking 'OK, this might actually work this time'. We're not showing a half-baked system.*

Mitchell concluded: 'We're a firm believer that the next generation of input devices will focus around VR.'

It was suggested that the enthusiasm generated by the 'Oculus Rift' was in part due to a lack of impressive details available on Gen-8 consoles for game developers and consumers hungry for real 'cutting-edge' entertainment. Speaking to the authors of this book, Luckey commented on applications of Oculus's technology in the DOE sector:

> *The higher budgets, larger spaces, and potential for trained attendants enable virtual reality experiences that are not possible in the home, at least not today. However, rapid technological advancement points to future in-home virtual reality systems being able to deliver the same kinds of experiences at a much lower cost.*

It is with great anticipation that the consumer-electronics industry waits to see the final reaction to the eagerly anticipated 'Oculus Rift' dev-kits, but there is an out-of-home element to many of the early adopters and supporters of the Oculus VR fund-raising effort. Chris Roberts, famous for the popular consumer space-combat game 'Wing Commander', who successfully undertook his own $2m Kickstarter campaign for a new space-epic game (called 'Star Citizen' including an intense space-sim), confirmed that the new company behind the project, Cloud Imperium Games, would be working to create a cockpit and motion base that would offer a hyper-realistic simulation of the PC-game experience using an 'Oculus Rift'. This simulator would initially be used as a promotion tool on a tour of the communities that backed the game.

This surge of popularity was observed by Nolan Bushnell:

> *What I have seen that interested me ... well there may be a place for the 'Oculus Rifts' in the public-space scene – for me, one of the touch-stones to gauging the viability of a product like this is if people like John Carmack and Tim Sweeny get excited – they are so damn good that I pay attention when they are involved in something. These are guys that are consistently breaking down technological barriers. Virtual reality has always been hurt by latency giving motion sickness. if you can get below 10-millisecond latency, then anyone can beat it – another factor to bear in mind is that you can train yourself out of motion sickness. I was on a ship for seven days recently and got seasick, so I focused and trained myself out of it and felt better the next day. The players are the same – what I have seen of the Oculus Rift gets me excited.*

Along with VR HMDs there is the issue of tracking (the ability for the computer to orientate the user's display to correspond with the virtual environment). Previously VR tracking technology has proven contentious. Over the years, however, better magnetic tracking has been joined to optical motion sensing. This technology appeared on the consumer-game scene: first with the motion-capture technology used in the Nintendo 'Wii' game console and later in 2010 with the launch of the Microsoft 'Kinect', based on camera tracking developed by PrimeSense. It is hoped that HMD technology can be combined with the cheap motion tracking used in the gaming and mobile-device sectors and CGI.

The placement of the individual in the virtual environment has driven much of the thinking behind the modern approach to VR, including the improvements in tracking. One such approach is from UK-based Mocap Games, a division of Animalive. The company uses their parent operation's patented and successful motion-tracking suit (eMove): players wear the upper-body sensor of the suit and a VR HMD and sit on a special swivel seat to play a networked shooting game called 'Sci-Shoota'. The eMove technology has also been applied to a non-VR experience. A rock-climbing simulator, 'Hang Tough', represents the user's arm movements on a virtual character who can climb, swing and traverse various obstacles.

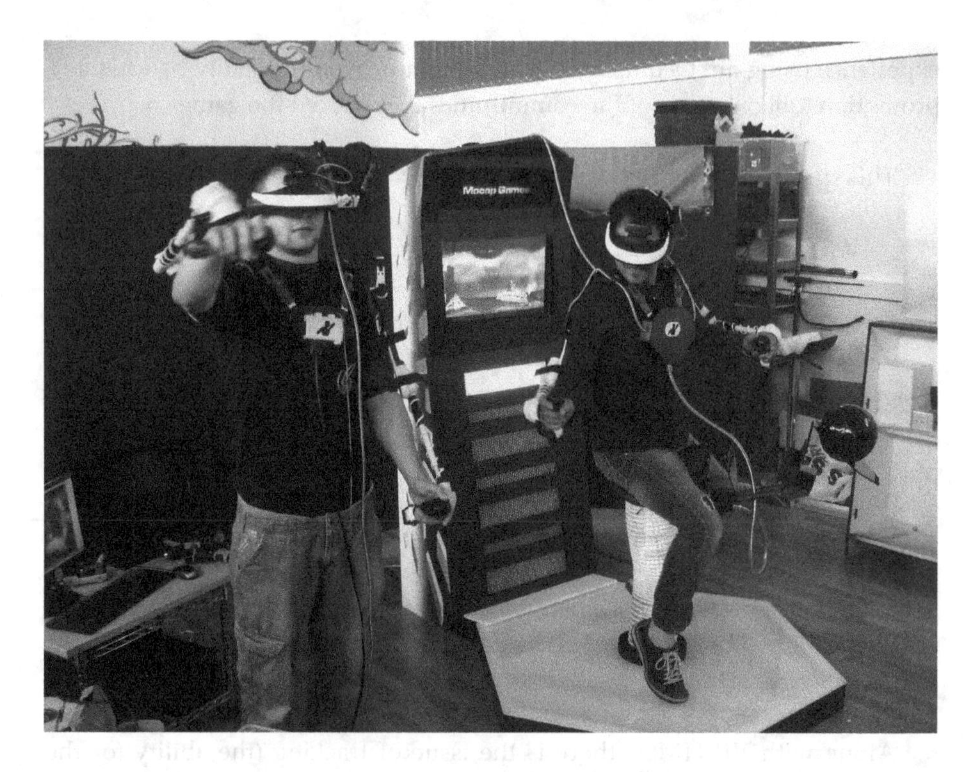

Figure 4.1 Development of MoCap Games' VR system: combining their leading mechanical motion-capture suit with the latest HMD

Asked why they had embraced VR, Paul Collimore, operations manager at Brighton Video Gamesuits Ltd., owners of Mocap Games, said:

> *With the advances in in-home digital entertainment, visitors to amusement centres have very high expectations in regards to video games. VR has always been regarded as the Holy Grail of video gaming, and our advances in technology means that we can now offer an arcade VR experience without letting the end user down.*

Regarding the unique elements of Mocap Games' system, he said:

> *The Mocap suit allows the player to control the whole upper body of the in-game avatar. So the player lifts his arm, the avatar lifts its arm, the player blocks with his arm, the avatar blocks with its arms. Mixed with the HMD, this provides a completely immersive experience.*

Obviously this is innovative technology and not easy to just drop into the amusement sector. Discussing the issues of working with such an advanced approach Collimore commented:

> *As our system is an operator-assisted attraction, we have experienced confusion from facilities that run conventional coin-op video games. They can't come to grips with the concept of having an employee out in the games area helping the players in and out of the system. On the other side of the coin, theme parks, holiday parks, and large FECs have embraced the system, largely because they have staff to man rides and attractions. They understand that modern players have high expectations, and if it takes a bit of man power to meet those expectations then they're ready to provide it.*

Coming from a background of advanced technology, Paul is struck by the lack of new technology in the theme-park and amusement sector. He observes that:

> *Augmented reality is underused by facilities, be it mobile apps or stand-alone distraction attractions. I think there's a real need for greater adoption of AR in these facilities and a linking of the technology to their social media platforms.*

While the application of the encumbered HMD application of VR stalled, development of projected virtual-environment viewing continued. The technology derives from the CAD and visualization sector used in automotive design and oil-and-gas exploration. Computer automated virtual environment (CAVE) enclosures use multiple rear-projection to represent the virtual environment on four or five surfaces of the enclosure. This technology has also been used as an immersive training environment for military and law-enforcement personnel. VirTra provide their versatile 'VirTra 3000' system, which offers 300° (five-screen) projection within a threat-training enclosure.

Walt Disney Imagineering used a projected virtual environment to realize remotely the planned development of Disneyland, Anaheim, California and its new 'Cars Land' attraction in 2012. Disney called their system the 'Digital Immersive Showroom' (DISH). It had four projectors creating a virtual environment that allowed executives to experience the planned attraction, ride the rides before they were constructed and make final changes. DISH presented the user with a 3-D representation of the virtual environment through special glasses and by tracking their head movements so that the scene would pan in the direction the user was going.

The limitations of placing visual technology on a user's head has triggered some new approaches to visual immersion within a virtual environment. A departure from VirTra is the approach taken by promotion and marketing company Aardvark Applications. The company has developed an audience-based multisensory theatre system using the individual 'Immersa-Dome'. High-definition imagery for the system is projected within a hemispherical display mounted on a seat capable of vibrating in synch with the visual stimuli. The user's head is placed in such a way that they are surrounded by the hemispherical display, offering a personal multisensory system.

VR has had an extensive life in marketing, especially in promotions by leading creative corporations hired to 'Wow' their clients' customers. One such example is Engage, commissioned by American automotive giant General Motors to create a branded space within Walt Disney World Resort Epcot Theme Park, in 1999. Engage installed 'Dream Chaser', a virtual simulator using special VR seats carrying 3-D goggles, wrap-around sound and movement. All the seats were fused together to create a 'flock' and therefore create an amazing experience for those riding the simulator as well as those in the queue.

Another UK company, Inition (a division of the Parity Group), has been a pioneering force in 3-D technology, production and creative services and has employed VR technology in a number of promotions. One cutting-edge VR application developed by the company was for the automotive manufacturer Nissan, who demanded an exciting experience for their presentation at the 2012 'Goodwood Festival of Speed'.

To fulfil this commission, Inition created a unique centre-piece attraction called 'Built to Thrill Wingsuit Experience'. They supplied their own VR HMD, fabricating the design through 3-D printing in-house (long before 'Oculus Rift') and developed a virtual sky-diving simulator, allowing riders wearing the HMD to navigate by their body movements on a multi-axis motion platform. All these specially developed components were blended together to create a one-of-a-kind recreation of a 6,500m plummet in a wingsuit with a game narrative controlled by the participant.

This was a unique attraction that had previously been the preserve of high-profile and heavily funded corporate marketing and promotion projects created for a specific campaign and then packed away. But, with the need for a greater level of entertainment from the promotional application of immersive technology, developers of these marketing experiences are now considering whether they can be turned into productized and usable entertainment systems. A wide variety of the latest immersive technologies are leaving the rarefied atmosphere of the research centre and prototype laboratory and entering the market.

AR and VR have been unwitting bed fellows, offering similar opportunities and restrictions: placing information in the user's vision can trace its lineage back to the research projects for the Apache helicopter, TADS technology and earlier NASA virtual-cockpit research. As previously mentioned, AR has continued to drive a sector of the out-of-home entertainment industry. Regarding encumbered applications, the sudden resurgence in popularity of AR, though projects such as Google's 'Project Glass' (a head-mounted display linked to social-networking apps), raises the expectation that those in the R&D sector of the attractions and amusement scene will consider this technology.

Visitors to large theme parks have already been seen using camera-enabled mobile phones to scan imagery only seen through the augmented display of their devices. It is expected that the AR window on the real world, will appear alongside the VR window on the virtual world, as compelling out-of-home gaming experiences.

Blending Augmented Reality and Mixed Reality with Live Theatre

Increasing experimentation with the fusion of AR or mixed reality with live theatre provides glimpses into the potential blending of the two media, although work in this area is generally embryonic.

One notable example of this fusion is 'Half Real', an interactive live theatre performance using spatial AR that was developed at the University of South Australia. The audience of a murder-mystery play were invited to vote on each step of the investigation process, with results displayed in a virtual 3-D environment. Live actors were integrated into the virtual world projected onto the set and tracked as they moved about. Projected content was activated based on their movements.

AR'istophanes, an experimental mixed-reality theatre project at the St Polten School of Applied Sciences in Austria, is also introducing mixed reality and AR into live theatre. It features 3-D animated characters that are tracked through motion-capture systems. The characters are currently viewed through 3-D glasses, but will be viewed through optical see-through AR glasses with head tracking by 2014. Audience members navigate the scenes and explore the stage using a controller. As such, the project is designed to place the audience in the role of director. AR'istophanes uses smartphone apps and real-time rendering.

The integration of virtual 'robot' characters into AR could lead to particularly intriguing entertainment and marketing possibilities. FlyBy Media (formerly Ogmento) has helped pioneer new opportunities for this hybrid form with its AR pet robot, OBOTO, a free app for the iPhone, which eliminates the need for 'initialization' and artificial tracking devices. It integrates a digital character called Oggie into real world settings, such as streets, tables and floors, and allows the user to 'pan, zoom, and explore' using 'natural surface tracking'. OBOTO can also be used for other applications such as virtual mascots and toys.

The Trends

The new immersive experience sector is not just built on cost-effective hardware but also on experiential hardware that provides the user with a fascinating experience within the virtual environment.

PHYSICAL INTERFACE

From the deployment of the Mocap's eMove suit to the use of a new generation of haptic gloves and interfaces, force-feedback and motion tracking have become important elements of the development of VR. The console industry's love-affair with motion tracking, especially apparent in Nintendo's 'Wii' and Microsoft's 'Kinect', has lead to greater use of cheap tracking technology in the market, but it also has to be remembered that developments in the mobile-phone sector, such as enhanced positioning and orientation technology, could have immersive applications.

IMMERSIVE DISPLAYS

Another aspect of the development of mobile-phone and tablet displays is the creation of increasingly effective flat-screen panels, used in new HMD and goggle systems along with superimposed displays to provide AR experiences. This ranges from the use of transparent LCDs creating virtual display units to the projection of HD imagery onto surfaces such as walls and floors for interactive experiences.

HIGH-FIDELITY BINAURAL AUDIO

One aspect of personalized display systems is the enclosure of the user with their own head-set and head-phones. Use of stereophonic audio in games has been limited, although the theme-park industry has installed binaural enhanced attractions, such as Walt Disney World's 'ExtraTERRORestrial Alien Encounter' in 1994. The future of new immersive platforms, possibly involving HMDs, will be linked with the re-emergence of this approach to user environment representation.

AUGMENTED ENVIRONMENTS

The ability to supply information to a user from the virtual environment superimposed on their real-world view has been a reality since the first head-up display (HUD) was deployed in fighter aircraft, a development of the early reflective gun sites of the 1950s. As mentioned previously, in the 1980s target acquisition and designation sights (TADS) projected information into the user's field of view, and this has become essential to high-workload situations, such as combat and commercial aircraft. But, with the use of see-through designs in mobile phones and tablets, it is expected that a new Graphical User Interface (GUI) lexicon will be created to support information superimposed on the user's vision, from glasses, overlaid windscreens or superimposed projection systems.

TOTAL IMMERSION

At this time, being totally immersed in a virtual environment still seems to be a dream to a large portion of those involved in VR. A small percentage of those embracing immersive entertainment are looking not to represent the user in a conventional virtual experience but to offer a total 'out-of-body' experience: the modern equivalent of the isolation tank. In its latest iteration, VR could offer a new means for social consciousness, creating a brand-new language of interfaces and definition of what can be seen as a game. At least two developers have created prototypes that offer an enclosure for the user to enter and immerse themselves in a hedonistic environment (e.g. the 'i-Cocoon').

SIMULATION SICKNESS

An aspect of VR that is little discussed is mild to severe headaches or more serious nausea, but it is essential to recognize the risk. The enclosed centrifugal simulator of Walt Disney's 'Mission: Space' attraction induced symptoms of simulation sickness in a small number of visitors (which the media jumped upon, forcing changes to the attraction).

Concerns have already been raised over long exposure to VR HMD systems with all-encroaching display media. In particular, there is concern that, although short exposure presents no problems, after 15 minutes susceptibility grows. This could raise serious questions about the viability for VR in the home for long games. The issue of overexposure and physical fatigue may force VR back to the short-play periods common in DOE.

As VR attempts to generate more revenue, the need for cheap technology that delivers on its promise is essential. At the time of writing, it is clear that 'Oculus Rift' and Google 'Project Glass' have captured the zeitgeist; however, how much of this technology will be realistically applicable for home use is another question.

MOVIE THEATRES EMBRACE THE INTERACTIVE HORIZON

Perhaps one of the most significant potential opportunities for games in the DOE market is in movie theatres, though many attempts failed to have much impact, often due to their contrived, canned interactivity and the burden of expensive infrastructure. Activity in this area has accelerated in the past few years, driven by the increasing use of smartphones and social media and the growing trend towards digital cinema.

Noticeably, many of these recent efforts have dispensed with audience control of movie scenes. One of the more striking efforts in recent years to allow the audience influence over scenes was *Last Call*, an interactive horror film shown in Germany in 2010. The film, which was developed by the horror channel, 13th Street, invited audience members equipped with smartphones to send a text in order to interact with the film. A randomly chosen moviegoer would then receive a call from a particular character in the film requesting advice on the next move they should make. The character then followed that moviegoer's direction, triggering the following movie scene with the help of recognition software and ensuring different endings to the movie.

Given the resistance of most moviegoers to paying for these games and interactive experiences in theatres, most on-screen games are offered free, and many are sponsored by major brands. That scenario is not likely to change much in the next few years, although some opportunities might

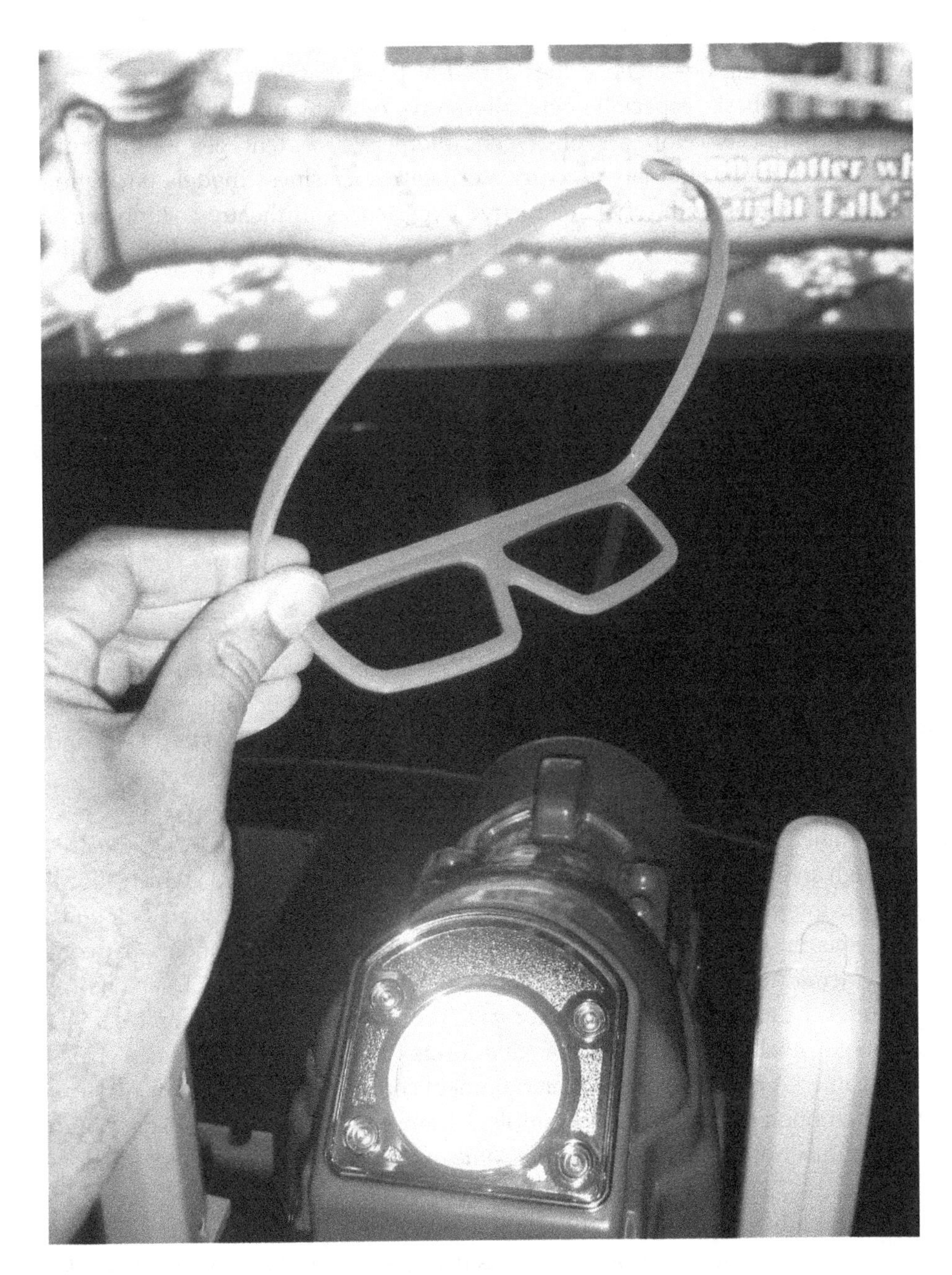

Figure 4.2 NAMCO Bandai's 'Deadstorm Pirates' 3-D shooting experience: 3-D has driven innovation in the movie industry and also found a home in the next generation of amusement systems

exist for offering on-screen games aimed at passionate game audiences on a pay-per-play basis, especially new, alternative or cult games, and a promising market might develop for on-screen interactive content geared to high-end audiences in alternative or private theatres. Business models packaging on-screen games with other interactive experiences in theatres or movies as part of premium theatre tickets or subscriptions are likely to fare better in the near future with the bulk of moviegoers.

A growing number of companies have enabled moviegoers to interact with and control games on screen through their body movements. For example, NCM Media Networks partnered Audience Entertainment Group and Disney Cruise Line in an AudienceGame interactive game experience called 'Aqua Duck' (using a gesture-based system developed by Audience Entertainment) as a promotion for the cruise line in NCM theatres in major US cities during the Christmas season of 2011.

Audience members essentially 'rode' with Donald Duck on a large-screen version of an aquatic ride, controlling the action on screen and navigating through the game by waving their arms in unison with other audience members and leaning left or right. Along the way, they encountered water blasts and could glide down a slide and pick up objects.

Tangibal Media has also brought gestural interactive experiences to theatres through an interactive floor projection system called 'Playground', which allows users to interact with games and other interactive experiences through their body movements. The system is a key component in an interactive media network for cinema advertising developed in association with Pearl & Dean, which includes theatres in the UK and Norway. The network also incorporates a 3-D technology called 'uPlay', which enables users to interact with on-screen effects and games. A number of major entertainment companies have used the network for promotional purposes. For example, Paramount Pictures used 'Playground' on a number of occasions to promote some of their films in UK theatres.

More often, recent interactive experiences in movie theatres have allowed audiences to participate from their seats using handheld devices. For example, Timeplay Entertainment has developed an interactive system allowing audiences to interact with games, ads and other content on the big screen using wireless handheld devices. In order to participate, they must download an app from Timeplay before the movie. They can play games with or against their friends and other audience members. Winners receive prizes, such as free drinks. Timeplay introduced a playful game to Canadian theatres in association with Koodo Mobile allowing audience members to throw snowballs at El Kabador, Koodo's animated character.

Some interactive experiences in theatres are linking mobile-phone content with large-screen movie content. For example, Mass Hysteria Entertainment announced in 2012 a venture with Patrick Greene and Alexander Harrington to introduce a system that will enable audiences to interact with films via smartphones using a technology called 'SideFlick' developed by Greene and Harrington. The technology will allow audience members to interact with content on their smartphones in conjunction with movies on the large screen. It is currently being tested and is reportedly due to be introduced commercially in 2013.

As mentioned earlier, new forms of laser games have recently been introduced into movie theatres, sometimes in connection with special events or festivals, such as the strategic and collaborative game 'Renga' from WallFour Studios. This type of experience is likely to play an increasingly important role in theatres in the near future.

As also mentioned earlier, 4-D and 5-D experiences are increasingly appearing in movie theatres, typically generating greater audience engagement and revenues. Interactive experiences in movie theatres are likely to become significantly more immersive in the next five to ten years, especially as technologies like mixed reality, VR and holography start to be used in theatres.

We expect the boundaries between movie theatres and LBE centres to increasingly blur, with theatres offering a wider range of interactive/immersive experiences. We anticipate that some of these theatres will exclusively or primarily provide specialized content targeted at passionate niche audiences, such as sci-fi and games. A number will likely incorporate a wide range of immersive and interactive experiences, including online games, gestural interactivity, mixed reality, VR and interactive lasers. For example, some of the VR experiences in these theatres might allow the audience to project themselves into movie scenes through characters of their choice, explore environments in those movies, help determine plot choices, and select or even create special effects for the movies at certain points. Another possibility is that a greater number of these theatres will serve as settings for location-based games, some of which might be connected with movies shown in the theatres, incorporating online games, gestural interactive experiences, AR and laser experiences, and probably 3-D printing, connected with the movies.

Andrei Severny, a noted filmmaker and artist, has presented a perspective on future movie theatres that takes some of these kinds of scenarios to their furthest extent. Envisioning a fluid, but often troubling world, he suggests that:

> *Theatres will evolve into large-scale public attractions or urban theme parks, where cinema will be only part of the experience. The most immersive forms of cinema will play according to the viewer's wishes outside of theatres and displays. There will be profound synergies between gaming and movies. At first, these experiences will be enabled through currently emerging technologies and systems, such as flexible screens, motion controls, haptic or tactile technology, smart glasses, virtual reality, and augmented reality. The merging of real and projected worlds will produce a seamless experience, creating a complete illusion of the user being a part of the film. We may reach a point where the real world becomes secondary. Landmarks and businesses will have stories, characters, sequences, and scenes attached to them, which will be accessible to visitors on the spot. This material will all be stored, affording potential experiences designed to increase one's relationship with the place. Every location or object will contain massive amounts of recorded information ready for playback.*

Apps in Amusement Parks and Movie Theatres

Given the widespread popularity of mobile phones, amusement parks are making increased use of multifaceted apps to attract visitors, disseminate park information more expeditiously and conveniently, and increase operational efficiency (especially by routing visitors better), brand loyalty and visitor engagement. Typically, these apps provide guests with up-to-date information on attractions and facilities, including waiting times for rides, directions to facilities and attractions, promotional information and ticketing capabilities. Increasingly, amusement-park apps are offering more entertainment-oriented experiences, such as games and links to such social-networking sites as Facebook and Twitter.

Apps geared to amusement parks have grown in sophistication and versatility. For example, Dogfi.sh Mobile developed an 'immersive' app for Legoland California that was aimed at extending park visits through enhanced park-visitor management, generating greater park revenue through ticketing capabilities, and promoting park features through mobile messaging and a custom call management system (CMS). The app, which works on iPhones and iPod Touch devices, includes a trip planner; information on operating times, rides, attractions, shows, games, park events, weather and dining and retail locations in the park; social-media links; a personal photo gallery; and ticketing capabilities; as well as interactive mapping features, including park map, satellite and AR map views, to help visitors find locations more quickly and easily. The app's cloud-messaging feature allows Legoland to deliver updates to visitors more quickly.

Amusement-park apps are delivering increasingly specialized and distinctive information on parks. For example, Theme Park Nerd developed an app for Flamingo Land Theme Park and Zoo that includes information on feeding times for animals in the zoo. In another effort to expand the capabilities of amusement-park apps, the company is developing a 'friend-finder' app that allows visitors to locate their friends on a park map.

The social-media capabilities of amusement-park apps are expanding considerably. For example, Walibi Park in Belgium offers an app called Walibi Connect that takes social networking in parks to another level. It allows visitors to post messages about their favourite rides and park experiences on Facebook without using smartphones or computers, thus bridging the real and virtual worlds. In order to access this free app, visitors must register on Walibi's website to receive a barcode that entitles them to special wristband at the park with a built-in RFID chip. The wristband can be used for any rides.

Game app features can be particularly effective in engaging park visitors. For example, Dogfi.sh Mobile's app for Gardaland in 2011 incorporated a scavenger hunt to better engage visitors.

The scope of pervasive media in public places is expanding to include more diverse non-game content. One of the more distinctive manifestations of that trend is 'Theatre Jukebox', an arcade-like device which combines animation, projections and binaural audio and delivers interactive stories through RFID technology embedded in postcards, which 'play' stories selected by users. As such, the device, which was developed by Lucy Heywood and Barney Heywood of the Stand + Stare Collective and refined in conjunction with the Pervasive Media Studio, offers an intriguing blend of low- and high-tech elements and is geared to theatres. A special application for the jukebox called 'Theatre Jukebox Presents: A World Elsewhere' was accessible in the foyer of the Royal Shakespeare Company's Swan Theatre in Stratford from January to April 2013 and was designed to foster greater engagement with theatregoers. It used cards inspired by the company's current programme as well as past productions.

Disney Parks has also placed a special value on games in their apps. Their Disney Mobile Magic app allows visitors to Disneyland and Walt Disney World to access a range of games using Verizon Wireless and their iPhones, including 'Disney Character Puzzle', which challenges visitors to guess a particular character before a timer expires, and 'Disney Character Quiz', which challenges visitors to identify which character most resembles them.

In some cases, park-game apps have been closely tied to rewards to induce greater engagement and park visits. For example, Six Flags partnered with Ask.com in 2011 to develop a mobile trivia game for iPhones called 'Skip the Line' aimed at users within two miles of their parks. Users answering questions correctly would receive points and a chance to win a spot at the 'head of the line' for rides and attractions at those parks.

Apps are also used to deliver extra content to moviegoers related to the film they are watching, such as background character information. The 'Horror Film' app, which was introduced in Holland in April 2012, is a free app synched with a movie. According to the filmmakers' synopsis, the film centres around a young student called Anna who becomes 'addicted to smartphones, apps, and social media, and discovers a mysterious app that provides a key to her personal life and friends. The app sends her cryptic messages and codes connected to the strange deaths of people around her' and the moviegoers receive the same messages. The app also allows moviegoers to access special additional content about the film during showings, such as photos and extra scenes that fit into the screenplay and are not available to non-moviegoers. All users of the app have access to the film's trailer, cast information and a set photos.

Apps at the Museum

Museum apps are demonstrating the capacity to change the relationship between visitors and museums and to transform museum visits into more meaningful and engaging experiences.

As Aaron Radin, former CEO of Toura, and currently senior vice president of partnerships and portfolio products at NBC Universal, sees it, museum apps are primarily designed to 'complement the museum experience' by 'providing visitors additional contextually relevant content that enhances their appreciation of the works' they are viewing. Toura is the developer of a platform called the Toura Mobile App Producer, which enables museums to create customized virtual museum tours that can be downloaded onto visitors' iPhones.

A key benefit of museum apps is their ability to involve museum visitors more. For example, many users of the Brooklyn Museum's API app are recommending objects at the museum to other visitors using the app's 'like' feature. In addition, museum apps can be very useful tools for securing museum sponsorships and funds. The Museum of Modern Art received funds from Bloomberg Art for an app that the museum's development department could use to attract donors.

The American Museum of Natural History (AMNH) has released three free apps so far: 'AMNH Explorer', 'Dinosaurs' and 'Cosmic Discoveries'. AMNH's main goal with the apps was to 'create a virtual mobile exhibition' for a 'global audience' and allow 'our audience to connect more deeply with objects and content in our museum', explained Linda Perry-Lube, chief digital officer of RF/Binder, formerly chief digital officer of AMNH. 'AMNH Explorer' allows visitors to 'virtually explore the entire museum' and choose tours or create their owns tour from a list of popular exhibits and share their museum experiences with family and friends by linking with their Twitter profiles. The 'Dinosaurs' app provided '800 photos of dinosaurs and stories of individual dinosaurs', and the 'Cosmic Discoveries' app currently provides '1,000 photos of astronomical phenomena, such as planets and comets, with 9 stories in total', she reports. Perry-Lube noted that the museum was 'continually updating and adding content to the apps' and, in fact, will be 'introducing iPad versions' of its 'Dinosaurs' and 'Cosmic Discoveries' apps 'soon'.

Toura has developed iPhone apps for various museums and exhibits, including the Art Institute of Chicago, the Smithsonian Institute's retrospective on Yves Klein and the Musee Guimet in Paris. Its platform has also been used by London's Imperial Art Museum. Toura charges visitors $1.99 to $5.99 for their museum apps and has not found much resistance to paying for them.

Some apps transcend conventional museum-guide models to engage visitors on a deeper level through play experiences, such as the game 'Tate Trumps'. This free app, which was commercially introduced in August, was jointly developed by Hide and Seek, a developer of 'social games and playful experiences' and Tate Media. It originated from an effort by the Tate Gallery to seek out projects that 'change the way visitors relate to the gallery space', explains Margaret Robertson, managing director at Hide and Seek. 'Tate Trumps' is geared to a wide audience, including those unfamiliar with the iPhone and video games, with play kept 'simple', she says. The app enables users to experience the Tate Galley in different ways through 'Battle Mode',

'Mood Mode' or 'Collector Mode'. 'Battle Mode' challenges users in an imaginary battle with physical artwork; 'Collector Mode' affords players the opportunity to create their own art gallery; and 'Mood Mode' allows players to select artworks they consider particularly menacing, exhilarating or absurd. The game has elicited a very positive response, with visitors spending on average 1–1¼ hours on the game per visit, says Robertson.

However, implementing apps in museums is often challenging. A key concern is 'apprising' visitors about the 'existence of apps' in museums and 'educating' them about the 'value of those apps', says Radin. Another potential drawback to museum apps is the lack of WiFi in some museums, particularly smaller museums, he notes, though he feels WiFi is not really necessary for museum apps.

AR museum apps promise to offer even more engaging and immersive experiences. 'Streetmuseum', an app offered by the Museum of London, gives an indication of the potential of AR in museums. It allows visitors to superimpose historical photos of London over modern ones in real time, affording them a unique and vivid perspective on the evolution of the city.

Augmented Reality: New Immersive Dimensions in Leisure Facilities

Extensions and variations of 3-D technology have been increasingly appearing in amusement parks and other leisure facilities. AR, one of those extensions, seems to have some of the greatest prospects in those facilities, because it is more transparent, cheaper than many VR technologies, less cumbersome and more rooted in reality.

Creating magic seems to be the mantra of amusement parks, and few technologies seem to exude 'magic' more than AR. But AR can and should be much more than a flashy bauble in parks and other leisure facilities. AR attractions should not overemphasize technology. They should be organic, accessible and improve the park experience, according to Chris Durmick, creative director at the Thinkwell Group, a California-based experiential design firm. In order for AR experiences to succeed, they must be based on content and storytelling, he stresses. He emphasizes that AR is primarily useful as a tool and toolbox, not as an end product.

Figure 4.3 Applying technology to the traditional telescope: Western Europe's tallest building, the Shard, uses these revolutionary AR telescopes to overlay information

One of the key problems with most AR games is that they are a novelty, fun for short periods of time, asserts Dave Cobb, creative director at the Thinkwell Group. But AR experiences in amusement parks cannot be a gimmick or a gadget, they must be deeper, given that visitors typically spend a whole day there.

Jon Snoddy, vice president of research and development at Walt Disney Imagineering, stresses that Disney's approach to AR is not about technology, it is focused on 'creating new experiences around our characters and stories' and 'making them as realistic and personal as possible through the use of such technologies as AR'.

Some experts believe AR will dramatically change parks. Chris Stapleton, president of Symiosis Real World Laboratory, sees AR completely transforming the entire amusement-park experience and the 'experiential entertainment paradigm'. He believes AR will 'change the way amusement parks do business' and 'create a whole new world for parks'. In his view, AR will change parks and other leisure facilities in three fundamental ways:

1. by providing the 'ability to tell infinite stories in a finite space';
2. by integrating virtuality into physical reality, combining the intensity of physical experiences with a virtual aspect and essentially 'melting the boundaries between the real and virtual worlds'; and
3. by extending experiences beyond the confines of theme parks and extending the breadth of experiences to other environments, such as malls, schools and recreational parks.

Stapleton points out that 'different audiences desire different experiences'. AR will allow for more 'personalized' experiences and 'different levels of engagement'.

From the perspective of Clark Dodsworth, managing director of Osage Associates, AR in amusement parks should be viewed as part of a broader trend towards 'contextually aware location-based services', driven by the delivery of personalized information geared to each visitor. These services will generate significant revenue for many sectors, beginning with amusement parks, because 'new heightened experiences offered by parks can be readily monetized. 'Hyper-personalized' experiences will be ideal for parks and generate considerable new revenue'.

Mobile AR has made some inroads in parks and seems well positioned to become a leading platform for AR in parks and other leisure facilities. Dodsworth contends that smartphones 'will serve as the baseline AR information and entertainment platform in amusement parks, delivering greater engagement with the licensed characters of each park, the way strolling costume characters now do, only with more knowledge of each visitor'. Likewise, 'apps for amusement parks will prepare visitors for attractions, and fill in gaps between experiences'.

One of the key driving factors for AR in amusement parks is the increasing 'buying power of millennials', whose life is centred around 'mobile platforms', says Michael McDermott, director of sales for Active Network. They use mobile devices for engagement and sharing experiences, he notes.

AR can be highly beneficial for parks on an operational level, according to Durmick. As he observes, mobile AR can offer users key park information, including information on queues for particular rides, locations of particular restaurants and webcams of particular attractions. Visitors can use mobile AR to learn about the availability of attractions and services in parks. As a result, AR will help to 'reduce queues to a very low level', observes Stapleton.

Nicolas Mollet, project manager at Futuroscope, believes 'the best application for AR in parks is service-related', providing visitors with information on attraction locations and waiting times via mobile apps, for example.

One of the most obvious applications of mobile AR in parks is 'way-finding', which involves 'capturing real estate for entertainment value', says Stapleton. In this vein, Thorpe Park in England introduced an AR app called 'Thorpe Park Official' last year, which offers guests a view of nearby 'attractions, restaurants, and retail units' in the park. Also, Resort Technology Partners launched RealParx last year, an AR prototype for the iPhone 3GS and other mobile devices that can serve as a travel guide for amusement parks and other leisure facilities. The platform allows users to find their way around parks and leisure facilities, geotag locations of interest, and share photos. For example, Resort Technology Partners developed an AR app for MGM in Las Vegas, which provides visitors with information about art galleries in the city centre, complemented by information on particular artists in each gallery. The app also allows visitors to book activities, make reservations and participate in social media.

AR can also open up key marketing opportunities for parks and other leisure facilities. McDermott feels that AR has considerable marketing value in leisure facilities and has found that the marketing departments of amusement parks have shown great interest in AR. In this regard, RealParx affords parks and other leisure facilities the ability to exploit location-based marketing opportunities, while users are present at particular locations and in the process of making purchasing decisions. AR can have significant use as a market-research tool for parks, allowing them to better understand their visitors, he points out. AR can be used for targeted promotions and registering park visitors with loyalty programmes.

AR can play a broader promotional role in parks, Bruno Uzzan, CEO of Total Immersion, concurs. For example, interactive advertising campaigns based around AR can induce people to visit theme parks after playing games online. AR apps allow visitors to continue their park experience at home on tablet devices, for example, says Uzzan. At the same time, McDermott warns that parks and other leisure facilities must be cognizant of privacy rules when gathering information on consumers through mobile AR apps.

Another key use of mobile AR is embedding a story in an experience, triggering physical elements and integrating them into the story, says Stapleton. Mobile helps 'melt the gap between physical and virtual elements' in his view.

Nicolas Bapst, former product marketing manager for Total Immersion, sees increasing use of AR in theme parks on mobile devices and the delivery of interactive games through mobile AR. Smartphones connected with AR will activate various activities in parks and establish a digital link with customers, he believes. For example, a special app could be installed on a smartphone with suggestions on new ways to spend the day in the park. The smartphone can be used to entertain visitors by providing pictures, mini-games and a magic-mirror feature. The iPad, in particular, allows parks to establish links with visitors and enhance their enjoyment of theme park experiences. He calls attention to the considerable potential of AR experiences driven by tablets, especially the iPad2, in amusement parks and museums. For example, these devices allow for the development of more social games in public places. Mobile AR devices can entertain park guests, provide more personalized experiences and entice visitors to parks.

But mobile AR faces some key challenges in parks. One of the potential drawbacks to mobile AR is that it can devolve into a 'piece of media and real estate' if it is not used properly, says Durmick. Another challenge is making the AR experience compelling enough for people to want to engage with others using mobile devices. The challenge with AR is ensuring that audiences are not isolated from each other by that technology, Durmick stresses. He believes the goal of amusement parks with AR should be to turn it into a social tool, making it more interactive with the environment.

In this regard, Stapleton believes social media will play an increasingly important role in AR in parks and other leisure facilities. For example, social media services such as 'Foursquare will be increasingly combined with AR' in parks, says Stapleton. Along these lines, Snoddy predicts AR will extend the excitement of roller coasters, drawing visitors into social networks through mobile devices, allowing visitors to 'bring their web of friends with them, wherever they're located'. He notes that 'theme park experiences are already social experiences'. AR allows those experiences to be 'extended outside the parks'. Ultimately, Durmick sees endless possibilities for mobile AR in amusement parks, including multi-player games, educational content and perks for repeat visitors.

One of the earliest AR attractions in parks was the 'Magic Mirror' at Disneyland, which debuted in 2008 and allowed users to try on virtual dresses and glasses, according to its developer, Ernie Merlan, CEO of Merlan Creative. The company also created the AR project for Innovention's 'House of Tomorrow' at Disneyland, which immersed users in a computer world where they could interact with different products in the house of the future.

As Bapst notes, another key AR application for theme parks is treasure hunts, which can be activated by smartphones using scenery from the parks as the background. In fact, the Kim Possible World Showcase Adventure at Epcot, which incorporates AR elements, was expressly developed by Disney as part of its exploration of new treasure-hunt games, which were favoured because of their great appeal with both children and their parents, reports Jonathan Ackley, senior director of Show Producer Interactive, for Walt Disney Imagineering. The attraction equips visitors with 'Kimmunicator' mobile devices at kiosks throughout the park, which they employ to carry out missions to prevent particular villains from taking over the world. Along the way, visitors encounter various Kim Possible characters who offer clues to help them accomplish their missions. The 'Kimmunicator' also allows visitors to take control of top-secret equipment in the World Showcase Pavilions at Epcot. They can play the adventure at seven of the pavilions.

Each adventure runs for 30 minutes and offers a different mission featuring separate visual events and a different super villain from the animated series. For example, in one adventure, visitors assume the role of a secret agent, pursue a criminal up the Eiffel Tower and point an 'old-fashioned camera' at the tower, activating a scanner that triggers a ray-gun blast that ricochets across the tower and hits the villain.

Another key aspect of the Kim Possible experience is that it takes photos of visitors and presents them as the 'cover model' for the fictitious Viking Fashion Agency, which visitors then receive on their mobile devices. Visitors also take pictures of an innocuous poster in the Norway Pavilion at Epcot. The 'Kimmunicator' scans the poster and reveals a hidden stolen masterpiece behind it. The attraction also invites visitors to take physical golf balls with a microchip inside to a sports shop in the UK pavilion, where they are instructed to drop the balls into a golf-ball washer, which then shows those balls on a screen and reveals the hidden plans of characters in the adventure.

According to Ackley, the attraction has been viewed very favourably and is generating significant engagement. A number of visitors spend several hours a day, and some even spend the entire day playing the adventures. Disney found that children particularly enjoyed Kim Possible for the game aspect, and parents liked it primarily for its wry humour.

AR can work well for certain types of rides, such as children's and dark rides, says Bapst. However, Uzzan does not feel AR is well suited to speed rides. One of the most popular AR rides is a dark ride called 'Les Animaux du Futur' for Futuroscope, which has drawn 'over 3 million visitors since its opening in 2008', according to Mollet. The attraction allows guests to interact with imaginary animals from three different eras in a futuristic landscape (5 million, 100 million, and 200 million years into the future), through the use of AR binoculars and sensor bracelets. It is based around the BBC TV show 'The Future is Wild'. Mollet notes that children respond very enthusiastically to the AR experience, while adults have exhibited a more 'mixed' reaction.

Another popular AR experience is 'Hitchhiking Ghosts', which Disney developed for its 'Haunted Mansion' ride at the Magic Kingdom in Florida. The experience, which was introduced in April 2013 and uses a projection system, takes realistic photos of visitors in the Doon Buggy and projects them onto an object that seems like a mirror in front of them (in actuality a video screen), triggering an animation of the Hitchhiking Ghosts around them. The experience allows for new interactions, with the ghosts even playing pranks on visitors, such as pulling off their heads and swapping them. It allows visitors to look into mirrors and see themselves in the characters. In essence, the ghosts come from a fantasy world and intrude into the real space, coming to life in the experience.

Discovery apps are emerging as key AR uses in amusement parks and other leisure facilities. For example, Thinkwell Group developed an AR experience in conjunction with the Fernbank Museum of Natural History for Fernbank NatureQuest in Georgia, which was introduced during 2013 and enhanced the discovery process for children at the centre. The company decided that AR 'was the best way to disseminate content'. As Chris Durmick notes, the AR element 'was truly hidden' at the attraction. Dave Cobb adds that the experience was completely transparent, and no touchscreens or other gadgets were used. Visitors used 'night vision goggles' to observe animals in their natural environment. Children could use 'binoculars' to track animals using real-time video images from cameras, which popped up on the viewscreen, providing information on animal habitats, such as beaver dams. The experience is highly intuitive and allows two people to engage with each other. It also incorporates magic mirrors. Response to the attraction has been very positive: it drew 232 visitors an hour in the first few days it was open, claims Durmick. Parents also found the AR element appealing and made many discoveries themselves using the app, he reports.

Nature exploration was also at the heart of the AR experience Metaio developed for the Sydney Aquarium as part of the 'Future is Wild' multimedia project for Sydney 2010, reports Lisa Murphy, former product marketing manager for Metaio, Inc. For that project, a webcam was used to capture visitor photos with the assistance of face-tracking devices. The AR feature allowed visitors to see themselves with scuba outfits swimming virtually with 'creatures and animals' underwater.

User-created experiences employing such technologies as AR are likely to become a more important part of parks in the future. Visitors 'will take ownership of experiences inside parks', and 'outside people will create experiences in the parks', ushering in a new age of 'user-created realities', predicts Stapleton. This, in turn, will generate 'increased repeat visits' to parks' and 'build regional aspects of destination theme parks', he believes. In fact, one of the key goals of AR in amusement parks should be to 'alter the entire content experience by allowing fans to create apps', contends Durmick. In this regard, he calls attention to a very popular app 'Wishing Stars' made by a visitor to Disneyland.

Bapst sees a major trend toward using AR to integrate customers into live shows, particularly in Asia. These experiences are particularly compelling because they build on 3-D theatres in such facilities as amusement parks, which are being used to showcase blockbuster movies. AR experiences help upgrade those theatres by creating events where guests can interact with live shows.

Essentially, they change 3-D theatres into interactive theatres, representing an 'easy upgrade of those theatres', says Bapst.

One of the more intriguing applications of AR in a live show was introduced in 2013 at Europa-Park in Germany. The experience was developed by Europa-Park, Total Immersion and Emotion Media Factory and uses a 'recorded system, which inserts the visitor in a holographic display'. The system is located in the 'Grimm Library', part of the newly developed 'Enchanted Forest' area, in which guests enter the world of the Brothers Grimm and have the opportunity to visit the 'Witch's Cottage', 'Sleeping Beauty's Castle' or the 'Grimm Library'.

The magic mirror is placed in the pre-show room and entertains visitors using AR while they wait for an introduction to the show's storyline. AR is used to incorporate visitors into the main show, which takes place in a theatre with 40 seats, and typically draws around 400 people an hour, claims Frederic Patuszak, project architect at Europa Park. A 3-D screen with HD holographic projection called 'Holoport' is used. During the show, which runs for six minutes, a witch and some giants emerge from a magical book, and only the wizard can save the audience. As the giants appear behind the windows of the show's set, visitors can recognize themselves. The magician's face is also one of the visitor's recorded by the magic mirror before the show. The whole object is to immerse visitors in the book's story, says Patuszak. Europa-Park also developed a second magic-mirror experience, which was used in the queue of the dark ride 'Piccolo Mondo'.

Costs for AR experiences in amusement parks vary widely: from $20,000–$30,000 for Total Immersion's magic-mirror app to a few million for an AR-centric ride, reports Uzzan.

The increasing integration of AR into multi-platform content and campaigns will likely have a significant impact on amusement parks and other leisure facilities in the near future, as those facilities use AR in a broader, richer and more organic manner. This trend clearly dovetails with the trend towards more story-based AR content in leisure facilities discussed above.

Key technological changes will have an impact on the application of AR in parks in the future. 'Voice interaction and natural gestural technology, such as "Kinect", will become the typical methods of interaction', Dodsworth predicts. Gestural AR experiences developed by such companies as Total Immersion and Snibbe Interactive are already evident today in amusement parks and other leisure facilities, he points out.

A key development likely to affect the future of AR in leisure facilities is the arrival of wearable AR systems with lightweight, HD glasses. According to Mats Johansson, CEO of EON Reality, once 'comfortable, lightweight, HD see-through glasses are available on a broad basis, they'll 'drive mixed reality forward more rapidly than practically anything else'.

A few wearable, lightweight AR systems with game and entertainment applications have been introduced onto the market. For example, Epson's Moverio BT-100 lightweight wearable Android AR HMD can be used for game and 3-D entertainment applications. The system, which offers HD resolution, incorporates multimedia capabilities, affording internet access, video viewing, streaming and downloading of movies and other content. A few entertainment applications have already been developed for the system. For example, MadMack's 'Rotation Locker' app enables easier and more enjoyable gameplay. A project developed by Thomas Sohmers fusing the system with the Parrot AR.drone quadricopter has some intriguing implications for amusement parks and other leisure facilities, especially because of the drone's existing game applications. Lumus has introduced wearable AR-display products with HD resolution, including its OE-31 and OE-32 lenses, which have consumer and entertainment uses. The lenses can be incorporated into standard glasses, such as sunglasses, and afford access to the internet, games, TV and movie content.

AR has strong potential in new hybrid game experiences in leisure facilities. For example, it is likely to be combined with such interactive entertainment forms as laser games. In a 2011 article, James Illiff highlighted the considerable potential impact of combining AR and laser-tag, thus bringing laser-tag into the virtual world and imbuing it with powerful new capabilities. To illustrate his point, he used scenarios of virtual versions of location-based games, such as laser-tag, proposed by Alberto Menache in his book *Understanding Motion Capture for Computer Animation*:

> *Essentially, a location-based game, such as laser tag, could be carried out in a virtual world. Users would wear motion-capture tags and a wireless stereoscopic head-mounted display. The virtual world's obstacles would match the real venue's obstacles, but all the decorations would be very different – the player's digital counterparts could take many different creature shapes. Weapons would also be greatly enhanced, resulting in a very realistic and immersive experience.*

In fact, a few recently introduced products are already fusing AR and laser games without traditional HMDs, such as Hasbro's iPhone Lazer Tag Blaster and the AppTag Laser Blaster game developed by Hex3 and released by Laser Blaster, though those game devices generally have rudimentary features and serious limitations, such as cumbersome configurations and sometimes blaring sounds at inopportune times.

The iPhone Lazer Tag Blaster, which was introduced in 2012, has slots for iPhone and iPod Touch units to be attached and incorporates a plastic gun with a built-in camera. The unit comes with a free app, which affords users views of their environment and graphic images of invading aliens. The game challenges players to vanquish the aliens by shooting at them with the blaster and can be played in single or multi-player mode. With each successful mission, players are awarded more advanced weapons for use in forestalling future alien invasions. The Lazer Tag Blaster can also be used for conventional laser games by groups of up to 23 people without iPhone devices.

The AppTag Laser Blaster, which was also introduced in 2012, operates for the most part in similar fashion, and comes with a companion app. It works with iPhones and Android smartphones, which can be attached to the device and used to monitor scores and other elements. The device's AR app, which is used in single-player mode, has the capability to integrate such objects as medkits, weapons and ammo packs.

Users load up the ammo app, attach it to the blaster and fire at their targets in real world surroundings. Unlike the iPhone blaster, the AppTag blaster does not require Wi-Fi or Bluetooth connections to communicate with smartphones, as it sends signals to those devices on high-frequency waves and employs an infrared beam and sensor for targeting.

Perhaps one of the more ambitious hybrid AR entertainment projects is LivePark, which incorporates AR, 4-D and user-generated content. LivePark is currently available only in a park in South Korea, though no further updates have been reported. In the near future, this kind of project is likely to have more limited use in amusement parks, though it might work well in museums and similar facilities.

Chapter 5
Social and Co-operative

Interactive Laser Experiences

Interactive laser experiences have become a key part of interactive entertainment in the DOE market, but they have much broader implications than many appreciate. In general, they allow users with laser guns, laser pointers, wands or other devices to control, manipulate or otherwise interact with laser beams as stand-alone experiences or as part of larger experiences, such as interactive dark rides. Interactive laser experiences can be particularly satisfying because they offer more physical and potent interactivity, empowering users and sometimes projecting them into fantasy worlds.

Traditionally, interactive laser experiences have been viewed as simply laser-tag games or as laser-gun elements incorporated into iDRs, and those experiences certainly represent a large portion of the market. But that narrow conception is changing, as the scope of interactive laser experiences in museums, amusement parks and other leisure facilities has expanded to include richer and more innovative laser games and such diverse interactive forms as laser graffiti, interactive laser attractions in planetariums and even laser harps. A key new element of some interactive laser experiences is their ability to allow users to engage in creativity experiences, by creating digital 'graffiti' with laser pointers, for example. This aspect is likely to expand considerably in the near future. Interactive laser games and experiences are being offered in a wider variety of leisure facilities, including location-based entertainment centres, amusement parks, bowling alleys and museums.

Laser games have been historically viewed as discrete experiences in leisure facilities, but they are becoming more integrated into a variety of interactive experiences in those facilities. They have also been primarily targeted at a young male audience, but some new forms of laser games and interactive laser experiences are aimed at a broader demographic and are geared to a wider range of leisure facilities.

Jeff Schilling, chief architect of experiences at Creative Works Theme Factory, believes interactive laser experiences have become more significant in leisure facilities largely due to the changing market for entertainment centres and amusement parks. Since consumers have less time and more choices, leisure facilities have been forced to make adaptations in the experiences they offer.

Interactive laser experiences have gained a foothold in planetariums and science centres. One of the leading pioneers of interactive laser experiences in science centres is SciPort: Louisiana's Science Center in Shevreport. The Sawyer Space Dome planetarium at the centre uses an Evans & Sutherland single-laser projection system (E&S migrated into the full-dome planetarium business, with their 'Digistar' system series, after their temperamental IG business failed). The system has three laser cavities housing red, green and blue lasers, explains Greg Andrews, planetarium manager. The planetarium's screen is tilted at a 45° angle to the guests, affording a view that is more directly in front of them. The centre introduced three main interactive laser attractions in November 2006: 'Birthday Skies', which is designed to show visitors 'on our 40-foot screen how the sky looked when they were born'; 'ISS' (International Space Station) shows, on computer stations and the planetarium screen, two models of recently retired space shuttles and allows visitors to 'dock the shuttle onto the International Space Station'; 'Constellation Quiz', divides the screen into five sections and challenges visitors to guess which constellation is in a given section.

'Birthday Skies' is the most popular 'by far' and 'appeals particularly to teenagers and young adults', reports Andrews. The interactive laser experiences run for 30 minutes and are offered 'in between scheduled programmes and shows' at the centre. Andrews estimates that about 10,000–30,000 visitors a year attend these and other interactive laser experiences.

Andrews believes laser-tag experiences would have great potential in museums and science centres, if such issues as insurance could be resolved, particularly because those experiences would appeal to young adults 'whose interest in science centres has waned'. He feels laser experiences would help bring back that audience to science centres and notes that his science centre has explored the possibility of introducing laser-tag games.

Laser games, and particularly laser-tag, have been the most successful interactive laser experiences in leisure facilities. In Schilling's view, laser games are increasingly attractive to leisure facilities because they have become cheaper and more effective, and they offer a greater range of colours. He believes laser technology will also have a greater impact in leisure facilities as it becomes 'quicker and faster'.

Laser-tag has become a 'dominant attraction' at leisure facilities, asserts Schilling. Creative Works offers laser-tag in 300 facilities, and attendance at those facilities has grown rapidly. In fact, a range of leisure facilities, such as bowling alleys and skating rinks, are retrofitting part of their facilities to accommodate laser-tag. Creative Works has partnered roller-skating rinks on the installation of laser-tag. The company has expanded the scope of laser games with 'Laser Frenzy', a 'very interactive experience' that Schilling describes as a 'mini-arcade game piece that accepts tokens and bills'. The game allows visitors to play at 'different skill levels' and lasts one minute. Many leisure facilities have incorporated it into their other experiences, using it to generate valuable 'additional revenue', says Schilling. He reports that leisure facilities have been averaging $1,500 to $1,600 a week in revenues from the game, which has been installed at 'about 100 locations so far in the last two years'. The game 'costs operators $30,000 and players $13 per play', occupies a '200 sq. ft area', and can accommodate 'up to 24 players' at a time.

Schilling sees real potential for laser games in museums. In fact, his company has been in discussions with two museums about introducing 'Laser Frenzy'. He believes 'Laser Frenzy' could attract a 'sizable audience' to museum exhibitions. For example, it could be applied essentially as an 'interactive display', showcasing laser technology and allowing visitors to learn about light and the measurement of light. Such interactive displays would help educate children about the technology behind lasers.

Schilling envisions a 'greater integration of laser-tag in dark rides' and believes that laser-tag experiences will continue to evolve.

The content in laser games is also improving, with laser games incorporating more diverse game themes and collaborative elements. For example, wallFour Studios have developed laser games for movie theatres and other public places that blend collaborative elements and extensive strategic play elements. Its audience-controlled laser show 'Renga' combines strategic-conquest-game elements as found in 'Civilization', for example, with arcade-style action. The game, which can be played by up to 300 people (using up to 100 lasers), allows the audience to interact through hand-held laser pointers. It challenges players to build a colony while fending off invasions. A key feature of the game is its length: 70–90 minutes. Also, players are awarded points for joining groups to meet challenges.

Figure 5.1 WallFour Studios' innovative audience-based interactive laser game: 100 laser pointers control the narrative on screen (demonstration at the 2012 Indicade, California)

Renga was premiered at the Broadway Nottingham theatre in the UK in 2011 and has been shown at such film festivals as TIFF and the New York Film Festival. WallFour has developed other innovative interactive experiences in public places, including a crowd-controlled interactive music experience and a special murder mystery.

The use of new technologies in laser games is also broadening the spectrum of laser-game play and opening up new markets for laser games. As mentioned earlier, some manufacturers have developed hybrid systems combining laser games with mobile-phone and AR technologies, such as Hasbro's multiplayer iPhone Lazer Tag Blaster.

Glenn Hill, creator and owner of Laserharps.com, is taking interactive laser experiences in a whole new direction with his line of custom-made multimedia laser harps, designed for museums, science centres and other institutions. Visitors can trigger 'an endless variety of' musical sounds and visual projections stored on OptiMusic software by 'breaking the laser beams', he says. Hill developed a 1m-tall laser harp with eight green lasers for the Trans Studio Science Center in Jakarta, Indonesia, which is due to be introduced in 2013. The harp is driven by a multimedia MIDI controller and incorporates a computer and stereo sound system. He also developed one to illustrate the story of King David for the Jewish Children's Museum in Brooklyn, which was introduced the same year. The harp has seven green lasers, and visitors can 'select one of three traditional Jewish melodies to be played'. In addition, he developed a 'new type of laser harp' with eight green lasers for the Ashland Science Works Museum in Oregon, which 'will shine the lasers across an entire room and allows adult visitors to break the laser beams above their heads and allows children' to do so with 'peacock feathers'. He notes that the harps use 'Class IIIa low-power lasers, which are FDA approved for public interaction'.

Laser-graffiti systems also seem to have potential in museums, amusement parks and other leisure facilities. Graffiti Research Lab Houston developed a participatory laser-graffiti experience in September 2010, with the University of Houston Cynthia Woods Mitchell Center for the Arts, for the opening night of the electronic arts festival 'Media Archeology: Texas Focus'. It allowed visitors to 'draw' on the side of the Meril Collection building using lasers. Sensaa's laser-graffiti system, which has been primarily used in event-based, 'non-permanent street installations', allows graffiti to be displayed on a building using a video camera and PC and a green laser pointer, which 'generates graphics based on its position near a building and then projects those graphics onto the building with a high-power video projector'. Typically, this laser graffiti has drawn strong crowd involvement, reports Angel Sastre, Sensaa's managing director. Sensaa has developed additional applications of its laser system, including a 'laser-based scratch-n-win game'.

Interactive laser experiences are likely to encompass a greater diversity of content and themes and offer wider-ranging, richer and more extensive capabilities, such as allowing users to fire laser guns at screens to trigger elaborate and striking simulations like volcanic eruptions. New opportunities are likely to develop in the near future for users to exercise their creativity further through interactive laser systems.

A key trend in amusement parks, museums and other leisure facilities is the wider application of user-generated and user-created content. For example, the Andy Warhol Museum in Pittsburgh offers its visitors varied opportunities to create and even distribute their own content based around Warhol themes and practices. Its 'DIY Pop' exhibit allows visitors to take photographs incorporating

Warhol's distinctive art techniques, and send them, via social media, to their friends. Its 'Create Your Own Screen Test' exhibit encourages visitors to create their own screen tests modelled on those devised by Warhol at The Factory, using such devices as a touchscreen computer, a modified camera and studio lights. Their screen tests are then transposed digitally to a custom webpage, where their material can be accessed and, again, spread via social media.

Applying Immersion to Education

The sophistication of the audiences that visit museums, science centres, planetariums and galleries has placed great strain on curators and directors looking to create appealing exhibits. Now, a new requirement is shaping their decisions: the need to monetize the museum experience. Many trusts are having to combat dwindling investment and soaring costs. However, audience handling and repeat visits are limited in traditional approaches. Now we see the education sector turning to the entertainment sector.

In what has been called 'edutainment', the educational narrative has been supported by the methods and technology of the visitor-attraction sector. This has seen a number of venues adopting 4-D attractions. Rather than just a fashionable euphemism, edutainment has become a serious means of generating not only new interest in such venues but also repeat visits. With sophisticated audiences familiar with digital gaming, it was only a matter of time before entertainment played its part in the heritage and museum experience.

Edutainment can be seen in three main areas of the museum sector: audience experiences, including the latest physical-effects theatres; simulator experiences, offering a recreation of various activities; and the incorporation of a game narrative into the exhibition space.

Innovations in audience experiences can be traced back directly to developments in the theme-park and attraction sector. This is best illustrated by the opening of the new 'Fly Zone' gallery in the Science Museum, London. A specialized space that includes a 4-D physical-effects theatre ('Red Arrow 3D') and simulator systems to offer an interactive narrative. The theatre uses 3-D film, Dolby 5:1 surround sound, smoke and smells and the motion of its 21-seat ride platforms, specially designed by UK firm Metropolis. But the passive film is now joined by an interactive experience. The 'Fly Zone' gallery also incorporates the 'Fly 360°' attraction, which has two-seat interactive simulators offering 360° motion on two axes and allowing guests to experience the thrill of piloting a jet fighter.

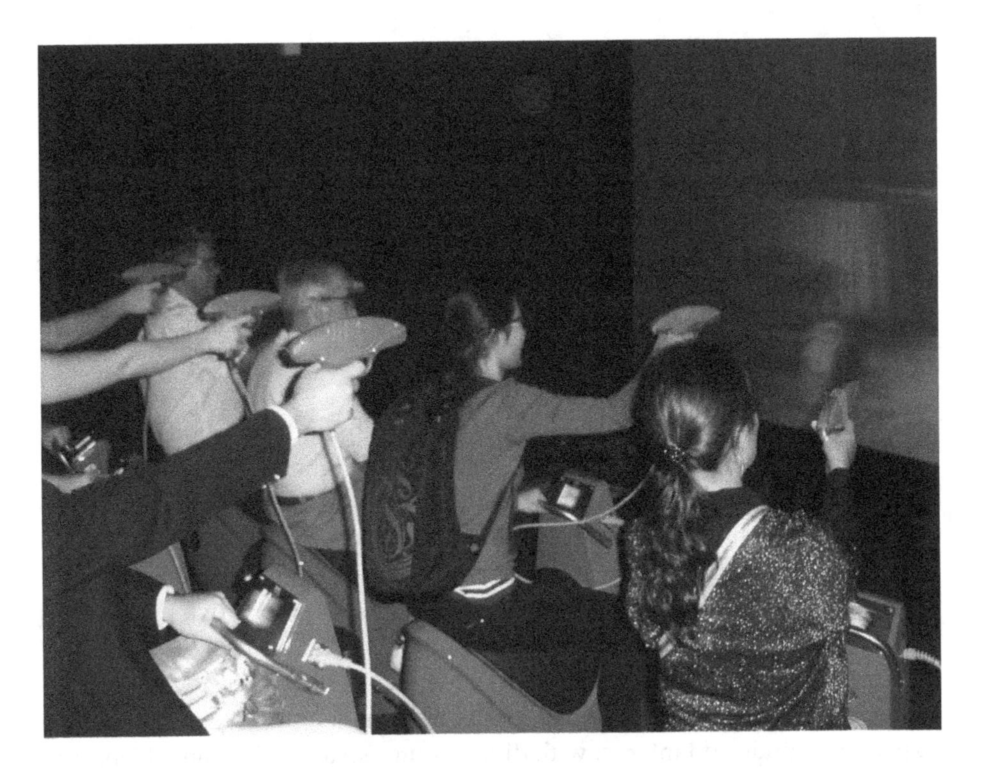

Figure 5.2 Alterface's 5Di Interactive Cinema: the audience takes parts in determining the narrative, which generates repeat visits

These simulators, manufactured by Maxflight, have become popular with aviation museums, heritage collections and visitor attractions, with game content created to suit their educational role and being attractions in their own right.

The immersive simulator experience has become an important component of edutainment and appeals to a wide demographic. US manufacturer ETC has developed 'Wild Earth: African Plains' at Philadelphia Zoo. A two-seater 'XSpeed eMotion' simulator allows guests to traverse the African savannah taking pictures of the wildlife. As mentioned earlier, companies such as Trans-Force have developed their own multiplayer interactive simulator attraction ('5D Attraction') for museums and visitor centres. An interactive game experience offers a informative narrative perfect for the museum environment.

The need for game and film content to match the educational message is opening up a new sector of the interactive-experience industry. To create an interesting and memorable educational experience, developers need to borrow from all aspects of video games, theme parks and computer graphics.

Developers now work with museum curators and specialists in particular aspects of heritage and historical studies, offering direction in the creation of compelling content.

3-D-mapping projections are being applied to a wider range of leisure facilities, including movie theatres. For example, Paintscaping, a specialist in 3-D-mapping projections, projected a holiday-themed 3-D 'paintscape' on the exterior of the Stone Theatre 14 in Morrisville, North Carolina in December 2012.

The trend towards offering multidimensional interactive options in a single attraction or experience and more diverse, deeper immersive attractions and experiences (relating to both content and technology) in leisure facilities is becoming increasingly apparent. A prime illustration of this trend is EonVision Idome, an edutainment dome developed by EON Reality and Vision 3 Experiential that will afford expansive, multisensory interactive experiences in a dome environment. The dome, which opened in November 2013 in Irvine, California, is designed to combine elements of feature films, VR, gaming, amusement-park attractions and museum exhibits. It allows visitors to experience, guide and interact with diverse outer-space and ocean adventures, including some set in pre-historic worlds. For example, they have the chance to explore our solar system, survive a black hole or meet, follow and help a baby humpback whale called Humphrey in deep oceans. The dome affords high-definition stereoscopic 3-D visuals and 3-D sound, combined with 4-D features, such as motion seats and ambient effects such as wind, heat and water. According to EonVision, the dome allows for deep immersion, more personalized interactivity and group collaboration. The dome seats up to 30 people and is semi-portable. It is designed for such diverse leisure facilities as theme parks, museums, science centres and shopping malls.

Another key effort to expand the boundaries of immersive theatres and merge museum exhibits, an amusement-park attraction, and interactive storytelling is Orbi Theatre 23.4, a high-tech theatre situated in Yokahama's 'Mark is Minatomirai' exhibition. The theatre, which was developed through a partnership between SEGA and BBC Worldwide, uses huge 40m-wide screens, 3-D sound, and features 'BBC Earth' nature documentaries, including a wildlife film specially developed for the theatre. It allows visitors to engage in multisensory explorations of animals and nature. Visitors also have the opportunity to explore other nature experiences in 12 themed areas before entering the theatre, including interacting with 'projections of life-size animals in the Animalpedia, [watching] footage of oceans on a fog screen, which causes the movie material to appear in thin air', experiencing the blistering cold of Antarctica and feeling the effects of wind in their face as they fly around the earth.

Next-generation immersive theatres are also incorporating greater real-time interactive and collaboration features. For example, Elumenati has developed Domecast learning events that permit 'simultaneous collaborative learning' experiences. These allow experts to give presentations, audiences to simultaneously help direct the discussion of those presentations and content to be displayed to the overall audience.

As in the digital out-of-home advertising sector, gamification is being used to increase audience interest and dwell time. The game narrative offers a means to educate through achievement, but it can also be used to manage large groups of visitors, inspiring them to take part in activities linked to exhibitions. EyeClick produces display-based game systems using motion tracking to represent the players' movements within the game. They installed systems in the Tower of David Museum in Jerusalem that projected images on the floor and windows of the facility and allowed guests to compete in creating and destroying virtual fortresses, bringing history to life.

There is also the application of game narrative to displays in conventional museums. Using the latest multi-touch screens, curators can create apps reminiscent of simple point-and-click online adventures to illustrate their cultural and historical message. A collaboration between MultiTouch Ltd., a Helsinki-based developer of software and hardware, and Snibbe Interactive, a digital-marketing and entertainment developer from San Francisco, led to interactive LCD multi-touch tables at the Mob Museum: The National Museum of Organized Crime and Law Enforcement in Las Vegas, enabling visitors to visualize the connections between mob bosses and casinos by placing markers on two side-by-side HD tables that called up images, video and text related to crime gangs and law enforcement.

As the video-amusement industry marks nearly 50 years since the first video game was developed, the games themselves find a place in the museum and digital out-of-home entertainment technology becomes the exhibit. The interest in exhibits charting the rise of video games was originally fuelled by travelling museum attractions such as 'Videotopia' in the 1990s, as well as a number of museum exhibits examining the emergence of video gaming (such as 'Game On' at the Barbican Gallery, London, in 2002).

Figure 5.3 'Fly 360°' at the 'Fly Zone' gallery in the Science Museum, London: interactive entertainment imparts an educational narrative

Most recently the Museum of the Moving Image in Astoria, New York installed an exhibit named after one of the first video games, 'Spacewar!', dedicated to charting the birth and rise of the electronic entertainment medium. The modern museum audience is now ready to be told the story of interactive entertainment, while expecting it from their leisure activities both in the home and out.

Originally seen as an oddity and distraction from the serious business of informing and educating museum and gallery visitors, the education sector now routinely uses the new tools of edutainment in shaping memories and passing on knowledge. Though still in its infancy, the skills needed to entertain can now be applied to education.

From Exercising the Mind to Exercising the Body: Exergaming

In the leisure and sports sector the application of a game narrative has been developed into what has been called 'Exergaming'. The technology borrows partly from traditional consumer gaming but also traces its roots back to the amusement scene. The application of the technology was seen as a great boon to tackling childhood obesity and a lack of fitness in youth. Many schools have joined gyms and leisure centres in using Exergaming technology.

As mentioned earlier, Konami's Bemani, and particularly 'Dance Dance Revolution' of 1998, was recognized not only as a compelling and highly popular game, but also as great exercise for the players. Other developers of similar dance games started to evaluate a game element that not only challenged the player, but also offered a workout. In 2002, Cobalt Flux created commercial dance pads that took game content from the amusement title 'Pump It Up' (Andamiro) and made it into an exergaming package for multiple users to simultaneously exercise through the narrative of the dance game. The system was even used in the West Virginia Obesity Study, with Cobalt Flux platforms placed in secondary education schools state-wide. However, due to the instability of the commercial exergaming market, the company failed in 2011.

Another exponent of a multi-player approach using networked dance pads is 'iDANCE' from Positive Gaming, who used a specially created game based on 'In The Groove' (Roxor Games, 2004) and tailored it to the needs of school and group exercise. The system was able to accommodate up to 32 users simultaneously with individual scoring (exercise levels). One of the earliest developers of wireless game pads, the company also supports the European Cup in the Machine Dance World Championship – a popular event for the dance-stage world community.

One of the visionaries behind the evolution of the dance-stage concept into exergaming is Ole Petter Høie, founder of Positive Gaming. Commenting on the emergence of this application, he said:

> *Positive Gaming recognized the great exercise potential in 2003, and we helped establish Machine Dance as an official sport in 2004 via*

the Norwegian Dance Association. The idea of developing a group training product from the dance-game concept came up when we displayed a Dancing Stage arcade machine at a fitness trade show in Holland in the autumn of 2004. … From this success we developed leading commercial exergaming products defined by the iDANCE introduced in September 2008; standing out in the way that it not only activates the user more in a physical and social way than any other exergame, but also in the way it offers a concept that makes the product more fun the more you play it.

Concerning the deployment of this technology in the market:

We have sold just over 1,000 multi-player systems since the first commercial release. About half of those are in the UK, primarily in schools, leisure centres and fitness studios. Our biggest market in 2012 has been the US, where iDANCE is prominent in schools, US Army camps, YMCA's, park districts, fitness studios etc. Our other more successful countries are Norway, Russia, Netherlands, Dubai and France, and we have partners that have purchased one or more systems in Australia, Germany, Croatia, South Korea, Finland, Switzerland, Spain, Belgium, Iran, Ecuador, etc. Schools are the biggest market over all, and the countries with most success are those that offer public funding for our type of products.

Commenting on exergaming content, Høie stated:

IDANCE was programmed from scratch as a multi-player product, while 'In the Groove' [ITG] was created as an arcade machine product. The team behind ITG knew what they were doing in general, and after our pilot project in 2005 through which we understood how to optimize the use of a multi-player dance-game system, the team behind ITG were able to apply most of our requested features into ITG, thus creating the ITG multi-player. This happened specifically based on our experiences. When we decided to create our title, we naturally brought along all we found to be relevant from the ITG multi-player, but since we started with multi-player in mind from the very beginning, our game was always much more custom made for its purpose. And via iDANCE 2, 2.1 and the upcoming iDANCE 3, a number of features never before seen in any other dance game have been introduced. Kyle Ward and Chris Foy, two of the key developers behind ITG, have also been important parts of developing iDANCE.

Figure 5.4 Pulsefitness's 'Dance Machine': an interactive game that increases fitness

Asked why Positive Games were still here while others failed, Høie answered:

> *Since we showed our first multi-player prototype in 2005, we have had more than 10 companies developing their own copies of the concept. This shows a bit about the success of our idea, one company even went onto the US stock market on the basis of a copy product. The main reason we have been more successful than all of those copying us added together, and the reason that we are still here, is that we are more than just a company making a game that can bring in money.*

As if to underline his word, as we were compiling this book, it was revealed that the originators of the Bemani concept were developing an exergaming variant of their own. In January 2013, it was announced that Konami Digital Entertainment and United Healthcare (a US-based health insurance and medical-care group) were to undertake a joint effort to reduce childhood obesity through exergaming in US schools.

The agreement was to use 'Dance Dance Revolution: Classroom Edition' (DDRCE), a specially created exergaming version of the original arcade system with many features of previous dance-pad platforms. The DDRCE system allows 48 students to simultaneously participate on wireless mat controllers that feature a smartcard reader that tracks each student's individual progress. KDE and United Healthcare launched the game at three schools in Longwood, Florida; Gainesville, Georgia; and Fresno, Texas. Participating schools used the game to track its impact on students' health, well-being and exercise habits. The data will go towards shaping 'Activate for Kids', a school health initiative operated by United Healthcare and United Health Foundation, in partnership with school systems throughout Florida, Georgia and Texas.

Traditional exercise machines have also been enhanced by gamification. The exercise bike was given the exergaming treatment with riders now able to steer their bikes through virtual worlds ('cyber-cycling') and compete with other users. In fact, 'exergaming' (or 'exertaiment') was first used to describe exercise bikes hooked up to video-game controllers with the 'Atari Puffer' prototype in 1982. Exponents of this approach include UK-based Instyle Fitness, with their 'Simultrainer Bike' that offers a high-level of interactive networked competitiveness in a real-world simulation. Another system using both advanced network capability and a detailed indoor training simulator platform is the 'Xdream' from Trixter. Developer Interactive Fitness and their 'Expresso' bike platform incorporates an international online leader board. The company developed a chasing game that offers a great workout with a strong fun element.

The other aspect of the exergame genre is motion capture and player tracking. Visual Sport, launched in 2000, produces interactive sports-based games using a camera-tracking system developed by Microsight that allows players to play virtual versions of golf, soccer, hockey, baseball, American football and basketball. TouchMagix is a developer offering a variety of interactive displays, such as 'Interactive Floor', 'Interactive Wall', 'Multi-Touch' and 'MagixFone' systems, which use gesture-based and multi-touch technologies. A dedicated fitness capability has been developed by Cybex International, a producer of commercial fitness equipment who released the 'Trazer' motion-tracking system.

Though exergaming was hijacked for a while by the consumer-game sector, new motion-tracking console-game interfaces gained popularity, and developers created fitness-oriented games promising increased levels of fitness. However, as proven by the professional fitness and health sector, more elaborate monitoring and instruction are needed for an exercise routine to be effective, and this curtailed attempts make this wholly a consumer product. The leisure and fitness industry has moved to regain control of the exergaming genre.

The application of exergaming goes much further than just the school gymnasium or leisure or fitness centre. Exergaming is also finding a home in hospitality, as part of rehabilitation after surgery or injury, as the game narrative offers a more conducive element to repetitive exercise. The play aspect of exergaming has also begun to be used with senior adults, as the enhanced exercise that it provides can delay cognitive decline more than traditional exercise, as demonstrated by Union College, Schenectady, New York. While Japanese amusement factories support nursing homes in Japan with specially developed amusement systems, offering elderly players the chance to use the systems as part of their exercise, the Japanese amusement trade, came late to the possibilities of exergaming but has started to catch up. 'E-Sports Ground' is a motion-tracked game system first released in 2011. The system offers a giant game of 'Pong', in which the player's body movements are tracked, and the player represented on the projected floor of the game enclosure as a giant paddle.

The use of the short distraction of interactive entertainment to make mundane tasks more interesting is a strong element of gamification. With exergaming, the ability of DOE to offer improvements in health and metal dexterity continues to prove the importance of this application of digital entertainment beyond the sedentary consumer alternative.

Chapter 6
Convergence

Channelling New Forms of Immersion with Gestural Signage

The 20th Century Fox motion picture *Minority Report* (2002) may have spun a fanciful concept about police centres fitted with futuristic gestural displays, but that kind of future apparently is not far off, judging by the growth and impact of gestural displays in shopping malls and other public places. The broader creative scope of gestural interactive experiences in stores, movie theatres and other public places and greater refinement of user interfaces for gesture-based experiences in those locations by such companies as YDreams and GestureTek have helped drive often high levels of user engagement. Gesture-based games in public places have had a particularly strong impact. As Antonio Camara, CEO of YDreams notes, games in public places have fundamentally changed, with visitors increasingly controlling video games through their body movements.

YDreams has made a special commitment to exploring and developing more intuitive, engaging gesture-based experiences in stores, movie theatres and other public places that have considerable marketing, entertainment and educational potential. It had significant success with the YSenses point-of-sale promotion developed for Compal at the 'World of Flavors' fair at seven Continente supermarkets throughout Portugal, according to Marta Vieira, former director of business development and operations for YDreams. For that promotion, a game was presented on a large plasma screen displaying an orchard populated with trees full of fruit. By purchasing four or more Compal products, users gained the opportunity to 'pick' as many pieces of fruit as possible from the orchard by clapping. The 'fruit' could then be exchanged for prizes. Reaction to the promotion was very positive, and it generated 'an average of 400 interactions per day', and 'customers who played the Compal Senses game were 40.3 per cent more likely to actually purchase the brand's products'.

YDreams also developed an interactive cinema campaign called 'Happiness Factory' for Coca-Cola that generated strong results. The campaign centred around a game designed to enable users to interact with the Coke brand and allowed them to control the main character's movements by waving their arms from left to right. In the game, the Worker ran from side to side, trying to catch as many Coke bottles as possible as they fell from the sky. An MC prepared audience members for the experience and mimicked the Worker during the game. Participants were interviewed afterwards: 300 said they were 'positively surprised by its innovative action', and 40 per cent more indicated increased 'brand awareness' of Coke compared to traditional cinema advertising.

YDreams elicited very positive results with an interactive 'advergame' it delivered in +Cinema theatres in the Greater Lisbon area to promote Vodafone's Duplex ADSL brand in 2008. The game, which was developed together with the agency Brandia Central, allowed users to control the movements of the main character (VodaRed Man) on the screen by waving their arms in the air. The character ducked left or right to avoid hazardous objects that were hurled at him and to retrieve as many ADSL packages as possible. Again, an MC prepared the audience and encouraged them to participate during the game. According to surveys conducted with moviegoers, those 'who played the Vodafone game were more inclined to purchase Vodafone products', reports YDreams. The surveys also found that brand recall and awareness of those products was higher than that generated by traditional cinema advertising.

YDreams created a special buzz with an interactive product promotion it developed for Dove Soap at São Paulo movie theatres in 2007, which afforded moviegoers the opportunity to play with soap bubbles that appeared onscreen. Webcams were installed at the back of the theatres to track the movements of the people while they were interacting with the bubbles. The moviegoers could push and burst bubbles on the screen through their gestures.

GestureTek has also generated a strong impact with its gestural interactive marketing systems. The company had 'great success' with a system it installed in the flagship store of Hudson Bay in Toronto with 'multisports windows', reports Vincent John Vincent, CEO of GestureTek. The system, which was situated at the corner of a window in that store, used 2.5m by 3.8m screens and featured special effects and ads for Hudson Bay.

GestureTek has witnessed growing demand for its retail digital-signage systems over the past few years, as shopping malls and other retail outlets seek new ways of making shopping a 'destination experience' and more enjoyable. The majority of malls installing GestureTek's systems are now using it for digital signage, reports Vincent. Most of the GestureTek experiences in shopping malls and retail outlets are entertainments, though they are ultimately designed to promote the brands of the malls and retail outlets and carry their logos. GestureTek's 'ScreenFX' system was an integral part of the launch of Charlestown Mall in Ireland.

The 'GestureFX' family of interactive display systems can project visual content onto any surface, including floors, walls, tables, countertops and bartops. Users control multimedia content and special effects by moving their hands and bodies without the need for other interfaces. 'GestureFX' uses GestureTek's patented video gesture-control software and special camera technology. The system, which was installed in a high-traffic location in Charlestown Mall, allowed users to interact with a 2.6m plasma display. GestureTek's 'GroundFX' interactive floor displays were also installed at several entrances to the mall. General feedback so far indicates that users have found it an 'enjoyable experience', says Vincent.

GestureTek's 'ScreenXtreme' system was used by the Spanish retailer Musgo-SXT. In a window promotion, customers were immersed in a multimedia interactive soccer game. Target Stores have used GestureTek's system in interactive billboards in an underground mall in Canada to great advantage: it proved to have a 'positive effect on store traffic', according to Vincent.

Some retail applications of GestureTek's systems are designed to promote specific products for particular companies. For example, Telefonica, a leading Spanish telecommunications company and part investor in GestureTek, is using GestureTek's multi-touch system to provide more information about its products and brand in its stores. This application, framed around the Telefonica Retail Window, affords users an opportunity to collaborate with others while interacting with content on the screen.

The impact of gestural interactive marketing in public places will be even greater in the near future, due to key new technological developments. One of the most important of which will be a greater convergence between gestural and mobile-phone systems, opening up even more expansive forms of interactivity in those settings, predicts Vincent.

3-D Building-Projection Advertisements and 3-D-Mapping Entertainment Projects

Perhaps one of the most ground-breaking innovations in digital experiential marketing was the development of 3-D building-projection advertisements. These large 3-D ads have a dramatic impact and foster greater viewer engagement. They typically project brand images onto building facades using multiple projectors and are designed to highlight certain architectural details. Their impact has been significantly boosted by combining the projections with interactive media. For example, mobile phones and iPads have started to be connected with 3-D video-mapping projection ads, allowing viewers of those projections to send photos of the projections to others on social media sites. Even more engaging and far-reaching interactive applications are being blended with 3-D building-projection ads. For example, users with mobile and tablet devices have the capability to 'wave their hands in front of motion detection devices like "Kinect" ' and 'spray digital particles' into 3-D-mapping projections, creating, in effect, 'digital fireworks', explains Rob Delfgauuw, general manager of Nuformer.

At the same time, striking entertainment-oriented 3-D building-projection attractions and shows have also had an impact in amusement parks, museums and other public places. For example, Disney introduced a new version of its 'Cinderella Castle 3D' projection show called 'Celebrate the Magic' at the Magic Kingdom Park in Walt Disney World in November 2012. The show, which runs nightly, projects effects onto the castle, creating a kaleidoscope of colours and incorporating sketches of Walt Disney and a display of Disney characters. While the new show includes scenes from classic Disney films shown in an earlier projection event called 'The Magic, the Memories, and You', it includes content from recent Disney films, such as *Brave, Wreck-it Ralph* and *Pirates of the Caribbean.* It also incorporates new music, stories and special effects and is updated seasonally.

In an effort to expand the scope of 3-D-mapping entertainment projects, Obscura Digital developed a 3-D projection-mapping event in conjunction with YouTube and the Guggenheim Museum in New York for the YouTube/ Play Awards Show in October 2011, combining internal and external projections of the 25 winning online videos from the show at the museum. The company projected the videos onto the museum's spiral staircase, and showed the videos on the exterior of the museum as well for the benefit of passers-by.

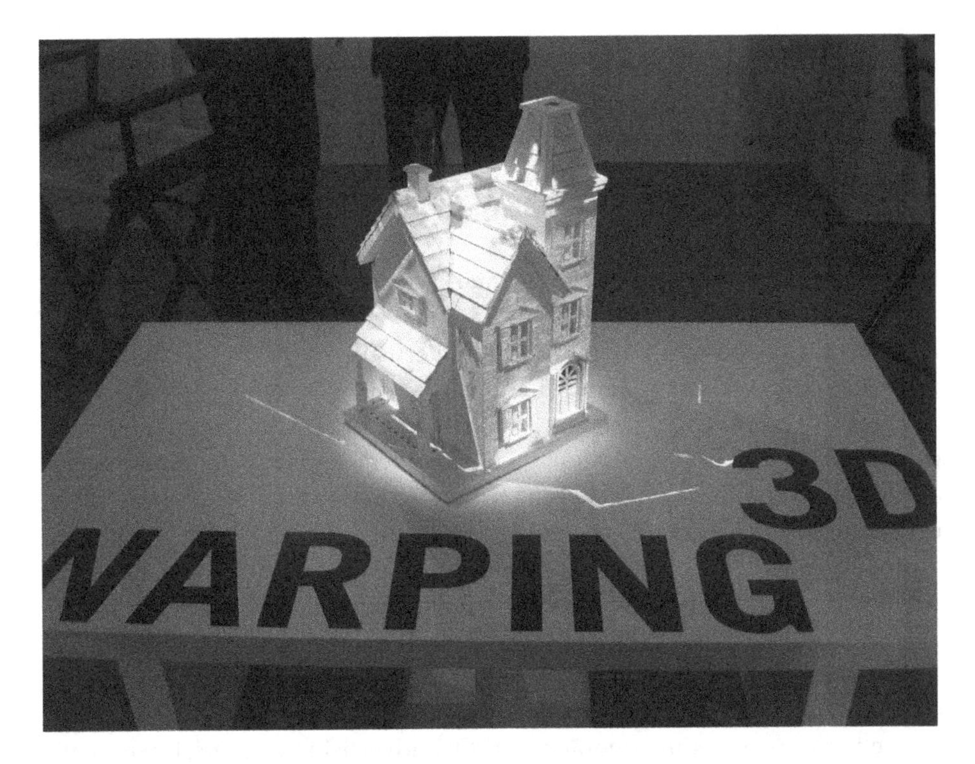

Figure 6.1 3-D warping: a model of a house demonstrates 3-D projection-mapping

3-D-mapping entertainment projects have also been designed to stimulate greater appreciation of and involvement with historical and cultural landmarks among visitors and residents alike. For example, Moment Factory developed a 3-D-mapping projection show with sound and light called 'Winter Sweet' for the Atlantic City Alliance, which debuted in December 2012. The 7½-minute show projected three winter scenes onto the city's Boardwalk Hall landmark nightly, including 'Snow and Ice', which heralded the arrival of winter in the city with images of dancing ballerinas, falling snow flakes and a train that appeared to run on top of a building; 'Winter Village', which included projections of sweets and candles; and 'Illumination', which highlighted elegant ornaments and intricate lighting that eventually melted away the surface of the building as spring approached. Moment Factory developed another 3-D-projection show called 'Duality' for Atlantic City, which ran from July to November 2012 and drew over 200,000 people.

3-D projections will appear in more and more public places and unexpected locations. Antonio Camara, CEO of YDreams, predicts that they will become larger and anticipates an increasing appearance of 'unique projections in bodies of water and even cloudy skies'.

Convergence in the Digital Out-of-Home Market

Historically, the digital out-of-home market was considered a discrete and narrow business far removed from traditional and digital advertising. That is dramatically changing, with DOOH advertising becoming an increasing part of cross-media campaigns. That shift has been driven largely by major changes in technology, content distribution, marketing strategies and consumer lifestyles. The increasing convergence of new technologies, such as mobile and online, and increasing synergies between physical and virtual experiences have opened up new opportunities for DOOH marketing, especially in terms of expanding audiences, enhancing brand awareness and developing new cross-promotional possibilities.

Convergent DOOH marketing fits in better with consumer-media consumption patterns, which are more fluid and varied. Multichannel marketing campaigns incorporating DOOH advertising also mesh well with the increasing trend towards experiential marketing and more expansive, multidimensional and user-centred brand experiences that foster a deeper, ongoing relationship with consumers. These experiences often incorporate a greater play element through games.

One of the most significant forms of convergence in the DOOH market is mobile digital signage, which exploits the mobile phone's ubiquity, interactive capability and immediacy. It allows users to interact with games, ads and other content on large screens via their mobile phones. Mobile digital signage has had a dramatic impact on brand awareness and creates a whole new context for interactive marketing in public places. The medium's key benefits are its ability to expand and target audiences better, provide more measurable advertising and deepen user interaction with brands, especially by tapping into social networking and linking the at-home and out-of-home interactive markets.

However, care must be taken to truly exploit this new medium, stresses Jeremy Lockhorn, vice president of emerging media practice at Razorfish. Not all brands or products lend themselves to mobile campaigns, he notes, and a clear and well-defined strategy is necessary to fully exploit mobile digital-signage campaigns. Adding mobile to digital signage enables the delivery of more targeted and personalized messages. From a broader perspective, mobile affords interactivity in the DOOH market, enabling interactivity through many different technologies, including Bluetooth and AR, according to Mike Cearley, senior vice president of social strategy at Fleishman Hillard. He believes mobile's greatest value in the DOOH market is its ability to bridge online and offline.

Another key advantage of mobile digital signage is its ability to provide measurability and accountability and to provoke an immediate response from its audience. It allows advertisers to quickly gauge the response to their ads. Measurability techniques have been particularly well developed for SMS, bar codes and proximity based marketing tied to digital signage, says Gurley. Dan Trigub, chief financial officer of Blue Bite, notes that more highly interactive mobile digital-signage campaigns offer 'greater data and accountability'. Although brand-impression measures in mobile digital signage have some value, they do not offer the level of accountability provided by measures of actual return on investment and audience responses, such as downloads prompted by the ad, he maintains.

A growing trend in mobile digital-signage campaigns involves prompting the audience to download mobile apps. For example, a DOOH campaign developed by Blue Bite and RMG Networks in airport locations in Los Angeles, New York, Atlanta and Chicago promoted 'Tripcase', an app for business travellers, reports Trigub. The campaign allowed travellers to download the app in a contextually 'relevant' environment where the 'app matters the most', he points out.

Trigub believes mobile digital-signage campaigns must offer either 'entertainment or monetary value' to succeed. He feels entertainment-based mobile digital-signage campaigns must offer 'unique content' specially designed for mobile users, such as 'behind the scenes movie trailers' and that monetary campaigns must offer something of tangible value to consumers, such as coupons.

Some DOOH campaigns have involved ongoing social-media campaigns, such as the campaign for Corona Light developed by Pereira and O'Dell for Crown Imports in Times Square. The campaign was designed to build on the success of a Facebook campaign for the beer, which generated over 90,000 users and was aimed at nurturing a long-term relationship with a younger audience in their twenties and early thirties.

One of the most innovative and user-centred mobile digital-signage campaigns was the multiplatform campaign run in Denmark in 2010 to promote Diesel's Be Stupid brand, which centred around the theme 'the relentless pursuit of a regret-free life'. The two-week campaign, which was developed by Comtech Experience A/S using Never.no's interactive mobile technology, used social media, digital signage and building-projection ads. The campaign was designed to take a bold, irreverent and playful approach, explains Karsten Solaas, Comtech Experience's managing director. In keeping with the Be Stupid theme, Diesel was perfectly prepared to allow 'anything to happen' and leave themselves completely open to the unexpected, as the campaign used 'real-time moderation', he noted. One of the key goals of the campaign was 'getting customers more involved with the Diesel brand', says Solaas.

People were invited to submit photos of themselves or their friends in amusing and playful poses to capture '15 seconds of fame'. The photos were then shown simultaneously on Facebook, digital signs in Diesel stores in Copenhagen and Aarhus, and on large buildings in Copenhagen. User photos were displayed on Fridays and Saturdays during the campaign. Postings of user photos to various locations in the campaign were done in a quick '15-second time' frame. The campaign, which was geared to a 17- to 30-year-old audience, drew 1,000 pictures and 5,000 participants, says Solaas. The campaign proved cost-efficient: less than £20,000 for everything.

As part of the campaign, street promoters with computers and screens on their heads walked around Copenhagen to encourage people to upload their photos via those computers. This proved to be a particularly effective tactic, as '5 times as many people sent in photos' through the efforts of these promoters than they did through other means.

Another key goal of the campaign was 'building a longer term relationship' with Diesel's customers by attracting more members to their Facebook group, which displayed photos from the campaign. Users were also encouraged to share their pictures with friends in the group. Ultimately, the campaign succeeded in generating 'a great deal of activity', reports Solaas.

Measurement techniques for mobile signage have been fairly effective, especially those through SMS and proximity based marketing, according to Steve Gurley, president and CEO of Pyrim Technologies, Inc. One of the greatest potentials in convergent DOOH forms lies in the integration of DOOH marketing with social media. Advantages include greater audience engagement and opportunities to create advocacy campaigns and offer consumers rewards, according to a whitepaper jointly released by Posterscope and LocaModa. That opportunity is greater now due to the rapid rise of DOOH screens that are web enabled. The combination of social media with DOOH displays has generated significantly greater exposure for the DOOH market, as evidenced by data gathered by Posterscope regarding the views and behaviour of UK's 'ardent social networking' audience. According to those findings, 30 per cent of the respondents reported 'informing others about customized posters they saw', and 31 per cent 'told others about digital out-of-home screens they saw'. Adding suitable user-generated content to this mix could increase user engagement even more and yield stronger brand impressions.

The Canadian Tourism Commission (CTC) launched a DOOH promotion dubbed 'Digital Storescapes' in 2010 that made extensive use of social media and took user-generated content in the DOOH market to a new level. The brand-building campaign, which ran in New York, Chicago and Los Angeles, centred around 'Twitter-based murals' providing a continuous stream of photos, videos and conversations relating to specific Canadian cities, cultural experiences and vacation packages. The campaign, developed by DDB Canada, eavesdropped on the key conversations Canadians were having about their country on Twitter. Both Canadians and Americans were encouraged to join in a Twitter conversation relating to the 'new' Canada via live billboards. Users could access images of the murals associated with particular tweets via touchscreens.

The campaign was designed to highlight the 'unique and compelling' qualities of Canada to American travellers and promote Canada as a 'hip' place to visit, explains Siobhan Chretien, former executive director of Americas marketing for CTC. It was an outgrowth of CTC's extensive social-media efforts and also part of a broader media campaign that comprised TV and online elements as well, she points out.

Responses to the campaign were very positive: 5,000,000 impressions were generated, 97 per cent of the participants in the campaign joined as Twitter followers of CTC's group, 20,000 people actively tweeted during the campaign, 5,000 pictures were posted and 40,000 views of CTC's YouTube vacation travel programme were generated, reports Chretien. To induce greater participation in the campaign, teams were sent out with iPads to sign up consumers in a travel contest offering the chance to win a free Canadian vacation of their choice. The contest had 8,000 entries, says Chretien.

An increasing number of museums have been expanding the boundaries of user-generated content. One of the most expansive, multidimensional applications of such content was the exhibit 'Our Space', which TePapa Museum in New Zealand introduced in 2008. This allowed citizens and tourists to express their feelings about New Zealand. The content at the exhibit was essentially co-created. Users first downloaded their content via the museum's website, which then filtered down to museum kiosks, where other museum visitors could remix the material.

User-curated content has also changed the dynamics of art selection and presentation in museums. 'Click! A Crowd-Curated Exhibition', which ran at the Brooklyn Museum in 2008, created a special context for visitor-curated content. It invited visitors to submit photos for an exhibition on the 'changing face of Brooklyn' and invited others to judge the submissions online without seeing the ratings of other voters. The selected photos were then exhibited in the museum in sizes corresponding to their ratings and were also shown online.

Some museums have developed more permanent, thematic and specialized materials based on user-generated content. For example, the Powerhouse Museum and the Brooklyn Museum culled user-generated content from visitors in community exhibitions and online projects at their museums to produce on-demand books.

Game-oriented mobile digital-signage campaigns have been particularly effective in raising brand awareness. For example, MegaPhone Labs developed a mobile campaign in 2008 for Adidas at the NBA All-Star game in New Orleans that combined 'out-of-home marketing, casual games, mobile marketing, and location-based services', according to Dan Albritton, MegaPhone's president and chief technology officer. The campaign used a 'branded van' outfitted with a 3m screen that was parked at a street corner near the game in order to add names to the Adidas mailing list, he explains. As part of that campaign, users 'received SMS messages' regarding special events and promotions at Adidas stores and were directed to the 'nearest Adidas' outlets. The campaign generated three times as many 'sign-ups' for the Adidas mailing list as the list at the game, reports Albritton. In addition, users participating in that campaign 'opted out at a much lower rate', he notes. Ultimately, the campaign was 'vastly superior' in terms of 'cost and response rate' and provided a very 'compelling' interactive experience, according to Albritton.

Response rates for blended social-media / digital-signage campaigns have often been significantly higher than traditional media campaigns. For example,

VH1 ran a brand-building campaign in New York blending social media with a DOOH element in connection with its show 'The Great Debate'. It combined viewer input from various locations and allowed viewers to respond to the programme's pop-culture trivia questions shown on digital screens via SMS, Facebook or the VH1 website. Audience participation was strong, with the show generating 'over 350,000 total messages', according to Steve King, former vice president of sales for LocaModa. Moreover, '1 per cent of the overall messages were mobile'. Significantly, 1 per cent of the votes cast were generated from the programme's DOOH audience, despite the limited DOOH footprint, and those responses generated the highest participation rate among all bought media channels.

It is clear that the DOOH market needs to expand beyond its traditional borders. For that reason, convergence will assume an even more important and broader role in the evolution of the DOOH market, continually expanding its scope and opening up greater opportunities for advertisers and marketers. Ultimately, DOOH advertising will become a more fluid element in the cross-channel marketing continuum, morphing into new and different forms.

Chapter 7
Future Trends

Implications of Location-Based Games for Leisure Facilities

Location-based games, mixed-reality games and AR games are likely to have a more significant impact on leisure facilities in the near future, especially because of their ability to fuse physical and virtual elements seamlessly and offer multidimensional game elements. A key catalyst for such games in leisure facilities is the increasing expectation of visitors for more meaningful and varied gameplay in public places, especially as at-home consumer-game genres have become more sophisticated and diverse and as leisure facilities serve more multifaceted purposes. Also, the burgeoning popularity of smartphones has made location-based games more attractive and accessible. Beyond that, these games can add new dimensions to more traditional storytelling and interactive experiences in parks and other leisure facilities.

Location-based games typically allow players to gather clues, follow stories and pursue missions in physical locations using mobile devices with GPS. They are becoming more sophisticated and expansive and are starting to incorporate such technologies as AR and encouraging players to venture further out into the real world. For example, Sprylab Technologies has developed location-based games incorporating AR features on its 'Tripventure' platform. The platform allows players to view and interact with virtual objects in real locations.

Location-based games tend to be more vital and energizing because of their rootedness in real-world environments, and, in some cases, because of their educational quality and facility for addressing social and political issues in lighter ways. Many location-based games also emphasize social interaction and team building, which also enhance their appeal.

Location-based games are extending further into the real world and adding key new dimensions. For example, the Tap Lab's 'Tiny Tycoons' 'geo-social' mobile city-building game allows players to take real-world jobs, buy real property and even hire their friends to help them with their new business. 'Shadow Cities', a ground-breaking location-based game developed by Grey Area Labs, also plunges players headlong into the real world and creates a wider web of intrigue. The free-to-play game pits players in two camps of Architects (nature lovers) and Animators (technologists) in a battle against each other on city streets using their smartphones. They are challenged to take over 'gateways' near local landmarks and use them as bases to seize control of their neighbourhoods. At the same time, they must counter threats and hold those neighbourhoods against attacks from the other team. One of the game's special features is its expansive collaboration process, allowing players from distant locations to exchange threat warnings and other key information that will enable them to complete their missions.

Location-based games and AR games have particular significance for leisure facilities because they essentially represent a key point of convergence between transmedia and the DOOH market, and they afford a more expansive and richer playing field for leisure facilities. Although the use of these games in leisure facilities is still limited and often experimental, there is growing interest among some amusement parks and other leisure facilities in this form of cross-media and cross-environment game play. One of the pioneers in the application of location-based games in leisure facilities is Millform Inc., who have developed a mixed-reality mobile game called 'Gbanga Ballenberg', which sends visitors on a scavenger hunt in amusement parks, museums and other tourist facilities, where they have to solve puzzles. Even some interactive live-theatre projects have incorporated elements of location-based games in their productions, such as 'Red Cloud Rising'.

Walt Disney Imagineering also initiated a project in 2012 called 'Living Worlds' to spur the development of innovative transmedia experiences and help foster a community for authors of transmedia works to gain more experience. The project invited developers to submit proposals for location-based narrative experiences at a reasonable cost that could run for at least two weeks and that afforded participants the opportunity to influence the story. These stories could not use existing intellectual property from Disney, as the participants retained ownership of the resulting intellectual property. As part of the project, Disney worked with selected creative developers to refine their programmes and prepare them for production. Currently, these works are still at a 'development stage', although 'they will be eventually transitioned to a production stage'. The company retains the right to a non-exclusive and perpetual licence of the programmes, presumably so they can be produced.

In perhaps one of the more intriguing examples of the convergence between games and amusement parks, Game Nation is developing a video-game theme park and related location-based entertainment experience that will incorporate game-based interactive rides and other interactive attractions and place visitors in the role of video-game characters. According to the company, Atari expressed an interest in licensing such classic games as 'Asteroids', 'Centipede' and 'Missile Command' for Game Nation's planned attractions.

Game Nation has adopted a fan-centric approach to its video-game theme park, according to Daniel T. Ruke, creator and co-founder of the company. Game Nation held a launch 'celebration party' in the second half of 2013 at the Fort Myers Convention Center in Florida, in order to roll out new 'technology and intellectual property', engage fans with high energy, distinctive video-game and music experiences and 'test market' their business concept, according to Ruke.

In selecting Fort Myers as the location for its launch party, Game Nation responded to strong fan interest in a Florida-based Game Nation park. The launch party, which was geared to 5,000 fans, began with 'Video Games Live', presented by Tommy Tallarico, and also included a '$30,000 League of Legends and Call of Duty' game competition and an 'interactive storyteller competition'. An adapted version of the event will tour the USA. Game Nation is considering opening parks in Florida and other parts of the USA.

Game Nation has created a 'Game Nation Assembly', which allows fans to vote on and share their ideas on attractions and other experiences they would like to see at Game Nation parks and events, explains Ruke. In order to participate in the assembly, fans must become members of Game Nation and pay a membership fee. All premium members will receive a lifetime pass to Game Nation parks and events. The company is planning to incorporate such transmedia elements as interactive fiction and e-sports into its attractions and event-based experiences. As part of its transmedia strategy, Game Nation released 'graphic novels', and its storytellers conducted storytelling events at Florida colleges to elicit 'true interactive stories of fictitious events', which were included in the August 2013 celebration after refinement by Game Nation storytellers.

Following a related path to convergence, NAMCO Bandai opened an anime theme park in 2013, based around the Shonen Jump manga franchise and incorporating a section with park employees donning costumes matching those of Shonen Jump characters.

The operators of 'Heart of Gaming', a video arcade that opened in London in 2013, have made transmedia an integral part of their business strategy. They created a Twitch.tv channel and are considering the possibility of establishing a radio station and developing their own sitcom or film. Regardless of the success of these spinoffs, the approach adopted by 'Heart of Gaming' reflects the deep roots of video-game culture and a more expansive multiplatform entertainment strategy for a video-game arcade operator.

Little attention has been given to the possible use of AR/location-based games with digital signage, but such a combination has some promising prospects, as it could allow users to gather clues from digital billboards and engage in various forms of gameplay with mobile digital signage.

The Niantic Project, a spin-off from Google, is also expanding the scope of location-based games with its multi-player AR game, 'Ingress'. The game, which is in beta stage, takes players into a world of shadowy characters, unusual new technologies, portals, XM satellite photos and abductions, while connecting with real-world environments. An app of the game will also be released. To heighten the game's appeal, Google has generated a massive viral marketing campaign.

In another extension of the trend towards combining physical and digital experiences in games, some location-based games require more physical activity and even exercise, such as the games of Team Action Zone. The company has developed what it calls 'outdoor exergames', in which players control gameplay by walking, running or engaging in other physical activities.

In the past, some location-based/mixed-reality games were hampered by thin, rudimentary stories and schemes. But the creative scope of such games is expanding significantly. For example, Six to Start's 'Wanderlust' 'experiential mobile story-telling platform' uses stories from such top writers as Tom Chatfield, Andrea Phillips and Alex Butterworth.

Mixed-reality/AR games are appearing in a wider range of public locations, including museums and libraries and offering more edutainment value. For example, the Smithsonian American Art Museum in conjunction with CityMystery broke ground with an AR game called 'Ghosts of a Chance' that they staged from 2008 to 2010, in which players hunted for hidden objects using treasure maps and text messages and by deciphering codes. The AR game 'Finding the Future', developed by Jane McGonigal, Kiyah Monsef, Nathan Baxter Applied Gaming and Playmatics, put a new twist on location-based games by requiring its 500 players to spend a night at the New York Public Library in April 2011 on a scavenger hunt for 100 artefacts and encouraging them to write a novel by collating their stories and thoughts about them. The game combined online and offline elements and required the use of mobile devices.

Another notable effort to bring games to new public locations was Yahoo's integrated marketing campaign 'Yahoo Bus Stop Derby', which it launched in 2010 with Clear Channel to promote some of its mobile games. That project has significant implications for multiplatform game approaches in the DOOH market. The games, which included 'Chatter Hatter', 'Snap Happy' and 'Sport a Pult' were offered at 20 high-traffic municipal bus shelters in the San Francisco area and allowed riders to play large-scale versions of the games on LCD touchscreen panels in the bus shelters against players at other bus stops. The games were well received, with over 80,000 commuters playing, according to Yahoo. In essence, the campaign transformed the bus shelters into social-gaming hubs.

Some of these games afford great flexibility in terms of location. The flexibility of Six to Start's 'Wanderlust' platform underlines the shift towards more varied venues in location-based games. The platform is not fixed to a particular location and allows Act I to be played in any cafe in the world and Act II in any bar in the world. Another key change in location-based games is their increasing incorporation of user-generated content, allowing users more input in the design of the games. Plenty of experimentation lies ahead for location-based games, which should open up many new opportunities for leisure facilities and creative developers from widely varying genres.

'Ambient' Interactivity in Leisure Facilities / Multi-Touch Interactive Tables and Countertops in Leisure Facilities

The concept of 'interactivity in a box', exemplified by standard kiosks, is undergoing a major transformation in leisure facilities and starting to recede, with the increasing development of ambient, embedded interactivity in such locations as bars, restaurants, clubs, hotels, museums, casinos and other public places. This new interactive form promises to fundamentally reshape the nature of interactive entertainment, marketing and educational experiences in those places.

According to Mark Foster Gage, founder of Mark Foster Gage + Associates and assistant dean in the Yale School of Architecture, 'ambient interactivity can add a deeper and more responsive element to architecture and content' and significantly expand and amplify environments. He believes ambient interactive design allows architects to fine tune the environments they create, especially by allowing spaces to be programmed and vary by time of the day and audience. 'It also offers the element of surprise', he asserts. 'Spaces become more comfortable, active, and engaging.' As a result, interactivity becomes easier and more transparent, allowing visitors to retrieve information more casually, he adds.

Eli Kuslansky, chief strategist for New York-based Unified Field, predicts that, in the next three to five years:

> *Ambient interactive forms such as responsive environments, embedded technologies, and interactive surfaces will have their greatest impact in public spaces when they're unified into an ecosystem integrating the built environment with multimodal sensors, media, big data, and social media networks.*

Overall, he sees the 'future of ambient interactivity in networked environments', though he notes they will not be 'as much technology networks' as 'people networks and resource and knowledge networks', allowing multiple informational and communications channels to be accessed.

Ana Monte, creative director of YDreams, Brazil, believes:

> *Touchable surfaces of all kinds of objects will be the next step in ambient interactivity. These surfaces will be combined with biometric recognition and devices controllable by apps to afford highly intelligent and customized environments.*

She feels that:

> *The internet of things is the biggest trend in ambient interactivity, because it allows users to control objects and environments. Through this technology, the whole environment is connected and controllable by many input devices and the environment itself must communicate with the user.*

Another key attribute of ambient interactivity is its capacity to serve as a platform for richer and more diverse user-generated content. In fact, user-generated content has generally proven to be one of the most popular forms of content delivered via ambient interactive forms.

Figure 7.1 A prototype large HD touchscreen display: the combination of object / image recognition with such screens is being considered for hospitality, retail and entertainment

Unsurprisingly, some of the more experimental applications of ambient interactivity have been offered in museum settings. For example, Hide and Seek created a unique context for ambient interactivity with a game it developed for the exhibition 'Joue le Joue' at La Gaite Lyrique gallery in Paris in 2012. The game allowed players to 'interact with different senses' of the building housing the exhibition. Players could 'make a sound the building wanted to hear, touch the building rhythmically and help the building see places' not accessible to its security cameras. The result is that 'the building told you what type of person it thinks you are' and 'let the player into a secret room where its heart lay, if the player was lucky enough'. In Kuslansky's view:

> *Ambient interactivity is revolutionizing the museum experience by offering greater context for exhibits. For art museums with extensive collections that can't be displayed due to space and resource constraints, multi-touch tables, gesture-based interactive experiences, and mobile apps serve as great ways to draw from a museum's broader collection, engage audiences, and generate new revenue streams.*

As he sums up, 'the most fundamental impact ambient interactivity will have on museums is transitioning the current model of discrete destinations to a twenty-first-century model of the networked community'.

He feels that 'the emergence of big data in urban planning and civic life is the next evolution of ambient interactivity in public places. Ambient sensors everywhere are collecting an avalanche of data every millisecond of the day.' In an effort to capitalize on this development, Unified Field 'has developed a concept to employ big data in the smart city called "Legible City", because it provides a means for people to tap into the data and mediate its flow for personal use, making it possible for citizens to interact with their environment and municipality in a narrative form'.

Intelligent interactive furniture has emerged as a highly transparent interactive paradigm in museums and other public places, as well as in marketing campaigns. New and more distinctive forms of intelligent furniture have emerged and afford more natural interfaces and transparent interactive experiences, removing distractions and barriers caused by such traditional user interfaces as keyboards and buttons. For example, YDreams has introduced a wide range of interactive-furniture products, including 'Interactive Benches', which afford visitors easy access to multimedia content in rest areas at museums and other cultural centres; the 'Interactive Table', a projection system enabling visitors to interact using physical markers; and 'Display Case', which allows visitors to access detailed information about the objects on display by tapping the display window.

Ambient interactivity can be applied to something seemingly as unexpected and mundane as lighting objects. That was the approach taken by Second Story, when it developed 'LYT', a 'collaborative lighting fixture', which allowed users to collaboratively draw in real time on light objects, select the size of the fixtures, and 'control the lighting via their smartphone', reports Daniel Meyers, AIA, creative director of environments, at Second Story. 'LYT' 'tapped into an innate citizen desire for crafting their own objects and controlling their environment.' (Users could 'connect via the web to a real-time RGB display embedded in a light fixture via a mobile phone' in the project, he notes.) Second Story used Intel's Galileo microcontroller board for the project. The aim of the experience, which debuted at the Maker Faire in Rome in October 2013, was simple fun, he explains. He characterizes the project as 'a DIY electronic dream' and essentially an 'experiment designed to test user reactions to drawing on a large canvas in big groups'.

One of the most vital and popular forms of ambient interactivity has been interactive windows, which constitute one of the most transparent user interfaces. Marcus Wallander, a digital creative official for Great Works, based in Stockholm, sees potential for interactive windows as retail tools because they serve as an 'excellent way' of attracting customers passing by stores. He adds that the 'media space afforded by interactive windows is very cost efficient, since the store or other property with the interactive window owns the space', and that the cost of producing content for interactive windows 'can be low' compared to other media.

Staat Creative Agency, based in Amsterdam, has worked on a number of innovative interactive window projects. In collaboration with Nike Brand Design, the company conceived and designed an interactive window for the Nike House of Innovation at Selfridges in London in June 2013, says Martijn Lamabada, partner and creative director for the agency. The window, which Staat developed with Random Studio, Jurlights and the Set Company, was designed not so much to market certain products, but primarily 'to showcase the diversity of Nike's products in a non-intrusive way, amplify Nike's brand image, and immerse passers-by in the Nike brand experience', he notes.

The window allowed visitors to experience diverse Nike products, such as its lunar shoes and metal jacket, in new ways. For example, 74 flashing strobe lights in the window and video art were employed to showcase a distinctive feature of the metal jacket. Staat also created a simple game connected with Nike's lunar shoes to enable passers-by to experience their special features. The game challenged passers-by to 'jump the highest', and 'Kinect'-based motion sensors were used to calculate the height and velocity of each jump. Staat observed that passers-by playing the game began to talk with others about their experience, making it a 'conversation starter between those people'.

Projection mapping has become a more significant element in ambient interactivity, adding literally new dimensions to it. Gage sees new vistas for projection mapping in urban environments, envisioning 'varying layers of technology built on existing notions of space to create new forms of architecture and urbanism'. In this regard, he points to an ambient design his company proposed to Samsung, which involved creating a canopy of one million balloons on the West Side Highway in New York producing a landscape of projected urban clouds

Another key element of the trend towards intelligent furniture is the growing use of multi-touch screens embedded in countertops and tables of bars, restaurants, nightclubs, hotels and casinos. They allow customers to play games and engage with other entertainment experiences, foster greater social interaction, deliver promotional and advertising messages, provide tourist information, drive greater sales, enhance brand loyalty, reduce operational costs and generally improve the operational efficiency of those facilities. In essence, they can afford more natural, fluid and satisfying interactive entertainment that is more competitive with interactive entertainment in the home market.

According to David Aichele, executive vice president of sales and marketing at T1Visions, the 'market potential' of multi-touch systems and interactive tables in bars and restaurants is probably in the 'hundreds of millions', especially considering the 'market isn't well established' yet. Echoing that point, Dax Patton, director of business operations for Digital Touch Systems, estimates that only a 'small percentage of bars and restaurants' currently have multi-touch tabletop systems, though 'the number has grown significantly in the past two years'. According to him, the first bar and restaurant adopters of multi-touch systems and interactive tables were 'sports bars', followed by 'casual dining restaurants'. Aichele observes that multi-touch tables tend to be used most by 'medium to high-end restaurants and bars that have digital-entertainment options such as TV or trivia games, including smaller restaurant-franchise chains and some independently owned restaurants'.

Patton acknowledges some entrenched resistance to these new devices, but he feels the markets are now 'more accepting of the systems'. According to him, multi-touch interactive tables have a number of key benefits for restaurants, bars and other hospitality facilities, including their ability to generate 'longer customer visits, greater recurring visits and increased sales' and to 'improve operational efficiency, thus lowering operational costs'. Patton notes another benefit of multi-touch interactive tables: by keeping customers in restaurants and bars occupied with games and other activities, they are less aware of or concerned with delays in receiving their food and drink. These systems provide a 'better customer experience overall', he sums up.

The sales impact of multi-touch systems and interactive tables in bars and restaurants is often significant. For example, Patton reports that Touch Café in Chisinau, Moldova, which uses his company's T3 interactive tables, experienced an 'over 14 per cent increase in sales' due to the use of the tables.

Digital Touch Systems' interactive tables include an interactive sports-bar table, allowing guests to post opinions on game plays and calls and interact with other fans in the bar; a touchscreen system for clubs, allowing guests to send song requests to the DJ from their tables; and customized way-finding systems, allowing guests to search for shops, restaurants, maps and weather information.

Aichele claims that his company's 'inTouch' multi-user, multi-touch interactive tables, which were first introduced in bars and restaurants during 2010, have been generating 'more revenue per table' at restaurants and bars using the systems. He adds that the tables with the highest percentage of occupied seats at restaurants using T1Visions' interactive tables are usually the interactive ones. To further highlight the impact of his company's tables, he cites a 2009 study conducted for the company at an undisclosed restaurant using the tables that showed '50 per cent higher revenues' at the company's interactive tables than revenues at the regular tables. T1Visions' restaurant and bar customers include Tracks and Records in Jamaica, partly owned by the Jamaican sprinter Usain Bolt; Mellow Mushroom in Charlotte, North Carolina; the Cowfish Sushi Burger Bar in Charlotte and Raleigh, North Carolina; BaJa Soul Taqueria in Charlotte; and Sparians Sports Bar and Bowling Center in Raleigh.

In order to be viable in bars and restaurants, multi-touch systems and interactive tables must be judiciously introduced. For example, typically restaurants using T1Visions' 'inTouch' system install it 'in 25 to 50 per cent' of their tables, reports Aichele. He notes that 'restaurants and bars can maximize their ROI [return on investment] at this level of adoption'. Multi-touch tables typically vary in cost from $4,000 to $20,000, depending on the 'size of the screens and level of graphical content'.

The popularity of features on multi-touch systems and interactive tables in bars and restaurants seems closely related to the nature of those facilities and the capabilities of the systems. According to Aichele, the most popular application on his company's 'inTouch' tables in restaurants and bars is entertainment, including 'interactive games and media viewing, such as pictures and video trailers'. The next most popular application is 'order processing', which allows restaurants and bars to 'order directly at the table and track analytics' for their customers, enabling them to collect data on the most popular food items on the menu and determine which 'ads and specials' to feature, he says. That has proven 'very effective' for those restaurants and bars.

One of the key issues affecting the success of multi-touch systems and interactive tables in bars and restaurants is how effectively system developers integrate their systems into those bars and restaurants. In that regard, the developers of E-Table multi-touch tables have an advantage, since they are themselves owners of Inamo restaurants in London, points out Neil Hunwick, CEO of E-Table and Inamo Restaurants. As a result, they 'know how to integrate the system' at their restaurants and can 'assure other restaurant operators that [their] system will work properly' at their restaurants, he maintains. In his view, one of the problems with many multi-touch table developers active in the restaurant market is that they 'fail to understand the operational requirements of restaurants'. Patton also emphasizes the need for developers of multi-touch systems and interactive tables aimed at bars and restaurants to be guided by their clients in the integration of those systems, since 'they know their customers better'.

E-Table introduced their first multi-touch table system at the Inamo restaurant on Wardour Street in London in 2008, and the second at Inamo St. James on Regent Street in London in 2010, reports Hunwick. E-Table has licensed their technology to the restaurant Izakaya and the Holland Casino Group in Holland and the restaurant Taste of Turkey in Turkey.

Some of the most popular features of the E-Tables in Inamo's restaurants is their 'tasteful images of food items, essentially sneak previews of the dish you're about to be served, and ordering capabilities'. According to Hunwick, games are also popular, especially 'Battleships': 'meaning you can blow up your own date', he reports.

Concerns have been raised about the possible negative effects of multi-touch systems on social interaction at bars and restaurants, but developers contend that the systems help foster social interaction not detract from it. In this regard, Hunwick feels that the E-Tables 'engender conversation' and serve as 'a talking point' at the Inamo restaurants.

Speaking with Mark Boyle, sales director of Compurants, founded in 2005 and the owner of the E-Table brand, the question of what their technology brings to the entertainment and hospitality sector was raised. Boyle stated:

> *E-Table provides increased efficiencies for the restaurant operator, allowing the potential to reduce staffing costs, provide real-time control over the menu and the ability to upsell, and the potential to turn tables more rapidly. The customer takes control over the ambience at their table by selecting from a gallery of charming 'tablecloths', projected from above; the system also gives guests access to an array of entertainment options, including games, and 'Chefcam', a live video feed from a camera in the kitchen.*

Going into the detail of the experience, Boyle was asked what lessons he had learned about how much media (social and entertainment) to place in front of the patron:

> *Our customers enjoy the E-Table experience, but they also want to taste our unique food, and to talk to their friends. The media on our tables is tailored to reflect the restaurant environment; for instance, our games are relatively simple and quick to play, and the two-player 'Battleship' is a particular favourite. The other applications on the table serve to assist our guests in enjoying the restaurant, by showing them the way to the washrooms, or suggesting local theatrical performances and clubs that they might enjoy after the meal.*

The question of what the future holds for this type of system was raised. Boyle commented:

> *Whilst the interactive ordering market is expanding rapidly, with new tablet-based designs becoming available by the week, the future of interactive ordering will be defined by radical innovation. E-Table is the only patented, downwards-projecting system on the market. Our team of developers are continually working to refine our existing systems, and to develop new solutions.*

Regarding the change in approach to the market, Nolan Bushnell stated:

> *I have seen all the developments in E-Table and the use of mobile devices to provide the content, sadly what we did not see coming was the tablets when we started uWink, we were too far ahead of the curve, by the time we had spent $10,000 to install an interactive table guests could get this on their mobile phone. Regarding providing the best content to guests I don't feel anyone has it figured out yet, all I know when you provide a worse experience than the guest has on their mobile, you are in a lot of trouble.*

The concept of ambient interactive entertainment was given one of its more unique twists by the Thinkwell Group in an interactive water-fountain show called the 'Show at the Pier' developed in 2006 for the Pier at Caesars in Atlantic City. The show combined coloured jets of water; lighting for most of the jets; 150 nozzles; rain, fog and other effects; and had an interactive system called 'Splash!', which used a network of cameras with computer tracking to follow visitors in the show area. Visitors could participate in three game experiences at the show, individually or in groups. In the game 'Follow Me', visitors were followed around the show area by the fountain using coloured lights and water. Another game called 'Paint the Fountain' projected 5 different colours of light around the edge of the pool and generated coloured blasts of water based on the number of people assembled in each light circle. When the crowds gathered near the fountain grew too large, the fountain would react by playing a game with a Gong Show-type spoof. Initially, water and light effects would follow the visitors, and the fountain would select visitors to participate in a mini-show randomly. During this part of the show, the fountain prompted visitors to dance (and play a musical selection). If the visitors did not participate, the fountain triggered a sound conveying disappointment. On the other hand, visitors agreeing to participate were treated to a choreographed show synched to the music they selected.

A futuristic immersive hotel-room concept called the 'IHR Room Xperience' developed by Serrano Brothers gives a sense of some far-reaching implications of ambient interactivity in leisure facilities. The concept involves touchscreen hotel-room 'walls' that can be accessed by guests via smartphone or touch. The walls will integrate Microsoft Surface tablets, touchscreens and interactive surfaces. The project was recently showcased at the Fiturtech International Tourism Trade Fair in Madrid.

The personalized social-entertainment terminal can trace much of its evolution back to the aspirations of the early touchscreen bartop terminals. One of those early developers, uWink, began in video amusement. It was founded by Nolan Bushnell and started as a touchscreen- video-terminal enterprise compiling original architecture and content. But it was the combination of touchscreen terminals and a restaurant with no waiters, just food runners, that established the 'food–drinks–media' mix.

UWink Bistro would go on to be established in three venues, all in California, that saw table service automated through the patrons touchscreen video terminal, building on firmware and content from the original uWink machine. Content also included new approaches to socializing the whole venue with at-table entertainment. After the first three venues the concept faltered, and eventually all the stores closed and the service was sold under the name Tapcode.

Nolan Bushnell gave his observation of this aspect of the sector saying:

> *I believe that people are playing more games than ever before, you look on the New York Subway and 60 per cent of the passengers are playing games on their mobiles. For the venues to compete with this they need to create compelling experience in bars that takes that natural design to best present games and take this to a whole different market all over again.*

Since uWink, the familiarity of social networks has added momentum to the multimedia experience in the hospitality industry. Services like Foursquare and Twitter offer promotional tools for venues to match to their clientele. The need to raise awareness of a venue on social media and to offer enticements to visit it are a major part of the promotion of modern social-entertainment venues. One new application is the ability to download apps onto customers' phones that can be used to enhance the experience of visiting. One of these has been developed by AMI Entertainment Network, who provide digital jukebox and touchscreen technology for bars and restaurants. The company has embraced the latest technology in launching their new 'AMI Bar Live', a mobile-phone app that offers personalized on-premises entertainment control via the phone, the user paying for the music or video through their handset.

Digital-photo-booth specialist Apple Industries partnered with AMI Entertainment to create the 'NGX Face Place' jukebox. This product combines the functionality of a networked digital jukebox with a digital photo booth mounted on the wall. With the Apple Industry infrastructure the photo-booth component is email compatible.

Apple Industries has also been advancing digital photos in the entertainment environment. Competing against the use of smartphones for the sharing of images, the company has developed their 'PixPlace' system that offers an 80cm-touchscreen kiosk that incorporates facial recognition and offers customizable recording of the visitor's experiences: both images and communication are shared via social media. Digital out-of-home entertainment in these environments has to offer something better than can be achieved with the plethora of devices carried by the modern consumer.

Allen Weisberg, CEO of Apple Industries / Face Place, stated:

> *Face Place photo booths feature Apple's brand-new cutting-edge 'Smile 2.0' software that links up to the internet and allows customers who have their picture taken to email their photos directly from the photo booth to any email address and to social networks such as Facebook and Twitter.*

All 'Smile 2.0' Face Place photo booths are internet-ready and can connect directly to customers' social-media pages. Customers can instantly upload their photo strip (containing the operators' logo on the fourth frame) from 'Face Place Photo Booth' to their personal page, spreading custom branded photo strips along with a message and a link to the venue's website. The average Facebook user has 130 friends, and customers show how much fun they are having at the establishment to all of them. There is no better way to advertise than to have the customer do it for you! Apple Industries have been in the photo, vending, coin-operated machine and event-planning industries for more than 30 years and are one of the leading providers of digital-imaging for retail environments. Their R&D team is headed by Mike Bloomfield, who commented: 'technology is one of most important elements in the modern amusement industry. The ability to support the latest trends in the social-networking sector can define future profits.'

Robotic Applications in Leisure Facilities

Although their use in leisure facilities will probably still be limited for the next few years, robotic devices are likely to become an increasingly important element in leisure facilities, especially in combination with other technologies, such as AR, smartphones, video games, 3-D and tablets, and they will be used for a wider array of applications. They will become more significant in leisure facilities because of their ability to afford more user-control and wider applications and because of the arrival of more compact, lightweight, multisensory and versatile personal robots and robot platforms, such as the 'PR2' from Willow Garage, 'Romo' from Romotive and 'Ballbot' from Bossa Nova Robotics.

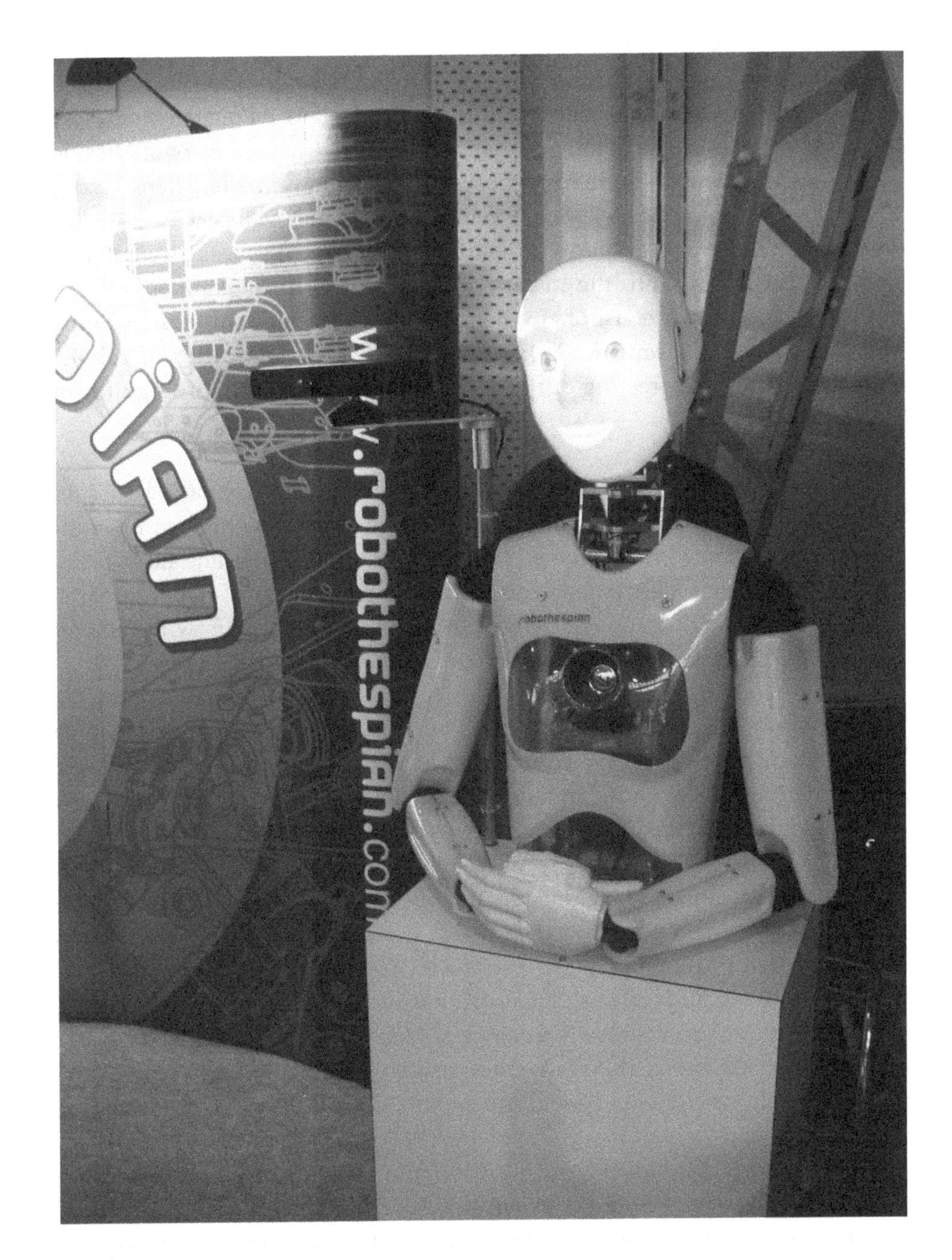

Figure 7.2 Robo-thespian: the life-sized humanoid robot can interact with customers, providing a fully interactive, multilingual and user-friendly platform

Moreover, Antonio Camara, CEO of YDreams, feels experiences centred around 'robots' will increasingly offer the important element of surprise in public places. In fact, YDreams has already used personal robots in one of its projects for way-finding purposes. The company made extensive use of robotics in the 'El Faro' visitor-centre project it developed in 2010 for Santander Group's headquarters in Madrid. The centre was designed to familiarize visitors with 'the history and presence' of the company. Small 'robots greet and guide visitors to their destination in the centre', says Filipe Vasconcellos, a spokesman for YDreams. Certainly, the application of 'robots' for way-finding and greeting purposes is starting to become more significant in public places.

One of the most ambitious projects involving the use of robotics in leisure facilities is Robot Land, a large amusement park due to open in South Korea in 2014. The park will be replete with robotic features and attractions, including robot cashiers, robot performances, robot-driven shopping carts, robotic competitions involving 'boxer-bot' battles, an aquarium with remote-controlled robot fish, and a giant robot arm connected to a rollercoaster.

An increasing effort is being made by some amusement parks to take a more light-hearted and playful approach to robots and foster greater engagement between robots and visitors. For example, Walt Disney has been testing animatronic robots that can play catch with visitors and juggle.

Another intriguing development in robotics for leisure facilities is the emergence of remote-controlled drones. For example, YDreams Acores recently developed an aquatic drone called 'Zipheus' that can be controlled by smartphones and tablets. It incorporates a built-in camera, allowing users to explore and capture footage of oceans, lakes and other underwater environments remotely. This kind of device is emblematic of the trend towards using small drones for educational and exploratory purposes.

Some efforts are underway to afford remote-controlled robots a more significant role in museums. For example, CSIRO and the National Museum of Australia are collaborating to develop and test a mobile 'telepresence' robot at the museum as part of CSIRO's 'Museum Robot' project. The robot will follow education staff through the Landmarks Gallery in the museum and allow remote visitors to take a virtual tour of the museum. The visitors will be able to interact with the educators via a broadband connection. The educators will guide the robot while the remote visitors will be able to control the robot's head and manipulate a 360° camera to view specific items in the exhibit.

The remote visitors will also have a chance to access AR images of the objects in the gallery in their original or restored form.

In light of these developments and broader trends in the DOE market, remote-controlled robots in general are likely to have a bright future in certain types of amusement parks, museums, aquariums, zoos and other leisure facilities for games, exploration, education and other purposes, as they afford visitors more control and involvement in attractions, exhibits and other experiences.

Although robotics has a clear place in some amusement parks and other leisure facilities, it seems doubtful that in the near future many visitors will be keen on completely robotic leisure facilities and would likely find them tedious, as most visitors seem to prefer a reasonable amount of human contact and a certain proportion of more conventional physical and digital attractions.

Whereas much of what is being considered regarding supported and autonomous robotic devices in the leisure sector is speculative, there are some companies that have made major strides towards application. Pal-Robotics strive to make robotics an integral part of daily life, with their 'REEM-Series' of humanoid robots. The company has developed an autonomous guide for public settings (an automated information service) and targeted the entertainment sector. Building on the popularity of animatronics in the theme-park sector, REEM systems could appear in DOE venues.

As robot use evolves in leisure facilities, they will likely be used for more exploratory and creative purposes and risky operations in parks, museums and other leisure facilities, such as stunts. Games and other attractions permitting increased teamwork between visitors and robots may also become part of leisure facilities further into the future.

Robots will likely become more closely connected with simulators and be charged with more elaborate missions in leisure facilities over the next five years. In addition, robots with more lifelike features will probably appear further down the road.

Potential of 3-D Printing in Leisure Facilities

The emergence of 'makerbots' driven by 3-D printing could open up intriguing creativity possibilities in amusement parks, museums and other leisure facilities, potentially allowing visitors to contribute objects and forms that could be integrated into attractions, exhibitions and other experiences. In fact, some leisure facilities are already capitalizing on the growing popularity of 'makerculture'. The Newark Museum, for example, has an attraction called 'Makerspace', which offers do-it-yourself learning using art and technology. It allows children to create their own forms and objects following their interests, with simple materials and tools and the help of 3-D printing technologies.

Defining the New Trends of Immersiveness

Some signs of transformation in the DOE market are emblematic of the rise of 'expansive' interactive-entertainment forms, which expand the scope of interactive entertainment in terms of time, place, content, personalization and immersiveness. These emerging forms of interactive entertainment can be described in some or all of the following ways: ongoing, fluid, multilayered, multidimensional, immersive, pervasive and convergent. Gestural technology, AR, holography, 3-D, 4-D and 5-D, AR games and user-generated content exemplify expansive interactive entertainment. They are markedly different from the fixed forms of interactivity and 'interactivity in a box' historically found in leisure facilities and public places, in that they are integral to and permeate those environments, as epitomized by 'ambient' interactive forms.

Perhaps one of the most significant trends affecting the DOE market is the growing convergence between real and virtual experiences, afforded by such interactive forms as mobile AR, location-based games and social media. New technologies, such as smartphones, and new consumer habits are hastening the increasing convergence of the interactive consumer and DOE markets in public places, and much greater convergence is likely to spawn huge opportunities in the next decade.

Another key element of expansive interactive entertainment in both the DOOH and interactive markets is the increasing application and integration of user-generated content and content co-created by amateur users and professional developers, including multilevel user-generated content. This trend is also likely to accelerate in the next five years. Event-based content will become an increasingly large part of interactive experiences in leisure facilities and public places and provide a platform for more varied and rich social-media experiences emanating from those locations.

World-based game models, such as that displayed by 'SimCity', will probably increasingly filter into public places and leisure facilities. These models have greater relevance (in modified form) now in leisure facilities, as those facilities seek to appeal to wider audiences beyond the typical young male demographic that represented the core video-arcade game audience and as blended real/physical experiences become more common in those facilities.

Social games have become more popular in location-based entertainment centres, amusement parks and other leisure facilities and will enjoy wider use in those facilities. In particular, they will likely centre around broader themes and topics and offer greater immersiveness in those facilities in order to reach wider audiences.

Games and other interactive experiences seem set to appear in a greater variety of new locations. Episodic interactive experiences have emerged in leisure facilities and are likely to play a more important role in those facilities in the near future.

Personalized interactivity is likely to become a much more significant factor in leisure facilities, as more customized interactive experiences, including customized interactive experiences 'on demand', assume a larger role. Alex Carru, CEO of Medialon, envisions 'mass customization becoming the norm' in amusement-park attractions and museum exhibits. Some current and future examples of that customization include:

> *Museums that remember you and your last visit and offer different experiences each time you come; museums that send you an e-mail with a summary of what you have or haven't seen and guide you through experiences where video interacts and speaks to visitors for a fraction of a second; and 'Kinect' interactive experiences incorporating videos synched up with the visitor's voice.*

In this new environment, elements of amusement-park rides and attractions could be altered practically instantaneously to suit different audiences, themes and content. To illustrate potential on-the-fly ride modifications and customizations, Joni Newkirk, CEO of Integrated Insight, explains: 'maybe the ride you take will be different every time you go on it. Or you'll be able to choose your own version: "princess or cowboy"'.

The increasing variety of leisure-facility forms, such as retail-tainment, eat-ertainment and hybrid entertainment centres (combining bowling alleys with laser-tag, for example) will provide key new opportunities for next-generation interactive experiences in leisure facilities. In addition, leisure facilities will be increasingly connected with the home market, enabling the development and delivery of more dynamic interactive experiences and extending interactive experiences in those facilities far beyond their confines.

Leisure facilities and public places have served as a laboratory and testing ground for new interactive experiences, technologies and applications. That role will likely increase significantly in the near future, but key challenges remain in this transitional period, including the all-too-familiar resistance to change and a need to devise effective new business and creative models, unshackle the DOE market from technology-driven interactivity, surmount significant market fragmentation and attract more diverse talent from outside the DOE mainstream, such as consumer-game developers, live-theatre producers and writers, traditional-event planners and video producers.

DOE seems poised soon to become a more integral part of cross-media projects. At the same time, content for that market will likely become more original and self-generating in the near future.

Business models for the DOE market will become more varied, encompassing diverse combinations of revenue streams. Those revenue streams might include pay-per-play, subscriptions, premium admissions, sponsorship, advertising and seasonal passes.

An increasing number of experiential marketeers and brands have been attracted to the special benefits of the DOE market and are using new tools to enhance brand awareness and increase product sales. As this book illustrates, there are many different facets to DOE. No one model is suited to all the different kinds of digital environments or content. The future of this market will largely lie in holistic, variegated interactive experiences that are regularly enhanced and expanded. Only a modest percentage of opportunities in the new DOE market has been tapped, leaving the market wide open to innovation and rife with opportunities.

One approach to the new DOE market is the productization of the latest developments in technology and being able to apply them to as many aspects of the market as possible. One exponent of this is D-Box, a leading manufacturer of motion systems who supply leading-edge applications in a package that can be used in a multitude of sectors. D-Box actuators have been used as motion bases for military simulations, but also as effective motion systems for the latest 'sim-racing' game-rigs. Amusement applications include the system used in Triotech theatre and attraction systems. The appeal of adding motion to a game can be seen in the casino and gaming sector: WMS Industries launched their 'Experience Motion Chair Technology' that has D-Box technology at its heart united with a 'chance-n-play' gaming experience.

Yannick Gemme, director of home and OEM division at D-Box, said of the corporation's involvement in DOE: 'D-Box is active in various field of the DOE and looking at this opportunity to get a vision at the market, with some thousand systems in the public sector.' D-Box has been working hard to exploit the opportunities in DOE: in health, military, theatre and attractions. This has recently seen the company support a drive to define the sector, becoming a member of the Digital Out-of-Home Entertainment Network Association to obtain networking opportunities and market data.

Some would see the console sector and the amusement sector as mortal enemies, but as has been revealed in this book, iOS apps, console-game booths, licensed content and the actual game developers from the consumer scene all play their part in the modern DOE sector. With the upheaval in the consumer-console sector and under pressure from the new generation of independent 'microconsoles' (powerful PC-based plug-and-play systems), independent consumer-game development studios and even the larger publishers are looking at broadening their product capabilities. Already consoles and PCs are vying against game decks, tablets and smartphones to be the release platform for the latest game content.

Nolan Bushnell stated:

> *The benefit from the apathy by players to the new generation consoles seems to show that they are lot close to end of life. When they start shouting 'my photo-realism is better than your photo-realism' you know you have problems. The manufacturers are hard pressed to make selling only slightly better graphics at an extra cost compelling. I perceive that development community people buy software they don't buy hardware. The developers have been so mis-used by console companies like Sony, I bet their authoring tools are not even translated into English. Kiss that off, and it will collapse so fast that it will make your head spin.*

Along with the latest in home simulator game-rigs, the sophisticated gaming audience is also looking father afield. This makes the consumer-game trade evaluate the possibility of targeting DOE as yet another platform they could support, as the opportunities to generate the same revenue from single-platform releases is affected by more systems and the transference from physical retail units to digital download content (DLC). Those in the consumer-game trade recognize that the extended console lifecycle has impeded a consumer rush to adopt eighth generation platforms. A high attrition rate in independent consumer-game developers with depressed game sales will lead many investors and publishers to focus on new opportunities, such as mobile-phone game apps and casual gaming platforms. The possibility of using already established development skills in a public-space environment (represented by DOE) is an opportunity worth considering in order to survive.

Conclusion
Living in the Dream

For many, the drive towards the interactive frontier in leisure facilities is the creation of a form of entertainment that has previously only been the plaything of sci-fi writers, best personified by the 'Star Trek' creation the holodeck. The dream of placing players within a totally synthetic recreation of a real or fictional environment that can be interacted with has become an vision of the pinnacle of interactive gaming.

Figure C.1 **Countering the stereotype of solitary and sedentary consumer-game play in a social environment**

The technology of the holodeck as well as its deployment in holosuites is an interesting plot device. Fictional recreational environments offer opportunities for the imaginations of the writers and the holographic technology of the twenty-third century strikes a resonant cord with the audiences of the twentieth (although other futurists and authors have postulated similar kinds of futuristic VR devices: William Gibson's 'cyberspace', based on what we now think of as VR, offering a comparison to the holograph).

As mentioned earlier, it is the ability to use simulation technology to hoodwink the user's brain into complete saturation in the virtual environment that has taken the idea of moving from just fooling the inner-ear and eye to deceiving the whole brain. Interest in the ideal of a 'complete-simulator' increased as the latest VR, AR and mixed-reality technologies gained momentum. The holodeck offers the opportunity not only of a recreational environment but also to take the technology to the next level and turning it into the next generation of human–machine interface.

The revolution in how people interact with their computers caused by the graphical user interface (GUI) is nothing compared to the effects the immersive user interface (IUI) could have in the near future. We have seen the use of computer automated virtual environments (CAVEs) in the automotive and petroleum industries and its improvements in how data is visualized and manipulated. The dream of a holodeck, in turn, looks beyond the most ergonomic placement of instruments in a car or the location of natural-gas seams in the North Atlantic and towards the new 'experiential' level of immersion.

Jet Propulsion Laboratory (JPL), whilst working for NASA, proposed developing the state-of-the-art human–system interaction: low-cost 'holodecks'. In a recent presentation the concept of 'telexploration' was introduced, using current immersive technology to represent the telemetry gathered from the hundreds of unmanned space-craft traversing the solar systems and representing this information in environments that could be explored and experienced not just by NASA mission scientists but by the general public. The aspiration was that immersive environments would allow users to perceive the reality of the environment as a distant rover does: virtual exploration for the masses.

In a presentation during the 2013 Game Developers Conference (GDC) Dr Jeff Norris of JPL told the assembled audience: 'We are the Space Invaders!' He then when on to state:

> *I want us to build a future of shared immersive exploration. Everyone exploring the universe through robotic avatars, not just peering at numbers or pictures on a screen, but stepping inside a holodeck and standing on those distant worlds.*

Though touching on much of the new immersive technology that has been discussed in this book, it is obvious that the game visuals are only part of what is needed to transport the player fully into a virtual environment. Physicality of experience has been a new and driving force in the gaming arena: first with force-feedback that attempted to simulate the loading imparted through a flight controller or steering wheel. This technology, mirroring the virtual world to the player, has been augmented by the use of 'haptic feedback', representing the solidity of the virtual world through special gloves.

The ability to navigate in this virtual environment has also seen the use of 'omnidirectional' treadmills and the latest high-definition tracking technologies. This near sci-fi technology has been nicknamed the 'human mouse' – allowing users to walk normally on a platform and be represented within the virtual world. Many of those developing this infrastructure are suppliers of technology for the defence sector. MSE Weibull is based in Sweden and are known to a select few for their revolutionary invention of the omnidirectional floor, which offered unlimited walking in any direction. After various projects the company has combined their floor with a unique 'virtual theatre' platform for deployment in infantry training as well as aspirations in high-end (prosumer) gaming, although as of yet they have not moved into the digital out-of-home entertainment sector.

The possibility of unencumbered freedom of movement within a virtual world has fuelled interest from start-up operations in many countries. One such company is Virtuix, which has prototyped their 'Omni', a treadmill that could become a low-cost consumer-game peripheral. Virtuix is hoping to attract Kickstarter crowd-funding. The success of the Oculus Rift Kickstarter campaign fuelling many aspirations in this field.

One of the most unusual omnidirectional systems is from VirtuSphere. Nicknamed the 'giant hamster wheel', it encloses the user in a special 3m sphere hooked up to movement sensors. The technology has been used by the military in infantry training, along with wireless HMD and gun interfaces. The entertainment and education sectors are now showing interest in the technology.

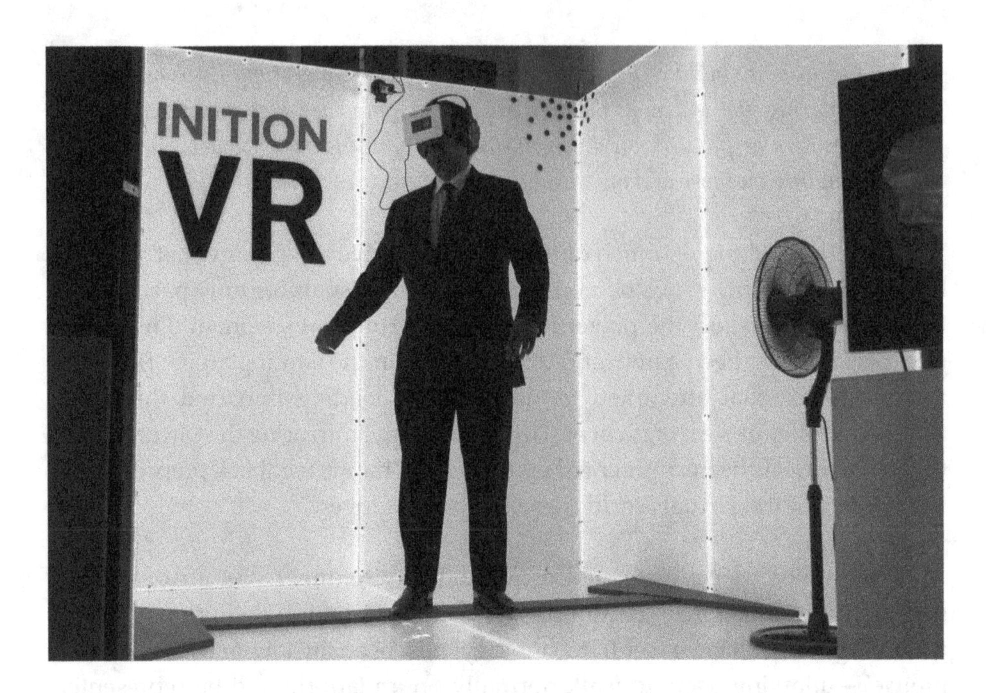

Figure C.2 Inition's vertigo simulator using an Oculus VR dev-kit: a compelling if unnerving example of the power of the immersive experience

But there is also the ability for the user's environment to be physically manipulated as well as having images projected upon it. One new piece of technology showcased recently was the 'HypoSurface', a dynamic wall and floor system that can achieve physical motion like waves and represent surfaces through a special interface. Though not the 'hard light' approach of sci-fi, all these technologies are driving towards a greater immersive platform to use the content on.

Designs like the 'i-Cocoon' offer a glimpse of the future. NAU of Zurich, Switzerland developed a conceptual prototype of a 360°, 3-D projected capsule. After selecting the desired experience, the user enters the capsule, and every move is captured and represented in the virtual environment, suggesting that game content for a system of this kind would be more experiential than competitive. This technology, like other 360° projection systems with tracked interfaces, is developed from current CAVE systems, like VirTra, with their 'V-3000' series for law-enforcement and military-weapon training applications, or Walt Disney, with their 'Digital Immersive Showroom' (DISH) for planning visualization.

The holodeck is also driving original entertainment projects that hope to apply the technology of the immersive display to visitor attractions. Corporations like SCALE-1 Portal are working to create a multiscreen environment for experiencing 3-D games in an ultra-immersive arcade environment: an ultra-low-cost CAVE simulator.

Regarding the implementation of their system Emmanuel Icart, founder of SCALE-1 Portal stated:

> *The infrastructure of our SCALE-1 Portal comes with dedicated gaming contents, ready for multi-player and multi-site features. Besides its gaming dedication, it is also open thanks to its software development kit, and makes in this state a perfect starting solution for any virtual reality needs.*

Regarding what is steering this development, Icart said: 'Innovation and fun, before all. We do think we are working on the most exciting gaming platform and we hope players will feel the same!' Icart was asked if he saw their system as a replacement for amusement machines or an evolution?

> *It's more like an evolution of existing amusement machines. Gameplay and even user workflow needs to be adapted in order to match the requirements of wireless virtual reality gaming.*

But, as is shown throughout this book, the game content as well as the hardware defines the experience offered by DOE above consumer development. On where SCALE-1 Portal will get its games from, Icat said

> *At first from our internal development studio. But the software development kit will allow any gaming studio to produce great contents for the Portal. An online distribution workflow will allow contents providers to publish their games to the online catalogue, after SCALE-1 internal validation and quality assurance. Owners of the Portal will be able to browse the games catalogue, grab updates or even try new games before buying them, straight from the Portal Center control application.*

The opportunity to step into a CAVE or a pod has been made achievable by an explosion in new projection technology. Developments from the commercial simulation sector being applied to the consumer scene have led to the latest digital video-projection technology, achieving greater resolution and image saturation (such as digital light processing systems). But it is the ability to create an all-encompassing projected image using multichannel projection that has been achieved with the latest blending of firmware for seamless immersive images from multiple projectors.

One of those involved in the application of the latest firmware to these kind of systems is Olav Sandnes of Univisial Technologies AB, a well-respected developer in the projection sector previously with corporations such as 3D Perception AS, Kongsberg Defence and Aerospace ASA and Miros AS. Speaking about his company he confirmed that:

> *Univisial supplies the 'Warpalizer' warp-and-blend software to developers like Polar Simulation AS, a company that delivers low-cost gaming rigs to the enthusiast gaming market. We focus on supplying software products that will bridge new technologies with existing concepts inside the mathematical constraints that will never change.*

The company's 'Warpalizer' software offers a simple solution to interactive simulation systems with an intuitive user interface, strong performance and a low-price that allows the entertainment sector to embrace immersive projection scenarios.

New developers are using this technology for their new entertainment simulator systems. SimPit Technologies has developed a range of two-, three-, five- and six-projector immersive simulators. Another developer is UK-based Motion Simulation, who developed the 'TL1', a 180° spherical projector screen system. Its stylish immersive cockpit was designed and developed in co-operation with the Ariel Motor Company for both the prosumer sector and sim-racing environments.

The creation of capsule or pod environments has gained momentum across providers of DOE technology. NAMCO Bandai had invested in immersive displays. In 2001, they experimented with 'ORBS' (Over Reality Booster System) and created a fully immersive cabinet. By 2006, they had released the network robot-combat simulator 'Mobile Suit Gundam: Bonds of the Battlefield': players competed in 'POD' (Panoramic Optical Display) cabinets, fully enclosed systems using immersive curved displays and full controls, reminiscent of VWE's 'Tesla' capsule. The 'POD' has been redeveloped for application in other new games from the NAMCO R&D stables, some of which will be seen outside Japan.

Acting as the perfect conclusion to this book, the authors were able to speak with one of those who has a unique perspective on the start of video-gaming and its future opportunities. Brent Bushnell is an engineer and entrepreneur, carving out executive roles in a wide variety of entertainment and technology start-ups, including founding Syyn Labs, a creative collective combining art and engineering to create high engagement for large brands, such as Google, Disney and OK Go. Most recently he is founder and CEO of Two Bit Circus, a think-tank creating products at the intersection of education and amusement, including a high-tech carnival to inspire children to pursue STEAM (science, technology, engineering, art and maths). Undaunted by the showdown with his father, Nolan Bushnell, Brent shares a passion for group games and out-of-home entertainment.

He was asked if his father's work with Atari or personal experience fed his passion for DOE:

> *I grew up surrounded by the games and out-of-home entertainment industries. I think I've been going to IAAPA [International Association of Amusement Parks and Attractions] since I was 5! Interestingly though, I didn't always know that I wanted to go into amusement. I took a circuitous route that included biotech, ERP [enterprise resource planning] systems and fibre optics before realizing that amusement was what I really loved.*

Brent has taken this love in some interesting directions, working on the start-up Virsix Interactive Entertainment, providing live-action gaming for public venues. Commenting on this aspect of his work, Brent described what drove the concept and his inspiration and more importantly if it would live beyond just being a concept.

> *Virsix came out of a lot of thinking my cofounder Eric Gradman and I had about the future of entertainment. We noticed the trend of increasing immersion from books to movies to video games, and how video games were trying to give players natural controls. With the falling price of sensors, the next step for us was the most high resolution experience of all … real life!*

Like his earlier 'MagiQuest', the first application of Brent's Virsix will initially be part of the Great Wolf Resorts operation ('Great Forest Challenge').

When asked what he had seen in the DOE sector that fired his imagination and interest, Brent said:

> *I really enjoyed my time at 'Sleep No More' in New York City. While not digital per se, it was a great re-imagining of the theatre experience.*

Expanding on the question to include what new user interfaces he thought would have the most impact on interactive experiences in leisure facilities in public places over the next five years, he stated:

> *The new interfaces and technologies I'm excited about are the Oculus Rift, the MYO [a low-cost gesture-control armband allowing the user to steer the experience like a physical mouse] and the Leap Motion controller. The Leap is a natural fit for out-of-home because it can be embedded in a kiosk or digital signage and requires no user contact to use it. The Oculus and the MYO combined open up a world of virtual reality possibilities that entire immersive environments could be built around. This time around, virtual reality is really going to work.*

Wrapping up the interview, it would have been impossible not to ask someone that was best placed to observe the birth of the video-amusement trade, why the market would seem, from a Western perspective, not to achieve its true potential:

> *Humans are jaded and get bored easily. In order to stay relevant, entertainment needs to evolve and captivate users time and again. So many of the entertainment staples are tired and just not interesting compared to all the other personal entertainment options available at home. Let me be clear, I believe people are social and absolutely would make the time to go out for compelling amusement, there's just not enough of it.*

The fundamental aspect of player immersion is fun. Something that has been repeated by many developers throughout this book. This aspect has to be considered alongside a mixed-reality approach (not just selecting one technology but including all of them), augmented displays superimposed over virtual environments, dynamic surfaces and high-fidelity visuals and audio in order to offer a gaming enclosure that is more than just fun, but also compelling to an audience looking for the next 'big thing' in how they play!

Supporting the Emergence of the New Horizon

Though we may be still working to achieve Jordan Wiseman's goal 'to create a legitimate entertainment format', moves have been made to create a foundation on which to build. The Digital Out-of-Home Interactive Entertainment Network Association was formed in 2011 and held its first conference the following year. The DNA was established as an international not-for-profit operation that could define some of the uncharted and vague aspects of DOE. The first element of its creation has been a map charting the fundamental business landscape of those working in the DOE environment.

Figure C.3 DNA Association Logo

The visionary behind this new rallying point for the future of DOE is the association's founding chairman, Kevin Williams of KWP (and co-author of this book), who has devised the Venn diagram in Figure C.4, the tangible visualization of the diversity of the DOE market and the influence of the various components.

This diagram is not the definitive shape of the DOE market, but offers the best representation of it available. The two most telling elements of the four Venn components are that they represent aspects influencing the DOE sector but are not supported by the association. The digital consumer-gaming sector is a vast and successful market as is the digital gaming sector (casinos and gambling). However, these sectors are represented by a plethora of trade associations focused wholly on their needs as are many of the sectors illustrated in the diagram.

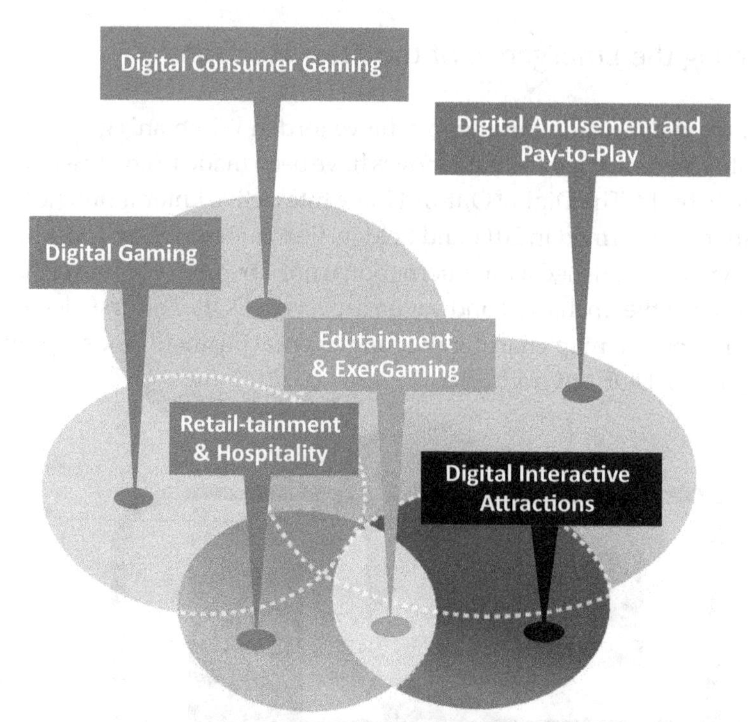

Figure C.4 Venn diagram of the DOE market (Kevin Williams)

Gaming and the consumer sector are profitable industries that have an obvious influence on the DOE sector, but they are influences rather than main areas of business. The first core sector of the DOE landscape is digital amusement and pay-to-play, representing the amusement industry that has been the launchpad for the immersive game experience. Likewise this has influenced the new digital interactive-attraction sector, applying gaming methodologies to the latest theme-park and resort-based attractions.

The final Venn element is the digital retail-tainment and hospitality sectors, representing the markets that are now turning to interactive entertainment as a new attraction for their venues, be they bars, taverns or shopping malls. For the DOE sector this is not the whole picture: it is through the interconnectivity of the various Venn segments that we see the emergence of growing new opportunities for the application of DOE technology. Between retail and attractions, we see the digital education and leisure sector embracing exergaming machines as well as the edutainment systems that bring gamification to a sophisticated audience. While between the amusement and attraction sectors, we see the development of new systems that offer unique interactive entertainments but in a package alien to the traditional approach. Immersion plays a major part in this application.

Figure C.5 The 2013 DNA/UK Seminar: attendees get to grips with what is needed for a compelling 3-D experience in DOE

With the transition from the traditional amusement mix to a new industry, the need for the DNA to chart this changing landscape and illustrate opportunities is great. At the same time the association has worked to create a number of resources for the exchange of information by those directly involved. Already conferences have been held in London and Los Angeles that brought together leading lights and innovators in all key sectors and many who look to new innovation. Along with this book, the DNA will include an extensive online repository of news and whitepapers that will continue to define the market.

This book represents the first foundation of what will be an industry that will overcome the current sedentary perceptions of video gaming and create a wholly compelling and immersive environment, such as an events space that could transport near-future audiences into a level of dimensional recreation and entertainment that we can only dream of. It would seem fitting that this book is being written as the video-amusement industry should be celebrating the fortieth anniversary of the first successful video game: 'Pong'!

Crystal-Ball Gazing

In this first book on the DOE sector, we have attempted to cover its core developments and new applications, but it would be a good idea at this point to look at some of the areas worthy of future observation, which could play fundamental roles in the short-term development of the industry.

First and foremost, we should look at future technology, in particular technology that could incentivize DOE in the key sectors. The development of the latest smartphone technology has had an impact on all emerging industries: the investment in R&D to create larger tougher touchscreens for mobile handsets has had knock effects on industries such as the VR HMD sector; the development of powerful built-in cameras and gyroscopic tracking has benefitted the VR and AR sectors.

The ability to enhance image quality in a VR HMD by employing the latest HD flat panels will prove important, though again the question has to be considered: Will the consumer-game sector benefit more than commercial applications in the DOE sector? Along with HD panels, the latest digital-projector technology has led to greater versatility and image saturation in recent years. The quality of the imagery has improved, the size and durability of the projectors have increased and the cost of projects dropped correspondingly. As with 'LivePark 4D' in Korea, a themed environment with high-quality digital projection is very appealing. The struggle to do things that cannot yet be achieved makes DOE such an important and innovative element of the entertainment landscape.

Secondly, as part of our crystal-ball gazing, we should look at emerging sectors of the industry. As mentioned earlier, there is a need for a wider perception of the various industries that are now involved in DOE. Some companies in the healthcare and rehabilitation industries are viewing gamification as an interesting opportunity to address the needs of injury, rehabilitation and senior-citizen activities. Where fitness was thought to have been the biggest user of exergaming, the slowing of investment in new equipment in the education and gym sectors has seen healthcare take up the mantle.

Another sector of the DOE industry that is worth closer examination is one that has yet to be defined in any detail by those outside the entertainment industry. The leisure and visitor-attraction sector comprises everything from tourist support in local areas to leisure-entertainment facilities.

Figure C.6 3-D-printed sculpture of a visitor: personalized memorabilia is one future application of technology in the theme-park (Disney Research)

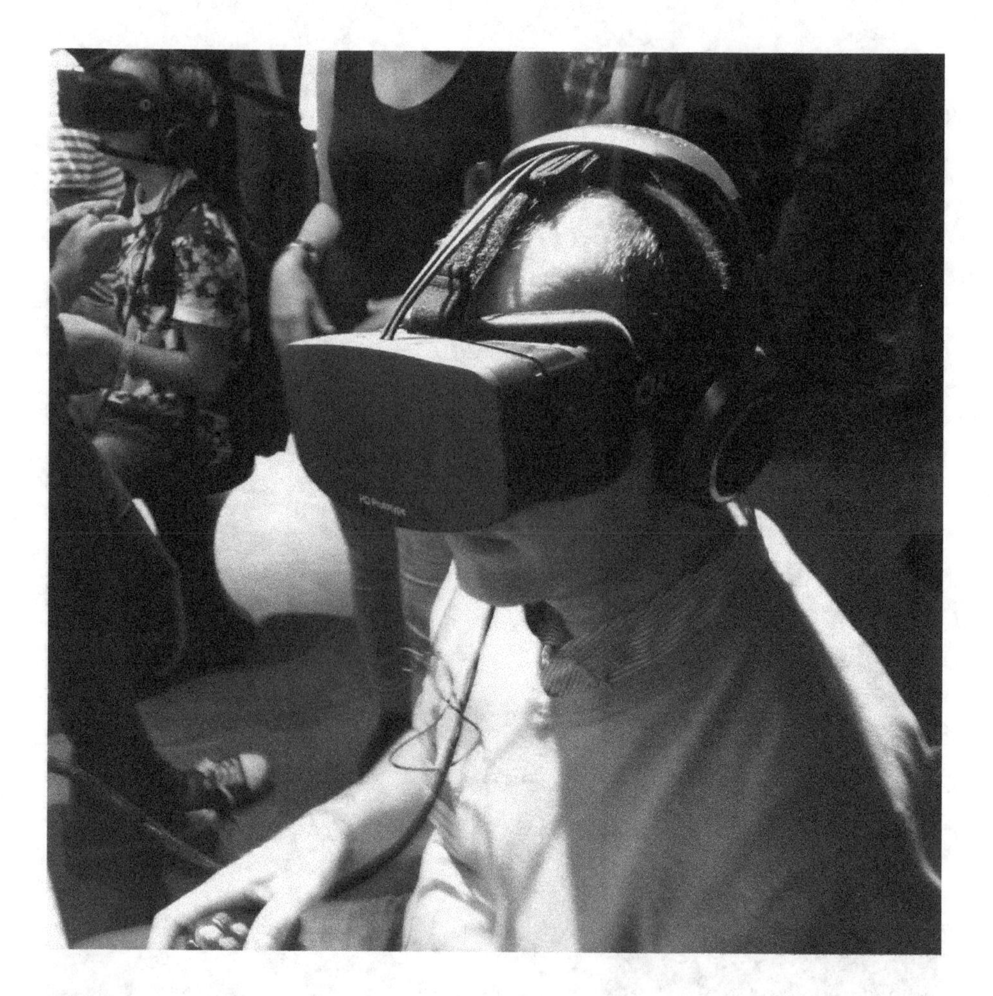

Figure C.7 Oculus VR's prototype HMD: part of the drive for greater immersion in the game experience

All sites that have a large throughput of transient visitors have an audience that can be offered entertainment experiences, which can be monetized to provide a new means of revenue for hard-pressed facilities.

There is one industry hoping to grow its investment in DOE that is keeping many very interested. The retail sector offers a vast array of opportunities for development, in particular there is a major interest in populating many of the available retail units at high-traffic shopping facilities with a new standard of entertainment venue not just mixed food-and-fun establishments but also repeat-visitor networked entertainment facilities like those developed by RaceRoom Entertainment. Questions still remain about the long-term profitability of this approach, though it feels more a matter of coming up with the correct marriage of technology and experience to draw a strong following, the correct approach could be a profitable trail blazer for the successful developer.

Finally, we turn to those who actually play the games. Currently DOE venues are mainly attracting 25- to 35-year-olds, but it is essential to attract a younger audience, rather than lose them to home gaming. The DOE sector offers a vibrant environment for a diverse audience in a variety of venues and locations. Future developments will affect not only how the market is perceived by other industries but also the reaction of the new audience it is trying to attract.

Index

Note: Figures indexed in **bold**.

3-D animated characters tracked through motion-capture systems 91–2
3-D building-projection advertisements 132–3
3-D entertainment applications 111
3-D experience in DOE **175**
3-D glasses 92
3-D mapping entertainment projects 132–3
3-D printed sculpture of a visitor: personalized memorabilia is one future application of technology in the theme-park (Disney Research) **177**
3-D printing in leisure facilities 159–60
3-D projection-mapping **133**
3-D projection shows 133
3-D screens with HD holographic projection 110
3-D sound 120
3-D technology 96, 102
3-D theatres 109
3-D warping **133**
4-D AR games 160
4-D enclosures 35
4-D entertainment 34
4-D experiences 35
4-D film content 33–4, 37
4-D systems 36–7
5-D theatre systems 35, 39, 45, 97, 160
7-D theatre systems 45

Aardvark Applications 90
Adidas mailing lists 138
advertising 27, 56, 76–8, 130, 134, 139, 162
Aero, Kenny 53
AET 35
Aichele, David 150, 152
Albritton, Dan 138
ALL.Net 18, 20, 30
Alterface 5-Di Interactive Cinema 43, **119**
ambient interactive entertainment 120, 145–6, 150, 154, 160
ambient sensors 148
America 15, 31, 33, 51, 63–5
American Museum of Natural History *see* AMNH
AMNH 101
'AMNH Explorer' 101
amusement 7, 13, 17, 29, 67, 171, 174
  indoor 63
  public 8
  traditional 28
Amusement and Edutainment Technologies *see* AET
amusement businesses 10, 69, 83

amusement centres 88
amusement collaboration between SEGA and Lucas ('Star Wars Arcade' simulator, 1993) 50
amusement developers 34
amusement devices 28
amusement environment 63
amusement experiences 31
amusement facilities 16, 25, 71
amusement halls 8
amusement industry 12, 79, 82, 84, 156, 174
Amusement Linkage Live Network System *see* ALL.Net
amusement machines 67, 169
amusement manufacturers 12
amusement network systems 63
amusement operators 85
amusement-park apps 98–100
amusement-park attractions 42, 120, 161
amusement-parks 11, 36, 38, 44, 56, 80, 98, 102, 104–7, 109–14, 117, 132, 142–3, 158–9, 161
amusement platforms 8
'Amusement Railway' 42
amusement systems **95**, 127
amusement theme parks *see* ATP
amusement trade 11–13, 18, 42
amusement venues 62–3, 69
  electric 33
  traditional 17
Andrews, Greg 114
Andy Warhol Museum 117–18
animation, concept of 99, 108
animation studios 40
animatronic characters 42, 45, 91, 97, 159
Apple Industries 155–6
apps 25, 29, 80, 96, 98–102, 105, 109, 121, 135, 144, 146
  ammo 112
  'AMNH Explorer' 101
  amusement-park 98–100
  companion 112
  consumer 83
  'Cosmic Discoveries' 101
  'Dinosaurs' 101
  discovery 109
  downloading of 96, 135, 155
  free 92, 99–101, 112
  friend-finder 99
  games 29
  immersive 98
  implementing of 102
  iOS 163
  mobile-phone 155
  multifaceted 98
  museum 100–102
  park-game 100
  social 29–30
  social-networking 91
  'Streetmuseum' 102
  tablet 75
  'Timeplay' 96
  video-game 29
AppTag Laser Blaster game 112
AR 40, 45, 52, 80, 89, 91–2, 97–8, 102, 104–12, 135, 141, 156, 160, 166
  elements of 107, 109
  as entertainment for visitors 110
  experiences of 92, 102, 104, 106, 108–10
  games 75, 104, 141–2, 144, 160
  telescopes **103**
  use of to integrate customers into live shows 109
  uses of apps 80, 105–6
The Arcade Experience: A Look Into Modern Arcade Games and Why They Still Matter 7
arcade games 12, 15–16, 21, 54, 76

Arcade Heroes (online service) 7
arcade industries 6
arcade machines 5, 11, 21, 65
arcades 1, 14, 17, 20, 33, 47, 63, **65**, 67, 69, 73–5
  classic 68
  darkened 5
  popup 73–4
  theme-oriented 75
  traditional 70
  upscale amusement 51
  virtual 5
  see also pop-up arcades
architecture 13, 18, 22, 83, 145, 150
Ariel Motor Company 170
AR'istophanes 91–2
art galleries 75, 102, 105
art museums 148
artificial tracking devices 92
Asia 25, 60, 63, 109
Asian PC Bang sites 30
Asian video-amusement scene 16
at-home console games 3, 23, 56, **57**
Atari Corporation 11, 15, 47, 54, 82, 143, 171
'Atari Puffer' prototype 126
ATP 51, 64, 80, 84
ATP and LBE projects 53
attractions 7, 10–11, 34–8, 40–43, 51, 55–6, 61, 84, 93–4, 98–100, 105, 108–9, 118–19, 143, 158–61
  28-player 61
  amusement-park 42, 120, 161
  building-projection 132
  compact 33
  digital 159
  interactive laser 113–14
  themed entertainment 53
  travelling museum 121
  visitor 8, 73, 119, 169
augmented reality *see* AR

Australia 51, 63, 124
aviation museums 119

Bachus, Kevin 66–7
Bally Company 13
BANA Passport 22
Bapst, Nicolas 106, 108–10
bar customers 151
'barcades' 69
bars 46–7, 56, 66, 68–9, 72, 75, 145, 150–53, 155, 174
  see also hotels, taverns
batting-cages 10
'Battle Mode' 102
'Battleships' 152–3
'Beatmania' 17
'beercades' 68–9
'Birthday Skies' 114
Bishop, David 71–2
blasters 112
Bloomfield, Mike 156
board games 48
Boeing 737 61
Bossa Nova Robotics 156
bowling alleys 10, 15, 62–3, 113, 115, 162
Boyle, Mark 153
brand-building campaigns 137, 139
brands 5, 13, 17, 24, 48, 53, 59–60, 67, 71, 94, 131, 134, 136, 162
  company's 8
  cyber arena facility 71
  luxury 59, 80
  showcase 73
Brighton Video Gamesuits Ltd 88
Brooklyn Museum 117, 138
budgets 8, 37–8, 86
buildings 44, 48, 81, 103, 117, 133, 136, 148, 155, 159
bus shelters 145
Bushnell, Brent 14–15, 171–2

Bushnell, Nolan 11–12, 65, 67, 87, 154–5, 163, 171
businesses 10–12, 14–15, 20, 29, 40, 45, 52, 56, 62, 67, 98, 104, 122, 174
  company's key 39
  consumer-game 75
  dark-ride 42
  entertainment-centre 71
  full-dome planetarium 114
  global 24
  mobile-gaming 76
  network of 20–21
  video-amusement 11, 22, 27, 29, 31, 71
Butterworth, Alex 144

call management system *see* CMS
Camara, Antonio 129, 133, 158
camera-tracking systems 126
cameras 80, 109, 153–4, 158
Cameron, James 45
campaigns 78, 90, 110, 130, 135–8, 145
  brand-building 137, 139
  digital-signage 134–6, 138
Canada 131, 137
Canadian Tourism Commission *see* CTC
cards 20, 22, 25–6
Carmack, John 87
carnival games 7
Carru, Alex 161
CAVE 89, 166, 169
Cearley, Mike 135
CEC 65–6
CGI 13, 16, 38, 40, 47–8, 56, 79, 87
CGI hardware developers 50
'Chameleon' entertainment system 54
Charlestown Mall 131
Chatfield, Tom 144
children 107–9, 115, 117, 160
Chinese companies 17, 23, 45
Chinese developers 23
Chuck E. Cheese Emporium **65**, 66
cinemas 10, 25, 35, 61, 72, 78, 96, 98, 130
CIS 35
Cloud Imperium Games Co. 86
CMS 98
Cobalt Flux platforms 123
Cobb, Dave 104, 109
coin-operated machines 156
Cold War 47, 53, 56, 79
'Collector Mode' 102
Collimore, Paul 88
'Comic-Con' show 74
'Commander' interactive capsule simulators 81
commercial airliners 62
commercial entertainment developers 56
commercial exergaming markets 123
commercial installations 58
commercial simulator developers 34
Commonwealth of Independent States *see* CIS
community exhibitions 138
'Compal Senses' game 129
companies 20, 22, 27–8, 34–5, 37–41, 43–5, 50–54, 61–3, 82, 125–6, 129–32, 142–4, 149–52, 158–9, 170
  breakaway 54
  console 163
  mascots of 82
  ownership of 23
  parent 52
  simulation-service 62
  support of 163
  T3 interactive tables 151

companion apps 112
'CompassQuest' 64
competition 3–4, 47, 49, 54, 58–9
  interactive storyteller 143
  lucrative 27
  prize 30
  realistic circuit-racing 58
  robotic 158
  traditional video-amusement business faces 11
'complete-simulator,' interest in the ideal of a 166
computer automated virtual environment *see* CAVE
computer-generated target information 80
computer-graphics companies 50
computer graphics imagery *see* CGI
computers **6**, 79, 87, 89, 99, 117–18, 136, 166
connectivity 27–8, 72
  Facebook 76
  player 30
console-game systems 73
consoles **6**, 10, 55, 73, 163
  home video-game 6, 77
  new generation 163
consumer apps 83
consumer devices 67
consumer-game developers 85, 162, 164
consumer-game media 5–6
consumer-games 31, 72, 78
consumers 9, 13, 50, 67, 69, 85, 106, 111, 114, 134–5, 137
  hungry 86
  interactive 160
  modern 156
  popular 86
  professional 58
  rewards 137
  sedentary 127
convergence 77, 129, 131, 134, 139, 142–3, 160
Core Cashless Co. 25
corporations 11, 26, 39, 42, 53, 72, 169–70
'Cosmic Discoveries' apps 101
costs 34, 38, 48, 55, 70, 142, 149, 152, 176
  for AR experiences 110
  development 50
  operational 150–51
  operators 115
'Create Your Own Screen Test' 118
creative developers 142, 145
Creative Kingdoms 64
Creative Works Co. 76, 115
credits, use of 20, 22, 24–5
Cruden BV 56, 58
CSIRO 158
CTC 137
customers 13, 20, 24, 37, 54–6, 61, 63, 74, 90, 106, 109, 129, 131, 150–53, 155–7
  bar 151
  Diesel's 136
  paying 66
cyber arena facility brands 71
cyber-cycling 126
'Cyber Dome Super Shooting System' 61
cyber-space 81, 166
cyber-space or stand-up (CS-SU) game platforms 81
cyberpunk novels 81
'Cyberspace Mountain' 52

D-Box Manufacturing Co. 162–3
'Dactyl Nightmare' 81

Dallas Museum of Art 75
'Dance Dance Revolution' 17, 123, 126
dance games 123–4
dance-pad platforms 126
Darim Control Technologies 34
dark rides 42–5, 108, 110, 115
  attractions of 41–2
  interactive 42–3, 113
Dave & Buster's (D & B) 66–7
De Pinxi 44
Delfgauuw, Rob 132
developers 15–16, 27, 29, 31, 35–6, 39, 41, 43–5, 56, 85–6, 100–101, 119–20, 126, 152–3, 170
  arcade-game 73
  CGI hardware 50
  Chinese 23
  commercial entertainment 56
  commercial simulator 34
  consumer-game 85, 162, 164
  creative 142, 145
  DOE 85
  early 123, 154
  FEC 63
  IG 53
  independent 58
  key 124
  legendary 35
  multi-touch table 152
  new 61, 170
  professional 160
  specialist 43
  successful 179
  system 152
  theatre 38
development costs 50
devices 26, 80, 91, 99, 106, 112–13, 118, 146, 156, 158
  artificial tracking 92
  consumer 67
  face-tracking 109
  futuristic VR 166
  game 21, 76, 112
  handheld **6**, 63, 96
  iPod Touch 98
  mobile 105–8, 141, 145, 154
  motion detection 132
  plot 166
  robotic 156, 159
  tablet 106, 132
  touchscreen 27
  using special 64
  using wireless 96
DeVincenzo, Jared 74
'Dido Kart 2' **68**
Diesel's 'Be Stupid Brand' 136
Diesel's customers 136
digital interactive-attraction sectors 174
digital media 42
'digital natives' 68
digital out-of-home *see* DOOH
Digital Out-of-Home Entertainment Network Association 163
Digital Out-of-Home Entertainment Network Association Conference 8
Digital Out-of-Home Interactive Entertainment Network Association 173
digital out-of-home markets 134
digital out-of-home technology *see* DOOT
digital signage 76, 131, 134–6, 138, 144, 172
Digital Touch Systems 150–51
'Dinosaurs' 101
DiNunzio, Joe 52
discovery apps 109
Disney 25, 43, 51–2, 80, 84, 89, 107–8, 132, 142, 171

Disney, Tim 49
Disneyland 42, 89, 107, 109
DisneyQuest 51–2, 84
displays 48, 81, 85, 132, 149
  field-of-view 83
  first head-up 93
  flat-screen 77
  heads up 45
  hemispherical 46, 90
  holographic 110
  immersive 77, 169
  interactive 115
  liquid crystal 84
  plasma 131
  real-time RGB 149
DNA 8, 173, 175
DNA Association Logo **173**
DNA/UK Seminar 2013 **175**
Dodsworth, Clark 104–5, 110
DOE 3, 8–10, 12, 24, 29–30, 42, 52, 67, 72, 76–8, 82, 94, 162–4, 173, 175–6
  developers 85
  environment 8, 173
  experience 8–9
  markets 94, 113, 159–60, 162, 173–4
  scene 6, 23, 30, 50
  sector 10, 31, 163
  sectors 59, 77–8, 86, 172–4, 176, 179
  systems 27, 35
  technology 170, 174
  venues 10, 59, 159, 179
Dogfi.sh Mobile 98–9
Dolby process 118
Donaldson, Bill 54–5
DOOH 27, 76–8, 134, 137, 139, 160
  campaigns 135
  markets 134–7, 139, 142, 145
  promotions 137
DOOT 7
Doron Precision Systems 39
downloading of apps 96, 135, 155
'Dream Chaser' 90
dreams 93, 165–6, 175
driving 38, 58, 167–9
driving games 45, 58
Durmick, Chris 102, 105–7, 109

e-payment systems 22, 25–6, 30
E-Table Co. 152–4
edutainment (visitor attractions) 8, 45, 50, 60–61, 118–20, 122, 144
effects 8, 33–4, 37, 39–40, 43, 45–6, 79, 96–7, 118, 120–21, 130–32, 153–4, 166, 176
  bubble 34
  digital 79
  in-seat 39
  interactive theatrical 43
  latest CGI 34
  negative 153
  on-screen 96
  physical 33–4, 45, 118
  sensory 45
  vibration 46
El Faro visitor-centre project 158
electro-mechanical games 12
entertainment 1, 6, 9, 24, 26–7, 29, 33–4, 41, 45, 54, 66, 81–2, 91–2, 152–3, 171–2
  applications 56, 80, 111
  centres 114
    hybrid 162
    location-based 113, 161
  companies 52, 84, 96
  digital 5, 65, 71–2, 88, 127
  elements 7, 72
  environment 1, 54, 155
  experiences 3, 9, 53, 150, 178
    interactive 80

location-based 143
modern out-of-home 8
multifaceted 74
regional 64
strong 63
total-immersion 60
facilities 25, 62, 68, 81, 178
immersive person-to-person 83
impulse 15
markets 9, 56, 58
platforms 105
modern 8
professional 59
sector 53, 56, 61, 80, 118, 159, 170
simulation 48, 53
experiences of 39
immersive 53
systems 39
systems 54, 56, 91
integration of 59
interactive 1, 77
new digital 69
technology 67, 82
venues 29–30, 33, 37, 50–51, 64, 73, 178
entrepreneurs 51, 53, 171
environments 8, 10, 42, 50, 68, 78, 84, 91, 97, 104, 107, 112, 146, 148–9, 166
immersive 79, 166, 172, 175
themed 42, 47, 64, 176
EON Reality 111, 120
Epcot 107–8
E&S 50, 114
Europa-Park 110
Evans & Sutherland Co. 50
event-planning industries 156
EXcape Entertainment Group 59–60
exercise bikes 126
exergaming 8, 123, 125–7, 176
genre 127
packages 123
variants 125
exhibitions 121, 138, 148, 160
museum 115
virtual mobile 101

face-tracking devices 109
Facebook 45, 76, 98–9, 136, 139, 156
The Factory 118, 133
'Faile Bast Deluxx Fluxx Arcade' **70**
failures 12, 14, 50, 55, 82
family entertainment centers *see* FECs
FEC developers 63
FECs 7, 10, 15, 23, 25, 29, 47, 62
Ferretti Industries 35
field-of-view displays 83
films 33, 37–8, 40, 76, 94, 96–8, 100, 118–19, 144
3-D 33, 35
4-D 33–5, 37
Fiorillo, James 60
fitness 123, 125–6, 176
fitness studios 124
flat-screen displays 77
flight-simulator operators 62
Flightdeck 61–2
'Fly 360' **122**
'Fly Zone' gallery,' Science Museum, London 118, **122**
Forest Lake, California 53
Foy, Chris 124
free apps 92, 99–101, 112
friend-finder apps 99
FROG 48
Frye, Bobby 75
funfairs 41
futuristic VR devices 166

Gage, Mark Foster 145, 150

'Galaxian 3 Theater 6' 61
gambling machines 29
Game Developers Conference *see* GDC
game devices 21, 76, 112
'gamebars' 1, 28, 68–9, 73
Gamerbase (UK retailer) 76
games 18, 25, 27, 66, 68, 73, 76, 141, 169–70
  'AppTag Laser Blaster' 112
  'Battle Mode' 102
  'Battleships' 152–3
  'Beatmania' 17
  casual 138
  classic 69, 143
  collaborative 97
  'Collector Mode' 102
  comic-based 74
  'Compal Senses' 129
  cross-environment 142
  cult of 96
  'Dactyl Nightmare' 81
  fitness-oriented 126
  free-to-play 73
  innovative 17
  large-format 67
  'Laser Frenzy' 115
  laser-tag 113–14
  location-based/mixed-reality 144
  'Mood Mode' 102
  network 18
  'Pong' 11–12, 24, 47, 127, 175
  popular 74, 123
  'Renga' 97, 115–16
  social 10, 101, 106, 161
  'Sonic the Hedgehog' 74
  'Space Invaders' 5, 12–13
  sports-oriented 71
  'Tate Trumps' 101
  traditional 29
  trivia 150
  'Video Games Live' 143
  'VTOL' 81
'gamification' 3, 8, 27, 76, 80, 121, 126–7, 174, 176
gaming 5, 10, 13, 66, 76, 84, 87, 98, 120, 144, 167, 174
GDC 166
Gemme, Yannick 163
genre 1, 3, **4**, 5, 10, 145
    at-home consumer-game 141
    exergame 126
    iDR 43
    new 17
Gerner, John 73–4
gestural interactive experiences 96–7, 129–31
gestural technology 110, 160
gesture-based experiences 129
gesture-based games 129
GestureTek Co. 129–31
Gibson, William 81, 166
Google 91, 94, 144, 171
graphical user interface *see* GUI
graphics 14, 117
Great Wolf Resorts 64
Greene, Patrick 97
'Grimm Library' 110
group training products 124
GUI 93, 166
Gurley, Steve 135–6

Haimson, Michael 35–6
Hale's Tour 33
handheld devices **6**, 63, 96
hardware 10, 25, 48, 58, 61, 81–2, 121, 163, 169
  complicated 54
  cost-effective 92
  dedicated 3
  expensive 50, 85
    amusement 15

CGI 14, 48
IG 50
temperamental 51
harps 117
Harrington, Alexander 97
HD 18, 77, 111
HD glasses 111
HD touchscreen display **147**
head-mounted-displays *see* HMDs
head-up displays *see* HUDs
health issues 126–7, 163, 176
hemispherical displays 46, 90
Heywood, Barney 99
Heywood, Lucy 99
high-definition *see* HD
Hill, Glenn 116–17
'Hitchhiking Ghosts' (Disney) 108
HMDs 46, 79, 81–3, 85, 87–8, 90, 93
Høie, Ole Petter 123–5
holodecks, technology of 165–7, 169
holographic displays 110
home game systems 14, 31
home video-game consoles 6, 77
hospitality 11, 15, 29, 46, 65–6, 68–9, 71–2, 127, 147
hospitality facilities 27, 151
hospitality industry 155
hospitality market 77
hospitality sector 28, 73, 153, 174
hotels 46–7, 145, 150
HUDs 93
humanoid robots **157**
Hunwick, Neil 152–3
hybrid systems 116

IAAPA 38, 40, 56, 171
Icart 169
ice rinks 10
iDANCE 123–4
iDR genre 43
iDRs 43–6, 113
IG 50, 54
IG developers 53
Illiff, James 111
image-generator *see* IG
Image Space Incorporated (software developer) 59
images 45, 121, 133, 156, 168–9
immersion 34, 41, 78–91, 120, 129, 166, 174
demands for greater 31, 178
of entertainment 33
increasing 171
love of 49
player 172
visual 90
immersive apps 98
immersive displays 77, 169
immersive entertainment systems 80
immersive installations 70
immersive simulator experiences 33, 56, 119, **168**
immersive technology 47, 91, 166
immersive theatres 120–21
immersive user interface *see* IUI
Imperial Art Museum, London 101
'In The Groove' 123–4
Inamo Restaurants 152–3
Incredible Pizza Company 65, 73
Incredible Technologies Co. 28
independent games 27, 75
independent operators 73
Indicade 2012, California **116**
industries 7, 11–13, 15–16, 23–5, 29, 40, 43, 63, 67, 76, 81, 175–6, 179
amusements 77
arcade 6
coin-operated-amusement 11
commercial-simulation 56
console-cartridge 16
console-games 13
consumer-electronics 86

entertainment 85
event-planning 156
in-home console-game 27
interactive-experience 119
motion-picture 79
motor-sports 56
petroleum 166
rehabilitation 176
simulation 13, 85
theme-park 93
infantry training 167
information 78, 91, 98–9, 105, 109, 131, 149, 166, 175
background character 100
baseline AR 105
computer-generated target 80
disseminate park 98
key park 105
personalized 104
projected 93
promotional 98
recorded 98
retrieving of 146
social 49
weather 151
infrastructure 22, 25–6, 167, 169
Inition (UK company) 90
Inition vertigo simulator **168**
innovation 6–7, 15, 17, 30–31, 35, 41, 77, 95, 118, 149, 162, 169
entertainment technology 41
'ground-breaking' 132
radical 153
innovative interfaces 30
Insert Coin(s) Interactive Nightlife facility 68–9, 71
installations 27, 34, 36, 38, 54, 73, 84, 115
bizarre 70
commercial 58
high-profile 54
immersive 70
non-permanent street 117
travelling 70
virtuality 67
interactive attractions 35, 43, 143
interactive consumers 160
interactive dark rides *see* iDRs
interactive display systems 131
interactive displays 115
interactive entertainment 1, 41, 44, 76, 113, 122, 127, 145, 150, 154, 160, 174
expansive 160
forms 111
imparts 122
imparts an educational narrative **122**
start-up Virsix 171
interactive experience industries 119
interactive experiences 44, 92, 94, 96–7, 113, 118, 120, 129, 141, 160–62, 172
compelling 138
customized 161
dynamic 162
extending 162
gesture-based 148
innovative 116
new 162
transparent 148
variegated 162
interactive floor projection systems 27, 96
interactive games 34, 54, 106, **125**, 152
interactive laser games 113–14, **116**, 117
interactive live-theatre projects 142
interactive marketing systems 84, 130
interactive products 55

interactive simulation systems 170
interactive sports-based games 126
interactive storyteller competitions 143
interactive systems 35, 96, 154
interactive tables 150–52
interactive theatres 40, 61, 110
interactive windows 149
interactivity 38, 41, 45, 61, 131, 135, 146, 160, 162
interfaces 30, 92–3, 131
  gun 167
  innovative 30
  motion-tracking console-game 126
  multi-touch 29
  tactile 81
  tracked 168
International Association of Amusement Parks and Attractions *see* IAAPA
International Space Station 114
investments 14, 16, 34–5, 37, 40, 52, 72, 78, 135, 151, 176, 178
iOS apps 163
iPads 106, 132, 137
iPhones 26, 92, 98, 100–101, 105, 112
iPod Touch devices 98
Iwerks Entertainment 35–6

Jackson, Michael 41
JAEPO 23
Jamele, Dan 37–8
JAMMA-compatible PCB kit 18
Japan Amusement Expo *see* JAEPO
Japan Amusement Machinery Manufacturers Association 16, 23
Japan-based leisure corporations 63
Japanese amusement factories 12, 16–17, 23, 71, 127
Japanese amusement trade 127
Japanese ATP sector 55
Japanese games 13, 23
Japanese video-amusement businesses 23
Japanese video-amusement factories 23, 51
Japanese video-amusement trade 17
Jarvis, Eugene 15
Jet Propulsion Laboratory *see* JPL
Jewish Children's Museum, Brooklyn 117
Johansson, Mats 111
JPL 166
'Jubeat' (Japan) 17

Kalff, Frank 56, 58
KDE 17, 22, 30, 125
Kee Games Co. 12
key park information 105
Kim Possible World Showcase Adventure 107–8
Kimmunicator' mobile devices 107–8
Kinetoscope, coin-operated 33
  see also peephole kiosks
King, Steve 139
King David (story) 117
Klein, Yves 101
Konami Digital Entertainment *see* KDE
Kondas, Kyle 75
Kuslansky, Eli 146, 148

LAI Games 63
Lamabada, Martijn 149
LaPorte, Christopher 69, 71
'Laser Frenzy' 115
laser games 111–16
  development of 115
  innovative 113
  interactive 113

new forms of 97, 113
laser pointers 113, 115, **116**, 117
laser-tag 10, 111, 114–15, 162
lasers 114–15, 117
LBE 1, 8–9, 26, 28, 47–9, 51, 54, 62, 142
centres 83, 97
concept of 78
digital 49
facilities 50, 61
markets 31, 55
products 55
sector 55, 61
viewed 53
Leisure Business Advisors 73
leisure centres 44, 123–4
leisure entertainment venues 35, 47
leisure facilities 102, 104–7, 109–11, 113–15, 117, 120, 141–2, 145, 154, 156–62, 165, 172
leisure sectors 29, 34, 159
Lilly Development Partners 26
liquid crystal displays 84
LivePark (amusement project) 112, 176
LocaModa Co. 137
location-based entertainment *see* LBE
location-based games 141–5
London Science Museum 45
London Soho Gallery **70**
Luckey, Palmer 85–6
luxury brands 59, 80
LYT 149

machines 8, 16, 23, 25, 27, 47, 66, 70–72, 124
arcade 5, 11, 21, 65
coin-operated 156
gambling 29
mechanical gaming 46
mixing ticket-redemption 15
networked 18
robotic battle 47
video-amusement 7, 31
video-game 29
Madame Tussauds, London 38
MagiQuest 64, 171
Maker Faire, Rome 149
'makerbots' 159
'makerculture' 160
'Makerspace,' Newark Museum 160
malls 15, 55, 72, 77, 84, 104, 131
Mass Hysteria Entertainment Co. 97
McDermott, Michael 105–6
McGonigal, Jane 144
media 13, 91, 94, 146, 149, 152–3
consumer-game 5–6
digital 42
MediaMation Co. 37
Menache, Alberto 111
Merlan, Ernie 107
Merlin Entertainment 64
metal jackets 149–50
Midway Manufacturing Company, Cactus Canyon **2**
Mikami, Katsuhiko 18, 20
military 34, 54, 79–80, 85, 89, 163, 167
military contractors 48
military helicopters 80
military-simulation 47, 50, 53, 56, 80, 163
military-simulator companies 34
mini-games 8, 106
mini-golf 10
Mitchell, Nate 85–6
mixed-reality/AR games 144
mixing ticket-redemption machines 15
mobile AR 105–7, 160
mobile devices 105–8, 141, 145, 154

mobile games 145
mobile-phone apps 155
mobile phones 9, 22, 30, 80, 93, 98, 132, 134, 149, 154
mobile technology 85, 136
MoCap Games' VR system 30, 87, **88**, 92
modern consumers 156
Mollet, Nicolas 105, 108
money 26, 63, 66, 125
Monkton, Terry 39–40
Monte, Ana 146
'Mood Mode' 102
Morrison, Scott 28
motion capture system *see* Mocap
motion detection devices 132
motion-picture industries 79
motion-tracking console-game interfaces 126
movie theatres 15, 76, 79, 94, 96–8, 115, 129
multi-player dance-game systems 124
multi-player products 124
multi-sensory technology 33, 45
multi-touch interactive tables and countertops in leisure facilities 145–56
multi-touch interfaces 29
multi-touch screens 121, 150
multi-touch tables 148, 150–51
  developers 152
  interactive LCD 121
  system 152
multi-touch tabletop systems 150
multidimensional 134, 141, 160
  applications 138
  experiences 44
  offerings 120
multifaceted apps 98
museum apps 100–102
museum exhibitions 115
Museum of London 102
museums 8, 37, 39, 44, 80, 100–102, 106, 112–22, 132, 138, 142, 145, 148, 158–9, 161
  art 148
  aviation 119
  transforming of 100
MYO 172

NAMCO Bandai 18–19, 22, 31, 95, 143, 170
NAMCO Bandai BANA Passport card system 19
NAMCO Bandai 'Deadstorm Pirates' 3-D shooting experience **95**
NAMCO Corporation 11, 13, 16, 18, 20, 82
NAMCO Entertainment 71
NAMCO Japan 20
NAMCO network system 20
NESiCA Card 20–21, 30
NESYS 20–21
Net Entry System *see* NESYS
networks 21, 35, 58–9, 96, 146, 154, 170
  interactive media 96
  server-based 59
  simulation 47
  social 107, 155–6
  social media 146
new generation consoles 163
New Reality for Location-Based Entertainment 8
Newkirk, Joni 161
NFC Cards 22, 25–6
nightclubs 68–9, 71, 150
non-permanent street installations 117

Norris, Jeff 166

OBOTO (robot) 92
Oculus, VR dev-kit **168**
Oculus, VR prototype HMD **178**
'Oculus Rift' 83, 86–7, 90, 94, 172
Oculus VR 85
on-screen effects 96
on-screen games 94, 96
online 12, 20, 29, 134, 138
  connected 22
  features 18
  projects 138
  registration 18
  services 7, 21
  submissions 138
online games 97, 106
  see also games
operational costs 150–51
operators 11, 14, 16–17, 20–22, 24–5, 28, 45, 69, 73–4, 76, 144, 156
  charging 25, 115
  flight-simulator 62
  independent 73
  restaurant 152–3
  video-arcade 14, 73–4, 144
out-of-home entertainment 9, 72, 171
  digital 3, 7, 11, 79, 156
  industries 91, 171

park-game apps 100
Parker, Kellie 74
partnerships 15, 41, 43–4, 100, 120, 126
PASELI (Pay Smart Enjoy Life) system 22
Patton, Dax 150–52
Paul, Robert 33, 89
pay-to-play 10, 76, 174
  entertainment's loss of relevence 31
  supplies 1
pay-to-view technology 33
paying customers 66
payments 26
  card-based 66
  cashless 25
  electronic 26
  methods of 26
  smart 26
  systems 74
payments infrastructure 26
peephole kiosks 33
personalized information 104
petroleum industries 166
Phillips, Andrea 144
photo-sensitive epilepsy 78
pinball machines 1–2, 15, 28, 74
pinball playing field **2**
planetariums 113–14, 118
plasma displays 131
player connectivity 30
player immersion 172
player interactions 30
player tracking 126
players 3, 7–8, 17–18, 20–22, 25–8, 36, 46–8, 64, 76–7, 87–9, 115, 141, 144–5, 148, 169–71
  challenges for 115
  multiple 52
  rewarding of 28
  uniqueness of 28
'Playground' (interactive floor projection system) 96
pods 31, 47, 54, 169–70
Polygon (games portal) 71
Pong 11–12, 24, 47, 127, 175
pop-up arcades **70**, 73–6
popular consumers 86
portfolio products 100
Positive Games 123, 125
Posterscope Co. 137

Pratt, Adam 7, 17
products 13, 18, 24, 35, 37, 55, 72, 82–3, 87, 102, 107, 111, 124, 130–31, 134
  arcade machine 5, 124
  commercial exergaming 124
  consumer 127
  group training 124
  interactive 55
  interactive-furniture 148
  large-scale simulation 40
  multi-player 124
  portfolio 100
  UNIS family of 24
  video 63
  wearable AR-display 111
professional consumers 58
projection mapping 150
projections 55, 89, 92, 99, 120, 132–3
    3-D-mapping 120, 132–3
    external 132
    high-quality digital 176
    using multichannel 170
    visual 116
projects 7, 36–7, 50, 52–4, 71–2, 84, 86, 91–2, 97, 101, 108–9, 111–12, 117, 142, 149
  ATP and LBE 53
  interactive live-theatre 142
  pilot 124
  promotional 90
  research 91
  retail 50
promotional information 98
'prosumers' 58, 167
publications 85
  The Arcade Experience: A Look Into Modern Arcade Games and Why They Still Matter 7
  Understanding Motion Capture for Computer Animation 111
Pulsefitness 'Dance Machine' (interactive game) **125**

Race Flight Club *see* RFC
Radin, Aaron 100, 102
Raw Thrills (video-amusement developer) 15
reactive monomer liquid crystal materials *see* RMLCM
real-time RGB displays 149
rehabilitation industries 176
'Renga' 97, 115–16
research projects 91
Resort Technology Partners 105
resources 20, 23, 146, 175
restaurant operators 152–3
restaurants 46, 56, 66, 71–2, 75, 105, 145, 150–53, 155
retail outlets 72, 76, 131, 178
retro games 74
revenue 5, 10–11, 22, 25, 27, 29, 73, 82, 94, 97, 104, 115, 151, 164, 178
revenue streams 25, 162
  new entertainment-facilities 14
  secondary 7, 10, 46–7
RMLCM 83
Roberts, Chris 86
Robertson, Margaret 101–2
robotic battle machines 47
robotic competitions 158
robotic devices 156, 159
robotic leisure facilities 156–9
robots 158–9
roller coasters 36, 107
roller-skating rinks 10
Roxor Games 123
Ruke, Daniel T. 143
Russia 35, 124

Salabi, Gabi 44

Sally Corporation 42–3
San Diego 74
San Francisco 53, 121
Sastre, Angel 117
SBG Labs 83
SCALE-1 Portal 169
Schilling, Jeff 114–15
schools 104, 123–4, 126
science centres 8, 37, 39, 44, 114, 116, 118, 120
Science Museum, London 118, 122
'ScreenFX' system 131
ScreenXtreme system 131
SD (sit-down game platforms) 81
Second Story Co. 149
sedentary consumers 127
SEGA Amusements 51, 82
SEGA Corporation 11, 13, 16, 18, 20, 22, 30, 34, 41, 50–52, 61, 74, 82
SEGA Gameworks 51
SEGA Gameworks venues 51
Sensaa Co. 117
Sensorama Simulator 33
sensors 112, 171
  based motion 150
  multimodal 146
  upper-body 87
sensory effects 45
Set Company 149
Shard **103**
shopping malls 8, 35, 39, 47, 120, 129, 131, 174
  see also malls
'Show at the Pier' (water-fountain show) 154
Silicon Motor Speedway *see* SMS
sim-racing 59
simulation industries 13, 85
simulation sickness 78, 93–4
simulation technology 47, 56, 79, 166
simulations 53–4, 79, 117
simulator (SIMNET) networking trainers 47
simulator systems 170
simulators 37, 55, 61, 79–80, 87, 90, 119, 159, 170
  'Dream Chaser' 90
  Flightdeck 61–2
  'Oculus Rift' 83, 86–7, 90, 94, 172
  Sensorama Simulator 33
Simworx Co. 39–40
sites 7, 47–9, 51–3, 61, 63, 69, 73–4, 80, 178
  Asian PC Bang 30
  early reflective gun 93
  planned LBE 50
  social media 132
  social-networking 98
  themed entertainment 64
  traditional location-based entertainment 60
  visitor-attraction 34
Slick Willy's World of Entertainment pool hall 66
smart payment systems 22
smartphone apps 80, 92
  see also mobile-phone apps
smartphones 8, 21, 74–5, 80, 85, 94, 97, 100, 105–7, 112, 141–2, 149, 154–6, 158, 160
SMS 54, 135–6, 139
Snoddy, Jon 104, 107
social information 49
social media 80, 94, 100, 105, 107, 118, 132, 136–7, 139, 155–6, 160
social media networks 146
social network technology 30
social networks 107, 155–6
software 55, 58, 61, 121, 156, 163
  development 48, 169

operating 56
patented video gesture-control 131
updates 54
Sohmers, Thomas 111
Solaas, Karsten 136
'Sonic the Hedgehog' games 74
Sony Computer Entertainment 13
SONY Entertainment 53
Sony Playstation Vita handheld games platform **6**
'Space Invaders' 5, 12–13
spring-suspension systems (GatorVision) 84
SR-2 systems 39
St. James, Inamo 152
Staat Creative Agency 149–50
Stapleton, Chris 104–7, 109
staycationers 29
staycations 8–9, 64, 68
stereotype of solitary and sedentary consumer-game play in a social environment **165**
'Streetmuseum' 102
Sweeny, Tim 87
swipe cards **19**, 25
Sydney Aquarium 109
system developers 152
systems 18, 20–22, 25–7, 35–40, 45–8, 77–8, 88–90, 96–8, 110–11, 123–4, 126–7, 130–31, 151–3, 163–4, 168–71
downwards-projecting 153
multi-player 124
multi-touch 150–53
solar 120, 166
touchscreen 151

T1Visions' interactive tables 151
tablet apps 75
tablet devices 106, 132
tablets 9, 21, 63, 73, 92–3, 106, 154, 156, 158, 163
Taito Corporation 5, 11–12, 16, 20–21
'Taito Net Entry System' *see* NESYS
Tallarico, Tommy 143
Tan, Steven 23–4
'Tate Trumps' 101
taverns 27, 46–7, 174
technology 10, 12–13, 43–7, 55–6, 61–2, 67, 79–82, 87–91, 96–7, 102, 104, 115, 123–4, 134–5, 166–72
application of 177
digital 10, 33, 53, 79
innovative 43, 89
interactive 43–4
latest 38, 155
digital-projector 176
digital video-projection 169
projection 77–8
smartphone 176
new projection 77, 169
revenue-enhancement 26
sophisticated projection 79
touchscreen 155
'Tekken Tag Tournament 2 Unlimited' *see* TTT2
Telefonica (Spanish telecommunications company) 131
theatre developers 38
'Theatre Jukebox' (arcade device) 99
theatre systems 37, 39, 46
audience-based multisensory 90
open-motion platform 35
theatres 8, 34, 38, 40, 45, 61, 94, 96–9, 109–10, 120, 130, 163
theme park experiences 52, 106–7
theme parks 1, 37, 39, 44, **65**, 80, 89, 104, 106–7, 119–20
construction of 34

destination 109
indoor 51
large 33, 91
urban 98
Thinkwell Group 102, 104, 109, 154
ticketing capabilities 98–9
'Timeplay' 96
Tiny Thumbs 75
Total Immersion and Snibbe Interactive Co. 110
Total Interactive Technologies 35
touchscreen devices 27
touchscreens 17, 29, 109, 137, 154–5, 176
Toura Co. 100–101
tournament infrastructure 28
Tower of David Museum 121
Tower of London 82
'Toy Storey: Midway Mania' 43
Trigub, Dan 135
Triotech Corp. 41, 43–4
TTT2 18
Twitter 98, 137, 155–6

'uBeat' 17
see also 'Jubeat' (Japan)
UNIS 23–4
United Healthcare 125
Universal Space *see* UNIS
Universal Studios Japan 26
US Army Armor School *see* USAARMS
US market 18
USAARMS 47
user-centred brand experiences 134
user-curated content 109, 138
user-generated content 112, 137–8, 145–6, 160
user interfaces 129, 148–9, 172
user photos 136
uWink 154–5
Uzzan, Bruno 106, 108

VAE 53
Veda Incorporated 54
Venn diagram of the DOE market 173, **174**
vibration effects 46
video-amusement
games 13
industry 5, 13–14, 28–9, 175
international 22
modern 15
new 24
traditional 24
machines 7, 31
manufacturers 31
projects 27
scene 16, 30
international 17
modern 30
socializing and competition **4**
video-arcade games 13, 73
video-arcade operators 14, 73–4, 144
video-arcades 1, **14**, 73, 76, 144
video-game apps 29
video-game machines 29
video-games 16–18, 23, 25, 28–9, 46–7, 65, 69, 72–3, 88, 101, 119, 121, 129, 156, 171
coin-op 89
consumer 62
distinctive 143
first successful 121–2, 175
network-based 25
production of 13
successful 12
'Video Games Live' 143
video-gaming 5, 16, 24, 65, 88, 121, 171, 175

video products 63
videos 11, 15, 43, 111, 121, 132, 137, 153, 155, 161
Vieira, Marta 129
Vincent, John Vincent 130–31
VIP visitors 60
VirTra 89–90, 168
'Virtual Adventures' 35–6, 50
Virtual Army Experience *see* VAE
virtual-reality *see* VR
virtual reality experiences 54, 86, 169
'Virtual Reality Theater' 84
Virtual World Entertainment *see* VWE
Virtuality (UK company) 67, 81–3, 104
virtuality installations 67
Virtuix Co. 167
Vision 3 Experiential 120
visitor-payment and ticketing infrastructure 25
visitors 41–3, 53, 80, 88, 91, 94, 98–102, 104–10, 114–18, 120–21, 138, 141–3, 148–9, 154, 158–9
  adult 117
  apprising of 102
  challenging of 100, 114
  entertaining of 106
  museum 101, 138
  registering park 106
  returning 66
Vissette (patented HMD technology) 81
VR HMDs 87, 90, 176
VR technology 46, 52, 81–94, 97, 102, 120, 166
VWE 47–50, 67, 170

WACs 48
Waldern, Jonathan 82–3
Wallander, Marcus 149
WallFour Studios 97, 115, **116**
Walt Disney Company 33, 39, 41, 49, 51, 76, 93, 132, 158, 168
Ward, Kyle 124
Warner Bros 43
weather information 151
Weisberg, Allen 156
Westfield mall, London 77
White, Randy 8
wide-angle collimated displays *see* WACs
WiFi 102
Wigboldy, Paul 61–2
Williams, Kevin 173
'Wing Commander' 86
'Winnitron 1000' 27
'Winter Sweet' 133
'Winter Village' 133
Wiseman, Jordan 48–50, 173
WMS Industries 163
Wood, John 42–3

X-D, technology 45
XBLA 5
Xbox Live Arcade *see* XBLA
'XD Theater' business 43

Yahoo 145
YDreams Co. 129–30, 146, 148, 158
YouTube 132

Zamperla 43–4